There's Life in The Word

You can be an over comer

You can reach the top of the Mountain

God will give you strength to climb

HILDA MARIE BARTON

Order this book online at www.trafford.com
or email orders@trafford.com

Most Trafford titles are also available at major online book retailers.

Printed in the United States of America.

ISBN: 978-1-4269-6220-2 (sc)
ISBN: 978-1-4269-6221-9 (e)

Library of Congress Control Number: 2011906124

Trafford rev. 04/28/2011

Trafford PUBLISHING www.trafford.com

North America & international
toll-free: 1 888 232 4444 (USA & Canada)
phone: 250 383 6864 • fax: 812 355 4082

Acknowledgement

I'd like to dedicate this book to my loving
husband Leon. He has been so faithful and helpful
to me as I have spent much time writing
this book and getting it together.

He's such a man of faith and has
inspired me over the years. He has such
love for Jesus Christ and for me. He loves the
work of the Lord and is faithful to it.

Together we make such a great team
and I thank God for him. Thank you honey
for standing with me and for being so
patient with me.

Hilda Marie Barton

There's Life in The Word

In the Beginning
was the Word and the Word was
with God and the Word was God ……
John 1:1

Contents

There's Life in

God's Word

you can be an overcomer

You can reach the top of

The Mountain

God

Will give you strength to climb

CHAPTER ONE

There's Life In God's Word

CHAPTER 1

There's Life in God's Word

Prov.4:20-23, My son or daughter, listen and pay attention to what I say, listen close to Me. Do not let them out of your sight; keep them within your heart. For they are life who find them and health to your whole body. Above all else, guard your heart for it in the well spring of life. The Word of God is life to you and it will keep you safe in Him always. It will bring health to your body and food to your bones. Keep My laws and commandments and you will live, keep My Words and store up My commandments within you. Guard My teachings as the apple of your eye. Bind them on your fingers and write them on the tablet of your heart. Prov.4:10-13, Listen to Me and accept what I say and the years of your life will be many. My Word will guide you in the way of wisdom and lead you along straight paths. When you walk your steps will not be hindered. When you run you will not stumble. Hold on to My instructions, do not let them go, guard them with your life. Prov.3:1-2. Don't forget My teachings but keep them in your heart for they will prolong your life many years and bring you prosperity.

Ps.119:105, David said, Thy Word is a lamp unto my feet and a light unto my path. We know the Word of God will last forever and will never change. Blessed are they that hear the Word and obey. The Word will preserve your life. We have seen in Proverbs that if we will obey the Word that it will prolong our life. It will keep you from falling. Joshua 14:11, Joshua said, I am as strong today as I was in the day that Moses sent me out at the age of forty and now I am eighty five. He went through many wars and battles and was a great man of God. God kept him through it all and He will still do the same for you and me today for He never changes. Joshua had a made up mind to serve God for he said, for me and my house we will serve the Lord. There's power in the Word of God. If you want a good life here on this earth then you will have to serve the Lord just as Joshua did. You have to love the Lord with all of your heart, mind, soul and strength. Give Him your all, your entire body and life. Jesus is still asking today, whom do you serve? There's life in Him for He is the Word. A Christian's life is exciting, happy and rewarding. Yes, there will be problems, trials, sorrows and tests but God will be with you to see you through for He said He would. Don't just exist in this life but live for there's life in the Word and Jesus Christ is the Word.

A Christian's life is satisfying

Ps.17:15, As for me I will behold, I will see Your face in righteousness and I shall be satisfied when I awake with Your likeness. Ps.63:5, You satisfy me more than the richest of food and I will praise You with songs of joy. Ps.16:11, You will show me the way of life granting me the joy of Your presence and the pleasure of living with Your favor. The Word of God will show you the ways of a good life. The joy of the Lord is your strength. Ps.103:5, Bless the Lord oh my soul, who satisfies my soul with good things so that my youth is renewed like the eagle. The eagle never grows old and his feathers stay the same. Ps.1:3, You shall be like a tree planted by the river of water, your leaf shall not wither and whatever you do shall prosper. Ps.92:14, Even in old age you will bring forth fruit and are fat and flourishing. For God satisfies the longing soul and fills the hungry soul with goodness. If you are hungry for the Word of God, He will feed you and you will be made full. Isa.58:11, The Lord will guide you continually and satisfy your soul even in drought and make fat your bones and you shall be like a watered garden and a spring of water whose waters fail not. If you will do your part and serve Him, you can rest assured that He will do what He said. He will not fail you, never. John 6:35, Jesus said,

I am the bread of life. Whosoever comes to Me shall never hunger and whosoever comes to Me will never thirst.

A Christian's life is promising

Isa.41:17, Even the poor and needy are rich in the Lord. When they call upon the Lord He hears them and does not forsake them. There are a lot of Christians struggling to survive through these hard times. Their money is gone, their health is not good and everything seems to be down on them. But the Word of God tells us there is life in the Word. There is help for all who will follow Him and be obedient to Him. All of the promises in the Word of God are for those who follow Him. If you obey His commandments and serve Him with your whole heart, mind, soul and strength then the blessings belong to you. Luke 11:9, Jesus promised that if you would ask He would give to you, seek and you will find, knock and it will be opened to you. You have to seek Him first of all, and then come to Him. You have to trust Him with all of your heart for He has all of these promises for you. He wants you to have what you need to survive and not have to struggle. If you are struggling, ask yourself, why? Are you giving your tithe? He only asks for ten percent of your first fruits. You see, a Christian has to do something to be able to achieve the promises of God. A lot of Christians are missing out on a lot of blessings because they aren't following God's Word. He never promised that we would be rich but that He would meet our every need if we were faithful to Him. If you're not reaping the promises of God then you need to check yourself to see why. It's never God's fault for He will keep His promises forever.

A Christian's life is eternal

John 10:27-28, My sheep know My voice and I know them and they follow Me. I give them eternal life and they will never perish. No one can snatch them away from Me. Draw near to God and He will draw near to you. He will give eternal life to those who persist in doing good and righteous, seeking after what God has to offer. He offers eternal life, glory and honor and immortality for all those who live holy unto Him, to those who love Him and are faithful to Him. The gift of God is eternal life through Jesus Christ our Lord. Titus 1:2, God promised eternal life before the world began. Jude 21, Keep yourselves in the love of God, looking for the mercy of our Lord Jesus Christ unto eternal life. We have to endure to the end to be saved.

When God made Adam and eve He made them perfect and all creation was made perfect. It wasn't His will that it would be sin in the world that He had made. He made man and woman to live forever for He made them in His own image. Everything was beautiful and perfect. Because they sinned and things changed God made another way for it to be perfect again. He sent His only begotten Son, Jesus to be born of a Virgin Mary and walk this earth teaching and preaching the Word of God. Then He was crucified and died and was buried. But on the third day He arose and He walked on earth for a while then He ascended up into Heaven where He is sitting at the right hand of the Father. He's been interceding for His children for all of these years and is waiting for the Father to tell Him to go get His children. He has made Heaven for all of those who are following Him to live forever.

A Christian's life is rewarding

Gen.15:1, God came to Abram in a vision saying, Fear not for I am your shield and your exceeding great reward. Our greatest reward is when we get to Heaven to live with our Lord Jesus Christ forever. We can see the rewards for His children while here on this earth in the Beatitudes that Jesus taught on the mountain. You can read them in Matt.5:3-12. We are blessed while we are here on this earth if we abide in Him and in the Word of God. Great are the rewards here for God's people and then we can be excited for the rewards in Heaven to come. We have a short life here on earth but Heaven will be eternal. The earth will be cleansed and we will live on a new earth forever with no sin, pain, sickness, sorrow, death or hurts. What a reward to look forward to a new life living with the saints and far better, we will live with Jesus Christ our Savior.

God's power keeps the saints

Gen.28:15, God is our companion in this pilgrim walk. Behold I am with you and will keep you in all places wherever you go. I will not leave you or forsake says the Lord. God is a sleepless watchman for He never slumbers or sleeps. The Word of the Lord will stand forever. Blessed are they that hear the Word and obey. John 17:11, Jesus prayed, Now Father I am no longer in the world but these are in the world and I come to You Holy Father, keep them through Your name all of those that You have given Me that they may be one as We are one. Jesus knew how hard it was to live in this world among all of the evil. He had such a compassion for His children and still does. He is ever interceding for His children to the Heavenly Father. II Thessalonians 3:3, The Lord is faithful and who shall make you strong and keep you from the evil one, the devil. God is our Almighty Guardian.

God is our protector in many ways

Ex.14:14, He is the God of our battles. The Lord shall fight for you and you shall hold your peace. So many Christians try to fight their battles without the Lord and they fail. He said we can hold our peace while God fights our battles. How many people do you see that have peace in their battles? We need to put it all in is His hands and get out of His way and just have peace like He told us.

Ps.31:3, He is our Rock and our Fortress. He can lead you out of the perils of this life. What kind of problem are you having that's causing you so much heartaches and troubles? David said that you don't have to worry or struggle with these things. Jesus will lead you right out of these perils in your life if you will allow Him to. Let go and let God do it for you.

Ps.17:8, He is our hiding place. David said to the Lord, hide me in the shadow of your wings. When we are in Jesus no one can harm us for He hides you from this evil generation. He is a blessed hiding place. There's such peace and comfort in Him. His arms of love satisfy us and keep us warm as He hides us.

Prov.14:26, He's our Refuge. He is a place of refuge for His children and protector. He gives us grace and glory. No good thing will He withhold from us. We can go to Him for safety and security. He's our refuge from the storms of this life. He's our helper and shield. He's our strength and our shield. I am your God and I will strengthen you.

Isa.46:3-4, Even in old age He is still our God and He will carry you. He said, I made you and I will bear you, I will carry and deliver you. In the New Living Translation it says this. Listen to Me, I created you and I have cared for you since before you were born. I will be your God through out your lifetime until your hair is white with age. I made you and I will care for you. I will carry you along and save you. Verse 9, I am God and there is no one else like Me. For I am God and there is none other. There has never been a God before Him and there will never be another God.

The Word is God

John 1:1, In the beginning was the Word and the Word was with God and the Word was God. Verse 14 And the Word was made flesh and dwelt among us. This was Jesus Christ. Heb.4:12, The Word is sharper than a two edged sword, it's the living Word and it is active. For it penetrates deep dividing soul and spirit, joints and marrow. It judges the thoughts and attitudes of the heart. It cleanses us and leads us in all righteousness. It corrects us, it gives us peace and it encourages. There's healing in the Word, it comforts and gives us patience. It also puts love in our hearts, strengthens us and gives us life. We could go on and on for there's so much more that the Word of God does for us. The Word of God is truth and power. John 8:31-32, Jesus said, if you hold on to My teachings you are My disciples. You will know the truth and the truth will set you free. Do you want to be set free? Just hold on to Jesus and He will set you free. I Pet.1:22-23, You have been purified, cleansed by obeying the Word of God. You have been born again through the living and enduring Word of God. The Word of God stands forever. Rev.19:11-12, Jesus is called the faithful and truth and His name is, THE WORD OF GOD.

Why not choose to serve God now because one day everyone will have to confess that Jesus is Lord of all and God Almighty. It will be too late to benefit any of His promises and rewards. Why would anyone not want to serve Him now and have a rewarding life here and then eternal life with Him and all of the Heavenly rewards? It will be too late for many when they stand before Him at the judgment when He tells them, Sorry for I never knew you. It will be then that they will have to confess that Jesus is Lord. It would be better to live your life on this earth believing there is God and then find out in the end there wasn't a God than to live your life here believing there was no God and then in the end to find out there is a God. What a terrible thing for many in the end. Isa.45:23, I have sworn by My name and I will never go back on My Word. Every knee shall bow and every tongue shall confess that Jesus Christ is Lord. I am God of the universe and there is none other. Everyone shall confess that He is Lord of all and king of all. If you wait until the judgment it will be too late. There will be only one place for those to go and that's hell with the devil and all the unbelievers. Don't put it off if you have not made that decision to follow Jesus Christ. For today is the day of salvation. Call on Jesus and repent and turn to Him with all of your heart, mind, soul and strength and He will save you. Get in His Word, read and study. Be ready for He is coming back for His children. Remember, there is no second chance after death. You have to make your plans here while you are living. Turn to Him and live forever and live a life more abundantly here on earth.

God's Word makes life work

II Pet.1:2-4, Grace and peace be multiplied to you through the knowledge of God and Jesus Christ our Lord. According to His divine power has given unto us all things that pertain to life and godliness through the knowledge of Him that has called us to glory and virtue. Whereby are given unto us exceeding great and precious promises that by these you might be partakers of the divine nature, having escaped the corruption that is in the world through lust and evil desires. We can be partakers of the divine nature and escape the corruption that is in this world of lust. Believing in God and His promises and being obedient to Him can help us escape all of the lust of the world. We can close our eyes, ears and our entire being from all of the evil and lust of their life if we keep our minds on Jesus Christ who gave His life for us to cleanse us from all sin. Our life would be much better, happier and more fulfilling if we would just listen to God's Word and obey it. God's Word truly makes life work. His Words lifts us up above ourselves and helps to keep a holy nature like His. It takes us out of a dead and lifeless life like we used to live when we were without Him in our lives. Without Him you would only be existing and not really living. God's Word is a weapon we can use for our spiritual warfare to protect us. Epe.6:17, Take the helmet of salvation and the sword of the spirit which is the Word of God. But in order to use it we must first read and study it. Always think about His Word , speak it, praise and worship Him everyday and always. His Word tells us how much He loves us and wants to help us. Nothing touches our hearts and souls or changes our lives more deeply than true love and His is the truest love you can ever have or get. The Bible is really a love letter from God. The Word of God teaches us that whatever we give up for His sake He will replace it with something much better and worthy. This kind of insight is only recognized in the Spirit of God. Without the Word of God in our lives we can do things that can and will destroy us. Without the Word of God in our lives flesh tries to do things to satisfy and find fulfillment in life but material things don't last. Then we wonder why we are not happy and contented in our lives. Without the Word of God and the Holy Spirit in us we find ourselves clinging to something or someone that won't last or really helps us. Instead, it causes us to fall deeper in sins and the things of this sinful world. His Word is dependable and unfailing. It fulfills our lives in the right direction and feeds our emptiness and enriches our lives to the fullest and the unseen power of God will cause His Word to grow deeper in your soul.

When we accept the Word of God and live it we are purged from our sins. Verse 10, says, if we do the things of the Lord we will never fall. We must have faith, spiritual knowledge, temperance, patience, godliness, brotherly love, kindness and charity, which is love. Having these good qualities in you makes you fruitful spiritually and you have spiritual knowledge of our Lord Jesus Christ. Without these qualities of life and beliefs you are blind and cannot see the things of God and you will fall and you will be worldly and live in sin. When we have the knowledge of God, grace and peace will be given you. Verse 2 says this, they will be multiplied to us, grace and peace. When we need grace and peace they will be there for us from God. God has given us all things that pertain to living a good and holy life, a Christian life in Him, a life that is pleasing to Him and fulfilling unto us. God has called us to follow Him. We can have Spiritual abundance in Him. God has called us to follow Him. We can have Spiritual abundance in Him. God's Word makes life work bountifully, beautiful, worth living and then eternal life after this life is over.

Why wouldn't anyone want a life like this? David said, happy are they who don't listen to the evil people or do what they do. They love the teachings of the Word of God and they think about these teachings day and night. They are strong like a tree planted by the river and they produce much fruit in their season and their leaves don't wither or die. Everything they do will succeed and prosper. You see, God takes good care of His children, those who truly follow Him. David is saying here that when you stay in God's Word and follow Him then you will be happy. You will enjoy reading His Word and will want to continue to read and study His Word. You will be strong because the joy of the Lord is your strength. Your limbs won't wither and die and you will be fruitful spiritually. You will prosper in what you do. So many try to find happiness in drugs, alcohol, sex, gambling and other things of this world but this is not what David said. He represents a total view, one that will always work and cause happiness. True happiness is found in avoiding sin loving and obeying God. The blessed stay away from the lust of sin and are obedient to the Word of God. Ps.16:5-15, David said, The Lord is all I need for He takes care of me. My share in life has been pleasant and my part has been beautiful. I praise the Lord because He teaches and advises me. I feel His leading me. I keep the Lord before me always because He is close by my side and I will not be hurt. I rejoice and am glad even my body has hope. Even when I am dead and in the grave you will not leave me . Being with You fills me with joy and at

Your right hand I find pleasure forever. You see, God does take care of His children so we can always rejoice and be glad just as David did. God's Word and His love are wonderful and powerful. Ps.19:7-11, The teachings of the Lord are perfect and they give you new strength. The rules of the Lord can be trusted and they make you wise. The orders of the Lord are right and make people happy. The commandments of the Lord are pure for they light up the way. Respect of the Lord is good and it last forever. They are worth more than gold, the purest gold. They are sweeter than honey even the finest honey. Keeping these Words of the Lord brings great reward.

Psalm 23 sums it all up. The Lord Jesus Christ is our great Shepherd and He takes good care of His sheep and His Word shows us the way. The Lord is my shepherd and I have everything that I need. He lets me rest in green pastures and leads me to calm water. He gives me new strength and leads me on paths that are right for the good of His name. Even if I walk in dark places and go through the valleys I will not be afraid because He is with me. His rod and His staff they comfort me. He prepares a meal for me in the presence of my enemies. He pours oil on my head and fills my cup to overflowing. Surely goodness and mercy shall follow me all the days of my life and I will live in the house of the Lord forever.

Why not give yourself to Him? Why can't you love Him and be obedient to Him? After all that He has done for you that's the least one could do. He doesn't ask too much of you just to love, serve and follow Him. There is no other way to pure happiness and fulfillment except in Jesus Christ and in His Word. Pray and ask Him to show you the way and how to live. He will teach you and guide you in all truth. You will receive mercy and grace from above. The Lord is good and He points sinner in the right way if they will just call upon Him and repent and turn from their ways and sins and walk with Him. You can enjoy life at it's best as you follow Him. The Lord is good and His Word is sweet and powerful. There's life in the Word. The Bible says to study the Word for in it you think you have eternal life. Just to think it is not good enough for you have to know that you have eternal life. You can know for the Bible tells you so. I have talked to some about their salvation and they will tell me, I think I'm saved. If you don't feel secure and know, then you should check your life out and make sure. For you can have the assurance that you are saved if you are saved. Please don't just think but make sure.

CHAPTER TWO

Spiritual Composer

CHAPTER 2

Spiritual Composer

To compose something you prepare it, write it and construct it to put into proper respect, you form a mold. Jesus Christ is the composer of the Word of God, the Bible. He has told us everything that's going to happen from the beginning to the end. It will all have to happen just like He said before He comes back to get His church in the rapture. The church is the Christians who are following Him and are ready to go.

Matt.24:6-8, You shall hear of wars and rumors of wars, see that you do not be troubled for all these things must come to pass but the end is not yet. For all nations shall rise against nations and kingdoms against kingdoms and there shall be famines, pestilence and earthquakes in divers places. All of these are the beginning of sorrows. Jesus said, don't be troubled, don't worry or be afraid because these must come to pass before I come again. He is trying to encourage His children with these Words so we can prepare ourselves to be ready when He come back to take His children home to be with Him forever. Verses 11-12, Many false prophets will rise and shall deceive man. But they that endure to the end shall be saved. Don't give up or give in to the devil or the devil's crowd. You will hear some teaching that these things aren't going to happen but don't believe them. We who read and study the Bible know the truth. God has told us the truth in His Word and we need to make sure that we believe and stand on His Word.

Luke 24:38, Jesus asked the disciples, why are you troubled? And why do you let such thoughts come in your thoughts and heart? He was trying to comfort and encourage them and He's still doing the same thing today. He is not with us in person but we have His Word and that never changes. He lives in every heart of a Christian and is leading you and me. When Jesus went away to Heaven He sent the Holy Spirit to comfort, guide and protect us on our journey here on this earth in the life we now live. Don't be worried about the world's economy system or what's going on because we live in God's system. God's economy system is a sure thing. Don't be worried about all of the wars, earth quakes, and sorrows going on in this world because God has it all in control. Look up for your redemption draws near, for Jesus is coming soon. We should be excited when we hear of all of these things coming to pass because Jesus has told us these things will happen. He said that He would protect His children. He said that He would never leave or forsake His children. He said He's go with us all of the way through everything that we have to go through. He will make a way where there seem to be no way. John 14:1, Let not your heart be troubled, you believe in God believe also in Me

With the entire affliction that Paul went through this is what he said. We too should feel the same way as he did. He went through lots of sufferings and trials. Acts 20:24, None of these things move me neither do I count my life dear to myself so that I may finish my course with joy and the ministry that I have been called to do of the Lord. I'm to testify the gospel of Jesus Christ and the grace of God is what he is saying. We have to finish our race just as Paul and others did with joy, knowing we are in God's hands. If we should lose our lives in any of these things mentioned here that the Bible teaches that's going to happen, we will gain. The Word of God says, to die is gain. It's gain if you are in the Lord and serving Him with your whole heart, mind, soul and strength. Verse 28, Jesus purchased our lives with His own blood. We are not our own for we belong to Him.

II Thessalonians 2:2, Be not shaken in mind or be troubled, neither in the spirit or by word or by letter from us as the day of Christ is at hand. I Pet.3:14-15, If you suffer for righteousness sake, happy are you and do not be afraid of their terror neither be troubled. Our testimony and holy living should be like this. Sanctify the Lord in your hearts and be ready always to give an answer to everyone that asks you a reason for your hope that is in you, with meekness and fear, and love. Having a good conscience and good conversation in Christ. You can be sure that all that Jesus said is true and will come to pass. We don't have to fear or be afraid. The fear of the Lord is the beginning of wisdom. We don't have to fear for the Lord is with us. I John 4:18, Perfect love cast out all fear, the only one we should fear is God who can kill both body and soul in hell. If you are one of His you will have eternal life and you can have no fear but love through Jesus Christ. The devil can hinder but he cannot stop the will of God from being done by His faithful followers or servants.

Bible, the Book of love and judgments

John 3:16-18, For God so loved the world that He gave His only begotten Son that whoever believes in Him shall not perish but have everlasting life. For God sent not His Son into the world to condemn the world but that the world through Him might be saved. He that believes on Him is not condemned but he that believes not is condemned already. God didn't say everyone would be saved but only those who believe in Jesus Christ. Verses 3 and 4, Jesus said, Verily, verily I say unto you, except a person is born again they cannot see the Kingdom of Heaven. Also, I say unto you that except a person is born of the water and of the Spirit, they cannot enter into the Kingdom of Heaven. First, Jesus said that you cannot see the Kingdom of Heaven unless you are born again. Then He said, you cannot enter into the Kingdom of Heaven unless you are born of the water and the Spirit. You have to accept Him and then be baptized in water and in the Holy Spirit. Lots of Christians back off of the Baptism of the Holy Spirit because the Bible tells us that speaking in other tongues is one of the evidences of being baptized in the Holy Spirit. When you are born again God's Spirit comes into you and you have Jesus Christ living in you. Being baptized in the Holy Ghost or the Holy Spirit, which are both the same, gives you power to do the things that Jesus said His disciples can do. If you are one of His then you are a disciple in Christ. There's power in the Holy Ghost.

Jesus Christ gave His all when He gave His life at Calvary on the cross for you and me. He wants your all and not just part of you. Praise God He didn't stop here when He died. But He rose again on the third and was ascended into Heaven shortly after and is sitting at the right hand of the Father interceding for you and me. He's now waiting for the time when the Father will tell Him, Go get My children. He's preparing a place for His children right now. He didn't leave His children comfortless for He sent the Holy Spirit to guide us, protect and lead us through this life we now live. Without the Holy Spirit we cannot make it. There has never been such love as this. He loves you so much that He doesn't make anyone serve Him but they have a choice. You are free to serve whom ever you want. There are only two ways and that's God's way or the devil's way. Choose today whom you will serve is what Joshua said. He said, but for me and my house we will serve the Lord. There's Heaven or hell, saved or unsaved for there is no in between. There's no such thing as straddling the fence as we have heard this statement said. How could a person ever lose if they served Him? You have a good life here with the Holy Spirit leading and taking care of you and then when you die or go in the rapture when Jesus comes after you and then living eternally with Jesus. It's not God's will that any should perish but that all have everlasting life. But He won't save you unless you want and ask Him. All have the invitation to come to Him and repent and be saved. My husband, Leon and I have chosen to serve the Lord many years ago and it's been a great life together and with Jesus Christ leading and keeping us. There's joy in serving the Lord. There's peace and comfort in living for Him. Yes, we have had some problems and gone through trials and testing but He brought us through them all. Paul told us that if we followed Jesus we would have trials and tribulations all the days of our life but that Jesus would make a way of escape to make things better so we could bear whatever we went through. God has done this for He has made many ways when there seem to be no way.

He's been better to us than we have been to ourselves. He's our life and we could do nothing without Him and I wouldn't even want to try. I would not want to get up a day in my life without Jesus Christ being with me. I know that the only good thing in me is Him and I can do nothing without Him. The only thing that is going to last is what you do for Jesus Christ. All else is vain and will pass away. Jesus said, Trust, try and prove Me and see if I won't do what I said I'd do.

I Corinthians 13 is the love chapter of the Bible. Love is the greatest gift of all. In this chapter love is spoken of nine times. This chapter shows the mark of love. Without love you are only going through formalism. Verse 2 says there is nothing but vanity without love. Verse 3, without love all sacrifice of giving is insufficient. Verse 4, Love suffers long and is not envious or puffed up for love is humbling. Verse 8, love never fails and verse 13, love is enduring and spiritual. Love is preeminent for it comes before all else. Love is the highest rank and most important. Love is the greatest gift of all. Love is what took Jesus Christ to the cross. It's because of His love that we are what and where we are today. It was love that held Him to the cross. He could have come down for He had the power but He died for you and me. There is no greater love than for one to lay down their life for another, or for their brother or sister or a friend. We know the Bible is a book of love but it's also a Book of judgments. It's better to be judged now than to be judged later in the end and be cast into the lake of fire with the devil and all of the wicked and unsaved. God does chastise his children just as parents chastises and corrects their children. This is done so you and I are better Christians and are going the right way. The right way is to live righteous and holy unto the Lord.

The greatest commandment

Mark 12:29-31, Jesus said this, The first of all the commandments is this, Hear O Israel the Lord thy God is one Lord and you shall love Him with all your heart, mind, soul and strength for this is the first commandment. And the second is liken to it, Thou shall love your neighbor as yourself. There is none other commandments greater than these. Epe.5:12, Walk in love as Christ has loved us. Col.3:14, Above all things put on love which is the bond of perfection. I John 4:16, God is love and they that dwell in love dwells in God and God is in them. The commandment is that we should love one another as Christ has loved us. Rom.8:38-39, Nothing shall separate us from the love of God. We can separate ourselves and our love from Him by being unfaithful and disobedient and not keeping His commandments but not His love from us. Nothing can stop His love for us. He doesn't love our sins and our sins can separate us from Him and He will not hear us when we pray. He still loves the sinner but not their sins. His love will always be there for everyone for He made us in His image. He showed the love He had for all when He gave His only Son Jesus Christ to die on the cross for all.

Epe.6:24, Grace be with them all that love our Lord Jesus Christ in sincerity. If you love Him sincerely than you will follow Him and be faithful and obedient to Him. You will follow Him all the days of your life and won't be on and off but will love Him with all of your heart, mind, soul and strength. This is sincere love and it's eternal. Rom.5:8, God loved us so much that even when we were sinner Christ died for us. He did this because He is rich in mercy, love and grace and He still loves you. I John 3;1, Behold what love the Father has bestowed upon us that we shall be called the sons of God. Love should be without dissimulation, deceit or hypocrisy. We are to love one another with pure love. We love God because He first loved us and gave Himself for us. We are to keep ourselves in the love of God. Just because bad things may be happening to you doesn't mean that God doesn't love you. Remember, all things work together for good to them that love the Lord and are called according to His purpose. (Rom.8:28) God has told us in His Word what love will do. If you love the Lord then you will keep His commandments and you will be true to Him. For love covers a multitude of sin. Love will even cause you to love your enemies. Love cast out all fear and doubt. Love will hold us all together. Love gives us grace and mercy of God. God loves us with an everlasting love. We are to love Him with the same kind of love. When you love one another this is proof that you are My disciple. You may say I can't love that person because of what he or she has done to me but if you are a disciple of God you have to love them and forgive also.

I John 3:10, If you don't love your brother you're not of God. Who is our brother? Any Christian man, woman, boy or girl is our brother and sister. Who is our neighbor? Anyone who is in need and everyone is our neighbor. It's not just the ones that live beside us but we are to love everyone. God said to love your neighbor as you love yourself. We are to love our enemies and all those who persecute and say all manner of evil against us for His name sake. Before we came to Christ we were His enemies and He still loved us. So if He loved us then we are to love our enemies as well. I Thessalonians 3:12-13, And the Lord make you increase and abound in love one toward another and to all people as we do toward you. In the end He will establish your hearts without blame in holiness before God even our Father at the coming of our Lord Jesus Christ. We should increase in love as we go along this life and it should grow deeper in Him. There's no hate in love.

Let's look at some of God's judgments

Isa.1:8. I The Lord love judgments. In the very beginning God designed judgments and justice. Gen.18:19, For I know Him that He will command His children and His household after Him and they shall keep the way of the Lord to do judgment and justice. This still has not changed today. We have the same Book of guidelines, the Bible and it never changes. You shall do no unrighteousness in judgment. It's a dangerous thing for a judge to bring unrighteous judgments in a court of law. It's a dangerous thing for any person to bring unrighteous judgment on anyone. God is a just God and we are to be just also. He is not a fair God but He is just. Deut.1:17-18, The Lord says, don't be afraid of man's judgments for you bring it unto Me and I will hear it and tell you what to do. God is the rock and His work is perfect, for all His ways are judgment, a God of truth and without iniquity and sin, for He is just. Job 34:12, Yes, surely God will not do wickedly neither will the Almighty pervert or misapply judgment. Job 37:23, Touching the Almighty we cannot find Him out. He is excellent in power, in judgment and in plenty of justice. He will not afflict for He is a just God and full of mercy, love and grace. Ps.33:5, God loves righteousness and judgment, the earth is full of the goodness of the Lord. God is a good God and He reigns down blessings upon His people. Justice and judgment are the habitation of His throne. Mercy and truth shall go before your face. Blessed are they that keep judgment and they that does righteous at all times. Prov.21:3, To do justice and judgment are more acceptable to the Lord than sacrifice. Isa.56:1, The Lord said, Keep judgment and do justice for My salvation is near to come and My righteousness to be revealed. We are born again when we repent and accept Jesus Christ as our Lord and Savior. But it's those that endure to the end that will be saved. He is our salvation and He will be revealed soon. Are you looking for Him?

Day of Judgment for the wicked and unbelievers

Mal.2:17-18, You have worried the Lord with your words. You say that anyone who does evil is good in the sight of the Lord and He delights in them or you say where is the God of judgments? Mal.3:5, I will come near to you in judgment against all who do evil. I will judge everything. Even against those who oppress the widow, needy and the fatherless, even for turning away the stranger from their rights and all who don't fear Me, says the Lord of hosts. Are you hearing all of this? Are you helping the poor, widows and the children that are without parents? Are you turning away the foreigners from having freedom? We are not to turn anyone away for we are to love and help everyone. Are you depriving foreigners from their rightful judgments? Are you holding back honest wages from your employees? Rom.2:26, God sees everything you do and you will be judged accordingly. Remember, He is the righteous judge and He is just and not fair. No where in the Bible does it say that God is a fair God. God loves everyone equally for He has no respect of persons. Rom.2:1-2, Judgment is forbidden to us. Therefore you are inexcusable who judge another. For you condemn yourself when you judge another's sin. For what you judge another of, you are guilty of the same thing. We are to pray for them and try to help them, show them the right way. We are sure that the judgments of God are according to truth against them which commit such things. We all will be judged by God for everything we do and say. Rom.12:33, God's judgments and His ways are unreachable and you can't find them out. The secret things belong to the Lord. When we stand before the Lord at the judgment we will be judged for all we do whether good or bad. God sees everything and knows everything. You may hide things from people but not from God. James 2:13, Judgment without mercy will be shown to anyone who has not been merciful. This sound hard but God is trying to teach us to show mercy to everyone and then He will show mercy to us. Being unmerciful to others can affect our Christian walk with God. Don't be so self righteous that you think no one else is good enough. We all make mistakes and praise God for His mercy, love and His grace toward us. When others make a mistake don't condemn them but pray for them and encourage them not to do the wrong things but don't condemn them. For if you condemn them then you are condemning yourself. Matt.12:26, We're going to be judged for every idle word that we speak. So be careful little mouth what you speak.

I Pet.4:17, For the time has come that judgment must begin in the house of God and if it first begins in us what shall the end of them that obey not the gospel of God? The Bible teaches that they that know much will be judged more. Luke 12:48, Unto whoever much is given much is required and to whom much have been trusted much more will be asked. If God has trusted you with His gospel then you will be required to do more than someone who is just trying to make it. We are to be good witnesses and to be a great testimony of the Lord Jesus Christ. If we fail, what is going to happen to those who are weak in the Lord? The Bible teaches another truth. Let there be few of you masters or teachers, for greater will be your condemnation or heavier judgment of God. If you are teaching or preaching then you best live what you preach and teach for God is going to hold you accountable for not standing up to what you teach. Don't use the ministry and the gospel of the Lord for self gain. Many are doing just this and I'm not judging but we see it all of the time. They are making millions of dollars from the ministry. God forbid. It does take money to do things but God doesn't call anyone out where He can't keep them and provide everything that they need. He said that He would supply all of your needs according to His riches in glory. Many are helping and spreading the gospel to the world but they don't need all of the money that they are spending on themselves. The love of money is the root of all evil and many love and worship their money and what it can buy. Why not help the poor and others in need instead of putting it all on self? It's not wrong to have good things or to have the best as long as you are doing all that the Lord said we're to do. The Lord supplies all of our needs so we should supply the needs of others as well. God is going to hold us accountable on how we spend our money and our time. God's judgment has already started in the house of the Lord. This doesn't mean the church or building you assemble in alone, but in your body which is the temple of the Lord if you're His child. We are to keep our temples holy unto God for it is our reasonable service unto the Lord. Ps.58:11, God has rewards for the righteous but He is a God of judgments also. II Pet.2:9, The Lord knows how to deliver the godly out of temptation and to reserve the unjust unto the day of judgment to be punished. The Lord is coming to execute judgment upon all ungodly and their ungodly deeds that they have committed and all their ungodly works they have spoken against Him.

Rev.20:11-15, Tells us about, The Great White Throne Judgment of Jesus Christ. All of the rest of the dead was raised from the graves and all were judged according to what they have done while living here on earth. Anyone's names not found in the Lamb's book of life was thrown into the lake of fire. This is the second death. Ps.9:16, The wicked is snared by the works of their own hands. Everyone chooses the way they go and what they do in this life here on earth. It's up to each individual what their end is going to be, Heaven or hell. People say if God was a loving God that He would not send anyone to hell. Well, He doesn't, they choose for themselves where they are going in the end. If you choose God's way then He has a place for you in Heaven and He will also carry you through this life and make a way for you in all situations. If you reject God then you have chosen the devil's way and you will end up where he will be and that's in hell. The only way to Heaven is through Jesus Christ. This is a short life here but Heaven will be forever. Don't you want to go there? You can escape the great white throne judgment if you will accept Jesus in your heart and live for Him. It's better to go to the judgment seat of Christ and receive rewards than to have to face Jesus Christ at the white throne judgment where He will have to say to you, Sorry for I never knew you, depart from me you workers of iniquity into everlasting damnation.

Matt.23:23, We will be judged for sins of omission as well as sins of commission. There are many things that we should be doing for Christ and in His work that we're leaving undone. We have lack of mercy, love and concern for others. Jesus went about doing good all of the time. We get caught up in our own little comfort zones at times and neglect our Christian duties. Ec.11:9, God will bring judgment upon everything you do, good or bad. 12; 14, God will bring every deed into judgment including every hidden thing whether good or bad. The Lord is a God of justice, blessed are those who wait for Him. Isaiah said, My reward is with my God, where is yours? We need to get busy in the things of God for time is running out here in this age. Time will be going on forever but we only have a little time to do what we're going to do for Christ. Pray and seek God to see what He wants you to do for His Kingdom. Don't ever turn back but keep going forward in Him.

If you don't know Jesus Christ as your Savior you need to accept Him today, right now for today is the day of salvation for tomorrow may be too late. Never put off until tomorrow what you can do today. He's standing at your heart's door waiting for you to invite Him in. He will not force His way in, for you have to open the door. Don't let this opportunity pass you by because you don't know whether you will ever have another one. He's coming soon so be ready and prepared. Amen

CHAPTER THREE

We Have The Victory In Jesus Christ

CHAPTER 3

We have the Victory in Jesus Christ

Rom.4:17, As it is written, I have made you a father of many nations before him, this is Abraham that Paul's talking about. The God who gives life to the dead and calls those things that are not as though they were. God called Abraham to be a father of many nations. God called things as though they were and Abraham believed Him. He had confidence in whatever God said. He had faith in God and didn't doubt for he had spiritual hope and he knew in whom he believed. He didn't ask Him any questions. Verse 21, And being fully persuaded that what God had promised that He was able to perform it. That's how we should be about whatever God tells us. So many times we question God, why, how or when. We need to be like Abraham, have faith in God in everything. Verses 23-25, All of this wasn't just promised to Abraham but to his seed. It is for us today also, all who believe on Him. Jesus Christ was raised from the dead for our offenses and was raised for our justification. He died for our sins and to give us eternal life if we would believe in Him and follow Him. Rom.5; 1, Therefore being justified by faith we have peace with God through our Lord Jesus Christ. When God told Abraham that he was going to be a father of many nations he believed Him because he knew only God could raise the dead and call things into existence. He made something out of nothing when He created the world. Abraham didn't live on the basic of what he saw but what God said He would do.

He didn't doubt God when He told him that he and Sarah were going to have a child in their old age. He knew that if God said it that it was going to happen. That's the kind of faith we need. A believer's walk has to be a walk of faith. Without faith you cannot please God. The just shall walk by faith. Rom.4:17, It is God that calls things as though they were. He called the world into existence in the very beginning of the creation. All He has to do is speak the Word. Epe.1:19-20, By the Word of His power, God can call into being or existence anything at anytime. He gave Jesus Christ this power when He raised Him up from the grave and seated Him at His right hand in the Heavenly realm. Right hand means power. No where do I find that He gave us that power to call things that are not as though they were. As I have said, God gave His children power and gifts to do other things but this one thing is the sovereignty of God Almighty and His absolute power and dominion.

Rom.8:24-25 and 28, For we are saved by hope but hope that is seen is not hope for what a person sees why do they hope for? But if we hope for that we cannot see then do we wait for it with patience? God works out all of the details in our life and all we have to do is wait with patience. He does all of the work and most of the time we Christians don't even have the patience to wait on Him. All things work together for good to them that love the Lord and are called according to His purpose. His divine purpose will never fail. Verse 37, We are more than conquerors through Him that loves us. We have the Spiritual victory in Jesus Christ. We have that blessed assurance in Him who died and rose again. We need to stop trying to call things into existence and let God do it. No where can I find that God told us to call things that are not as though they were. If we could do this we would never have to go through anything unless we wanted to. There would be no sick or hurting people. We need to stop playing God and be obedient children to Him, our Father and God. Yes, we are to look for a better future and always hope for good things but only God has the power to call things that are not as though they were. Men and women have formed their opinions but we need to stick with the Word of God. God has given His children that are baptized in the Holy Ghost, power to do a lot of things but I can't see this one, which we can call things into existence that are not. We pray and ask God and have faith like Abraham did in Him and things will come to pass that we ask for. It is God that calls things that are not, into existence. He called everything into existence in the beginning, for He created all things that were created in the beginning of the world. Gen.1:3 and II Cor.4:6, The justified and salvation of sinners, the calling of the Gentiles, that had not been a people were graciously called of things, which are not as though they were, giving being to things that were not. God made the Gentiles to be something out of nothing when He grafted them into the fellowship of Jesus Christ. This expresses the sovereignty of God and His absolute power and dominion, a mighty stay in faith when all other props sink and totter or fall. It is the faith of the all sufficiency of God for the accomplishment of that which is impossible to anything but that all sufficient sovereignty of God Almighty the Father. He made light to come out of darkness, He made the light to shine in our hearts to give us the light of knowledge of the glory of God in the face of Christ. We make too many mistakes but He never makes a mistake. He knows what we need and why we need it and the right time to give it to us. Christians many times miss God's calls and mess up what His plans are for them. We need to keep a firmer listening ear and heart to His instructions. If God says it, believe it, stand on it for it will come to pass. Our victory is in Jesus Christ the Son of God. So claim your victory in Jesus name.

Get out of your rut and claim the victory

Deut.1:6, The Lord our God spoke to us in Horeb saying. You have dwelt long enough in this mount. You have been in this rut long enough. Get up and get out and claim the victory over all of your problems. Stop your worrying and start trusting Me and lean on Me. You can have all of the blessings that I have promised you. You will always have some kind of problems but look to the Lord for your help. He is a very present help in time of troubles. Verse 8, God told them to go in and possess the land which He had promised Abraham, Jacob, Isaac and their seed and has given His children earthly inheritance. The devil loves to keep God's children in a rut so they can be miserable, down and out, discouraged, sad and worried.

God wants His children to be happy and enjoy this life in Him. Even when we go through troubles and trials we can still have the joy of the Lord. The joy of the Lord is our strength. We may not always be happy but we can still have joy. Ps.37:21-22, The righteous shows mercy and gives and they will be blessed and inherit the earth. You don't have to be in a rut, get up and get out. Verses 23-24, The steps of a good person are ordered by God and he delights in His ways. Even though they may fall the Lord picks them back up. They are not utterly cast down because the Lord upholds them with His hand. God is our divine support at all times and in all things that are of Him. Acts 20:32, Look to God and to His Word for His grace is able to build you up and give you an inheritance. He knows what you need even before you ask and He has it ready for you. He's concerned about everything that concerns you. Acts 26:13, He will open your eyes and turn you from darkness to light and from the power of the devil.

In order for you to get out of your rut you have to be dissatisfied with the ways things are and want them to change. There are several things that can keep us in a rut and cause us to be down and out, discouraged and feeling hopeless. You can't get the victory as long as you dwell on the problems and not the problem solver, Jesus Christ. Prayer may no longer be a vital part of your Christian walk. Prayer is the key to Heaven but faith unlocks the door. In order to get to Jesus you have to talk to Him through prayer. You need to talk to Him often when you need something and when you don't need anything. He wants us to talk to Him, praise and worship Him continually. Praise and worship brings about many miracles from God. You may be in a rut because you have Bible knowledge but don't apply it to your life. Some people know about Jesus but they don't really know Him and have a personal relationship with Him. We have to be a doer of the Word and not just hearers only. If you're not trusting God and leaning on Him and you're leaning on your own understanding then you will put yourself in a rut. If going to church has become a chore or a duty and you don't delight in it anymore then you may be in a rut. If entertainment has become a large and important part of your life, more than going to church to worship God then you are probably in a rut. You allow anything or anyone to come before God and your time with Him whether at home or in the church it will put you in a rut sooner or later. If you indulge in sin and not be convicted or feel it is wrong, then that's the worse rut you can be in for sin separates you from God. God said that He would turn His face from you and will not hear you if you are living in sin. If you love the things of the world more than you love God then you are in a back sliding position and in a deep rut. If material things are more important than Spiritual things then you are surely in a rut. If living a holy and righteous life is not your greatest desire then you're in trouble and it will bring you to a deep rut. If you have lost your joy in living a Christian life and you are adjusting to the world's way of living and doing things that make you feel good then you are headed for a deep, deep rut. If your greatest desire is not to serve the Lord and your tears has dried up for lost souls and your worship to God is gone, you're on a down hill slide to a very deep rut that may cause you to lose your soul. If it doesn't bother you that your entire family is not saved and is serving the Lord and they are dying and going to hell then something is badly wrong with your life in the Lord. You are in a bad situation and you are headed down hill and will fall into a deep pit and rut. You need to make your way back to Jesus Christ to get up out of your rut. Verse 6, The Lord told them that they had been in the rut long enough. He said, You have been in this mount or place too long so get up and get out and claim your victory. Be anxious and deliberate in changing your direction toward the Lord and get out of your rut or the place that you are in. Verse 7, Turn and take your journey. Take the journey that I have shown you and follow Me.

In order to get out of the rut and get the victory you have to change things in your life. You have to put Jesus first in you heart and life. He won't be second place, for you're either for Him or against Him. There is no in between or living on the fence so to speak. Stop making excuses and reasons that keep you from Spiritual things and living. Don be content in the way you are living and the things you are doing. Get in God's Word and study more and talk to him. Have a close relationship with Him. Make sure that you sin not because God doesn't put His permission on any sin no matter what you think or the reason you may be using to sin. Verse 8, behold I have set the land before you, go in and possess it. God has made many promises to His children and made the way and all we have to do is claim them. He gives but it's up to you to accept what He gives. You need to be determined to accept and obtain the best from God. So, what is keeping you in a rut? Give it up and give it to God and go His way.

You will find in God's Word how to live His way. You will find His direction for your life. You can have all of the promises and gifts that He has promised all who will follow Him and do His will. So there's no need for anyone to be in a rut that is following Him. When we are weak then we are strong in Him for He is our strength. David said the joy of the Lord is my strength. We are weak without Him and you will never get out of your rut without Him. Check your life and heart and see what's falling apart. **IF YOUR BIBLE IS FALLING OR TEARING APART THEN YOU'RE NOT.**

Salvation through Jesus Christ

II Tim. God has saved us and called us with a holy calling not according to our work but according to His own purpose and grace which was given us in Christ Jesus before the world began. This was manifested by the appearing of Jesus Christ our Savior who has abolished death and brought life and immorality to light through the gospel. We can see that it is nothing that we can do to be saved except through Jesus Christ. It is by His love, mercy and grace that we are saved. We can't work for it neither can we buy it. Once we have accepted Him in our heart and life then we have to be a different person for He has washed us from all of our sins and now we are a new creature or person in Him. We have to make a complete turn around to be like Him. You can't be of the world and in Him at the same time. If you are of the world then you are none of His. The old person is dead and now you have a new life in Him. Some people are so blind that they think just because they believe in Jesus Christ that they're ok now. Believing only is not enough for you have to be a doer as well as a hearer. The devil believes and trembles. Faith without works is dead. You can't have faith without works. Don't be blinded by the devil in thinking that you can do what you want to after you are saved just because you believe.

Matt.7:22-23, Many will say to Me in that day. Lord, Lord have we not prophesied in Your name? Have we not cast out devil in Your name, and in Your name done many wonderful works? Jesus will have to confess to them, I never knew you, depart from Me you workers of iniquity. Does Jesus know you today? Are you really one of His? This will be a terrible thing to think that you are one of His and you are even doing His work but you really don't know Him and then He will have to say to you, Sorry I never knew you. You can do His work and still be lost. That's the Word of God not mine. Epe.2:8-9, By grace are you saved through faith and that not of yourself it is the gift of God. Not of works lest anyone should boast. Your works will and cannot save anyone. Titus 3:4-5, After that the kindness and love of God our Savior toward men appeared. Not of works of righteousness which we have done but according to His mercy He saved us by the washing of regeneration and renewing of the Holy Ghost.

How we have to change

Ps.34:14, Depart from evil and do good, seek peace and pursue it. Trust in the Lord and do good so shall you dwell in the land and surely you will be fed. Heb.13:16, But to do good and communicate, and forget not, for with such sacrifice God is well pleased. Never forget the things that God has done for you. We have to communicate with others about what He has done and what He is doing for God is please with us when we do these things. James 4:17, Therefore to them that know to do good and doesn't do it to them it is sin. If you know you are to be doing something good for someone in the Lord and don't do it, James is saying that you have sinned. That's what you call sins of omission. Col.3:2, Set your affections on things above and not on things on earth. Luke 21:34, Take heed to yourselves unless at anytime your heart be over taken with carelessness, drunkenness and cares of this life and that day come upon you unawares. We need to stay sober and alert for we don't know when the Lord is coming back and we have to stay ready at all times. Titus 2:12, Teaching us that denying ungodliness and worldly lusts we should live soberly, righteous and godly in this present world. Paul said in Rom.12:2, Be not conformed to this world but be ye transformed by the renewing of your mind that you may prove what is good , acceptable and perfect will of God. We cannot live as the world does and please God for we have to be different. I John 2:15, Love not the world nor the things in the world. If anyone loves the world the love of the Father is not in them. So you see, you have to be different from the world if you are a child of God. Epe.5:11, Have no fellowship with the unfruitful works of darkness but rather reprove and correct them. David said, depart from me all ye workers of iniquity for I will keep the commandments of the Lord. If you let the sinners and evil ones know where you stand they will stay away from you. That's why you lose your old friends when you get saved because they don't have anything in common with you anymore. But you will gain new friends in Christ Jesus. I Cor.6;17, Come out from among them and be a separated people said the Lord and touch not the unclean thing and I will receive you. We are not to be socializing with the unsaved and workers of iniquity, the sinners. We are to live a life that they can see pleases God and we have to love them. This is the Lord's Words and He knows what's best for His children. There's too much temptations when you mingle with the unsaved. We are to love them but not to associate with them. II Thessalonians 3:6, Now we command you brothers and sisters in the name of the Lord Jesus Christ that you withdraw yourselves from every brother or sister that walks disorderly and not after the tradition which they received of us. Paul is saying that He was a good example as well as Jesus Christ to show us the right way and we are to follow them. When you are doing something, saying something or going some place ask yourselves, would Jesus do, say or go to these places? If the answer is no, then you should follow the same example. We are to follow Him in everything and always. Isa.52:11, Depart and go out from among them and touch no unclean thing. Go out from anything that's evil all of you that bear the vessel of the Lord. Your body is the temple and the vessel of the Lord if you are truly one of His children and are serving Him. Jesus Christ will not live in a dirty temple. You are to keep it holy and righteous in Him at all times. The devil and the Lord will not live in the same temple together. One or the other in living in your heart and temple. Save yourselves from this evil and forward generation. Col.2:20, Since you died with Christ and with the basic principles why do you act as though you belong to the world and submit to its rules? Why do you still do the things of the world and all of its evil if you are a true Christian? If you are still doing the same things as the world is doing, what makes you any different? What's makes you any different than you were before you accepted Jesus Christ in your life? THINK ABOUT IT. Verse 21 says, Do not handle, do not taste and do not touch. Verse 22, Anything that you can handle, taste or touch are all going to perish with use because they are based on human commands and wants. Anything that is not of God and His commandments are going to perish and anyone who deals with things ungodly will perish with them. This may sound hard but it's the true Words of God. Only the things of God and what we do for Him will last. You need to choose whom you're going to serve and love. Joshua said, as far as me and my house we will serve the Lord and we need to be like him. He told the people to choose this day whom you will serve. You may not have another day so you need to do it today. My husband Leon and I have made this choice many years ago whom we were going to serve and we are still serving Him and always will. We're not going to turn back now this is our life for there's no life outside of Jesus Christ. There's life in God's Word and it's a happy and prosperous one. We do go through some bad times as well as good times but we still have the joy of the Lord.

Final separation by Jesus Christ

Matt.13:30, Jesus is going to separate the righteous from the wicked and unrighteous. The tares are the evil ones and they will be bundled up and burned but the wheat which are the true Christians will be saved. They will both grow up together but Jesus will separate them at the judgment. Matt.13:49, At the end of the world as we know it, the angels will come and sever, cut the evil and wicked from among the just, which are the children of God who are born again and have been living for Jesus Christ and serving Him. We know that the world will not end for it will continue on but all things will be different. There will be no more sin, sorrow, trouble, pain or death.

Rules for holy living

Col.3:1-10, Since you have become a child of God you should set your hearts on things above. Set your minds on things above and not on earthly things and cares of the world. For if you are truly a child of God your life will be hidden with Christ Jesus in God. Do away with whatever belongs to your earth by nature like, sexual immorality, impurities, lusts, evil desires and greed. God's wrath is coming down on all of these things. You once walked in these ways before you accepted Christ in your life but now you have confessed Jesus as your Savior so now you are a child of God and you must not have any sin in your heart and life. Things like anger, rage, malice, slander, filthy language from your lips and lying to one another. When you come to Christ you have to do away with your old self and become a new person in Him. You are to be renewed everyday in Him and in the knowledge of Jesus Christ for you are made in His image and you are to be like Him. Verses 12-17 tells us of the Christian's graces. We are to be clothed with compassion, kindness, humility, gentleness and patience. Bear one another's burdens and forgives just as the Lord has forgiven you. Most of all we have to love because love binds us all together in Him. Let the peace of God rule in your hearts. All Christians belong in one body and are called to peace. Be thankful in all things. Let the Word of God dwell in you richly as you teach and admonish one another with all wisdom. Whatever you do whether in deed or word do it all in the name of the Lord Jesus Christ, giving thanks to God the Father through Jesus Christ. Verse 23, Whatever you do, work at it with all of your heart as working for the Lord and not for man. It is the Lord that you are serving and not man or people. Col.4:2, Devote yourself in prayer always. Have a close relationship with the Lord and walk with Him daily. Verse 5-6, Be wise in the way you act toward outsiders and make the most out of every opportunity. Let your communications be always full of grace. Do whatever you can to see the lost saved. Let everyone see Jesus in you no matter what the situation that you may be in. Let them see the joy of the Lord in you and the love of Jesus in you.

Separation from the worldly people or hypocrites

I Cor.5:11, Do not keep company with any man that is called a brother and is a fornicator, covetous, hypocrite, slanderer, drunkard or a swindler. With such a one do not eat with. These are called hypocrites because they confess one thing but do another. God says to stay away from these kinds of people. II Cor.6:14, Be not unequally yoked together with unbelievers for what communion has righteousness with unrighteousness? What communion has light with darkness? There is no darkness in light for Jesus is the light. Ps.1:1, Blessed is the man that walks not in the counsel of the ungodly nor stands in the way of sinners nor sits in the seat of the scornful. You have to take your stand for what's right no matter what your position may be. When you sit around a table with important people making decisions you have to always remember to be just and righteous for God is going to hold you accountable. Your decision may not win among the people but you are a winner in Jesus Christ. I Cor.15:33, Be not deceived, evil company corrupt good morals. I tried to teach my children this when they were young. Bad company can cause you to be tempted to do the wrong things and make the wrong choices. Many times good morals fall into this trap. This doesn't mean that you don't love them but you can't keep company with them or associate with sinful people if you are a child of God. You have nothing in common with them. God loves everyone but He hates their sins. We are to pray for them that they will turn to God just as we have and change their lives. We are known by the company we keep. How can you have fellowship with someone that you have nothing in common with? Either you are being deceived or you're making a fool out of yourself. You can't serve God and the devil too. You have to choose right or wrong. Ask yourself, would Jesus say, do or be where I am? If the answer is no then you best heed to His Words and do His will.

False profession

Luke 6:46, Why call Me Lord, Lord and do not the things I say? They profess that they know God but in works they deny Him being abominable or hateful, disobedient and unto every good works reprobates or worthless by the way they live, they deny Christ. Just because you confess with your mouth that you love Christ doesn't mean that you are one of His. Your works has to show it as well. Faith without works is dead. Titus 2:12, We are instructed to turn from evil and godless living and from sinful pleasure in this evil and live in this evil world with self control, right conduct and devotion to God. We don't have to live as the world lives and do what they do for we are different because we have Christ living in us. Maybe if the world saw more of God in us then it would make a great impact and more would be saved. It's a sad thing to say, but so many who are called by the name of the Lord are living like the world and people don't see any need to believe and live for God for they see no change or difference in the ones who call themselves Christians Be careful of your testimony for someone in watching. James 3:10, Out of the mouth precede blessings and curses, my brother this should not be so. II Tim.3:5, You have a form of godliness but deny the power thereof from such turn away. Matt.7:21, Not all that call Me Lord, Lord shall enter into the Kingdom of Heaven but only them that do the will of My Father which is in Heaven. People may think that they are doing right but God examines the heart. He judges you from your heart and He knows all about you whether you are just confessing false professions or are true to Him. You can't fool Him for He knows everything. You can confess that you are rich in this world's good but if you don't have these riches it's a false profession and it will never do you any good. The same way with your profession in Christ. Just talk will never pay off and you will not gain eternal life.

Warning about drifting away from God

Heb.2:1-4, Listen carefully to the message of truth or you may drift from it. The message of God has always proven true and the people as well as the angels were punished for every violation of the law and every act of disobedience. What makes you think that you can escape if you neglect this great salvation of God that the Lord has spoken about from the beginning and have been confirmed to us by them that has heard Him? The angels were kicked out of Heaven, one third of them for not being obedient to God. Man has been made a little lower than the angels so who do we think we are if we're not faithful to Him in all things? If we confess that we know Him then we should live for Him and act like it. Our actions shall be proof that we love Him and want to do His will. Actions speak louder than words.

Warning to us about getting to Heaven

Heb.4:1, God's promise of entering His place of rest still stands today as it did for the Israelites. You should tremble with fear that some of you may not make it to Heaven. Anyone who fails to obey the Lord as the Israelites did will fall. The Word of God is full of living power. Verse 12, It is sharper than a two edged sword or the sharpest knife, cutting deep into our most inner being, thoughts and desires. It exposes us for what we really are. Nothing can be hid from God. Everything is exposed right before His eyes always. What can we do to stay in Him or when we fall away? Verse 16, Come boldly to the throne of our gracious God. There we will find mercy and we will find grace to help us when we need it. We always need His love, mercy and His grace for we could never make it without any of these. We always need His forgiveness for our sins and our weaknesses. We could never make it through this life without Him and His help. He is our strength, salvation, healer, keeper and a very present help in time of trouble. We don't have the power on our own to survive. In order to enter into the Kingdom of Heaven we have to strive to be like Jesus all of the time. We are to live holy and righteous without sin.

We should grow spiritually

Heb.5:11-14, There's so much more that we'd like to teach you but you don't seem to listen so it's hard to make you understand. You have been a Christian a long time now and you should be teaching others. Instead, you need someone to teach you again the basic things a beginner must learn about the scriptures. You are like babies who drink only milk only and cannot eat solid food. A person living on milk can't get very far along in the Christian life and doesn't know much about doing what's right. Solid food is for those who are mature and have trained themselves to recognize the difference between right and wrong and then do what's right. Are you in this category? Are you still on the milk of the Word? Then you need to grow so the Lord can teach you more about what He expects of you and show you how to live for Him. Stop having to go over the basics of Christianity and become mature in your understanding. I am surprised how little so many Christians know about the Word of God. They seem to be satisfied with just being saved and are not concerned about anything else. We all have a work to do and we need to have wisdom and understanding of the Word of God to do His Work. How can you grow spiritually unless you are learning more about Him? We learn by reading and studying the Word of God. Heb.8:12, God said, I will forgive their wrong doings and I will never again remember their sins again. We must strive to be like Jesus for He was perfect. We're not perfect but we are to strive to be. We have to work on it. When we do sin we can go to Him and ask forgiveness and He will forgive and forget. He doesn't expect you to go and do the same sin again. Don't sin willfully for you will be like the Israelites. Verse 9, The Israelites did not remain faithful and obedient to My commandments and My covenant or laws so I turned My back on them says the Lord God. There are times when we may sin through ignorance but when we pray and ask God to search our hearts, He will tell us and if we ask forgiveness He will forgive because of His love, grace and mercy. We should always pray and ask God if there's anything in our heart or life that's not pleasing to Him or if there's any sin that we aren't aware of. He will show it to you and then you ask for forgiveness and He will forgive. We are still living in this fleshly body so we have to be careful not to sin. We can live above sin when we stay in God's Words and have a close relationship with Him. Draw near to God and He will draw near to you, resist the devil and he will flee from you. The more you love God the more you will serve Him.

We need to persevere, hold fast to our profession to Jesus Christ

Heb.10:19, We can boldly enter Heaven's most holy place because of the blood of Jesus Christ who died for us at Calvary. He rose again and He lives and is coming back for His bride, the church. All who are living for Him and are watching and waiting for Him. We can go right into the presence of God with true hearts fully trusting Him. Never waver or doubt what God can do for you. He will do what He said. Verses 25-26, Do not neglect the assembling of yourselves together as some people do. We are to encourage one another and warn others, especially now that the day of His coming back is drawing near. This is important to every Christians. Verses 30-31, God said, I will take vengeance, I will repay them that deserve it, the Lord will judge His people. It is a terrible thing to fall into the hands of the living God. If we sin deliberately and willfully after we have received the knowledge of the truth there is no sacrifice that will cover these sins. Jesus died once and for all and we have to live by His ways and commandments. Don't throw away your confidence and trust in God no matter what happens. Remember the great reward that it brings you. There are blessings that come out of sorrows and distresses. We will all go through many trials and tribulations in this life but Jesus is with us so hang in there and don't ever give up or give into the evil of this world. We have need of patience to keep enduring so then we will receive the promises of God. For just in a little while He is coming and will not delay. Praise the Lord. The just, who is the righteous person, shall live by faith. God says He has no pleasure in anyone who turns away. You can't live on yesterday's salvation for today is a new day. You are to renew your mind, heart and life everyday. We have to endure to the end in Jesus Christ to be saved. If you should fall away then you will not make it into the Kingdom of Heaven. We have to die daily to self and live for Him. Do we make mistakes, yes, but He is faithful to forgive us and lead us in the right way.

We must have faith to persevere

Heb.11:1, Faith is the confident assurance that what we hope for is going to happen. It is the evidence of things not seen. Having faith doesn't exempt us from having problems, pain or sorrows, but it will give us strength to fight our battles. Without faith you cannot please God. The just shall live by faith. Faith in God will carry us through whatever we have to go through in this life. Faith that He will keep

His promises to us if we stay true to Him. God has done everything to show us the right way to live holy, righteous and acceptable unto Him. Heb.12:1-3, Let us strip off every weight or sin that so easily besets us or hinders our progress in serving the Lord. Let us run the race with endurance, the race that God has set before us. We do this by keeping our eyes on Jesus whom our faith depends on from start to finish. Don't become weary and give up. The Lord loves them who He disciplines and He punishes those who He accepts as His children. Just as parents discipline and punishes their children so does God His children. His discipline is always right and good for us because it means we will share in His holiness. Verses 12-13, Take a new grip with your hands and stand firm on your shaky legs. Mark out a straight path for your feet. Try to live in peace with everyone and seek to live a clean and holy life, for without holiness you won't see God. Look after each other so none will miss out on the special favors of the things God has for all who will serve Him and obey Him. The Bible teaches us to correct and abase. There are times when we should lift others up and then there are times that we should correct them. See to it that you obey God in everything. Verses 27-19, Only the things done on this earth for God will last. Let's be thankful and please God by worshipping Him with holy fear and awe. For God is a consuming fire. The Kingdom we're receiving cannot be destroyed. Continue to love each other with true Christian love. Show hospitality to strangers because they may be angels. Don't forget those in prisons, suffer with them as though you were there or it was you. Share with those who are mistreated and cast down. Give honor to marriage and stay faithful. Stay away from the love of money. Remember those who first taught you the Word of God. Verses 15-17, With Jesus help let us continue to offer sacrifice of praise to God. Do good and share with those in need. This is all pleasing to God. Obey your spiritual leaders and do what they say. Their work is to watch over your soul and they know they are accountable to God. Give them reason to do this joyfully and not with sorrow. This is not just your preachers but any spiritual leader of God. It could be your mother, your earthly father or anyone who is called of God to minister to you. If they are called then they have a work to do and God will hold them accountable. If they fail to tell you the truth and you are lost then your blood will be required on their hands by God. If they warn you and you are not obedient then they will not be accountable if you are lost. They can just shake off the dust on their feet and move on. Study the word of God so you will know the truth when someone confronts you. The truth shall set you free. Pray and seek God for the truth. Jesus is the Great Shepherd of the sheep, an everlasting covenant signed with His blood. To Him be glory and honor forever. Amen

Salvation belongs to the Lord, blessings belong to His people

Ps.3:8, Salvation belongs to the Lord. Thy blessings are upon Thy people. From the Lord comes deliverance but His blessings are upon His children. His children are all who believe on Him, accept Him and do His will. Only God has the power to shield us and keep our salvation eternally safe, for He watches over His children always. The only way we can be saved is through Jesus Christ. Ps.27:1, The Lord is my salvation and my light, whom shall I fear? The Lord is the strength of my life, whom shall I fear? We don't have to fear or be afraid of anyone else or anything because God has promised to keep us safe in His care always as long as we serve Him. He is our salvation, shield and stronghold. Our protector, guide and our Lord and Savior. He is a very presence help in time of trouble, for He's always with us. You have seen that I use this scripture lots in my book for I lean on it. He is my help and my strength in times of troubles. Ps.37:39, The salvation of the righteous is of the Lord. He is their strength in time of trouble and you can lean on that as I do. We are to trust Him in everything at all times. Don't ever try to do things on your own without consulting Him first. He knows the right way to lead you for He never makes a mistake and He's always on time. We mess up many times when we try to do it our way and not wait on the Lord. I have had to reap a lot of bad seeds that I have sown because I didn't wait on the Lord or consult Him first. We are going to reap what we sow whether good or bad. Reaping can be a hard lesson not only for you but for others as well. Our mistakes don't just affect us but others too. Our children have to suffer lots of times because of the bad seeds that we as parents have sown. If we want them to be blessed of the Lord then we need to lead them in the right direction. To lead them right, we have to follow the right way before them. God wants to bless us, our children and their children also. His blessings are for all generations that follow Him.

Isa.25:9, Even Isaiah was looking for salvation of the Lord. He said, we have waited for Him and He will save us. We will be glad and rejoice in His salvation. Jesus had not come but He was promised to come and they believed and waited for Him to come. Zep.3:17, Zephaniah told the Israelites, don't fear and don't be slack in what your hands can do, for the Lord is in the midst of you and He is mighty. He will save you and rejoice over you with joy. He knew that God was going to restore them and they would receive the salvation of God. He encouraged them to wait on the Lord for their salvation because He's the only one who has the power to save. God still saves today and it is His will that none perish but all have eternal life. God is our salvation and our only salvation. We can't buy it neither can we work for it for it is free to all who will believe in Him and accept Him in their hearts and lives and then serve him with their whole heart, mind, soul and strength.

Matt.10:22, We have to remember that it is those that endure to the end that will be saved. Confess with your mouth the Lord Jesus and believe in your heart that God has raised Him from the dead and you shall be saved. Whosoever calls on the name of the Lord shall be saved. God wants all people to be saved and come to the knowledge of the truth. Luke 3:6, And all flesh shall see the salvation of the Lord. This is a universal call of God. Those who do not receive His call will be eternally lost. In the end all will see and then know that Jesus Christ is the Lord of all and they will have to confess that but it will be too late for them. They will be doomed forever and cast into the lake of fire where the fire burns forever and it will never be quenched. Why not accept Him now and escape the fires of hell while you have time. God gave His only Son to die for everyone what more could He have done? Titus 2:11, For the grace of God that brought salvation will appear to all. Accept Him now and receive the gift of God, salvation and all of the blessings that He has promised His children here in this life and then eternal life with Him. Every eye shall see Him and know that He is the Christ but for some it will be too late. Matt.6:33, Seek ye first the Kingdom of Heaven and all of these other things will be added unto you. Seek His righteousness and then all of His blessings will be given you. There are many Christians missing out on the blessings that God has for them because they're not being faithful and obedient to Him. The blessings of the Lord are rich. Ps.133:3, The Lord commands the blessings even life forevermore. May the blessings of the Lord be upon you, all those who serve Him. Our prayer to the Lord should be this. Lead me in Thy truth and teach me for You are the God of my salvation and on You do I wait all the day. Show me Your ways O Lord and teach me Your paths.

How can you belong to the Lord and receive blessings of God?

John 3:7, first of all you must be born again. No one can see the Kingdom of God unless they are born again. For God so loved the world that He gave His only begotten Son that whosoever believes in Him should not perish but have everlasting life. You must believe in God and His Son. We are saved by faith through grace and that not of yourselves for it is a gift of God not of works lest anyone should boast. What is faith? Believing what you cannot see or prove but what we hope for. Heb.11:1, what we trust to be true. By faith we are saved because we believe what the Word says. Acts 2:38-39, Peter said, repent and be baptized all of you in the name of Jesus Christ for the forgiveness of sins and you will receive the gift of the Holy Ghost. This promise is for all of you and your children and all who are afar off, for all the Lord our God will call. John 3:5, Jesus said, you must be born of the water and of the Spirit. You must die to self to be born again in the Spirit.

How can we stay saved?

Col.3:2-17, Set your minds on things above and not on earthly things. For you died and your life is hidden with Christ in God. Put to death whatever belongs to your earthly nature such as, sexual immorality, impurities, lusts, evil desires and greed. Do not make idols of anything. Rid yourselves of such things as, anger, rage, malice, slander and filthy language from your lips. Do not lie to one another. Put on a new self which is renewed daily in knowledge in the image of the Creator. As God's chosen vessels clothe yourselves with compassion, kindness, humility, gentleness and patience. Bear one another's burdens and forgive one another just as the Lord forgives you. Put on love which binds us all together in unity. Let the peace of God rule in your hearts as you were called to peace and be thankful. Let the Words of Christ dwell in you richly. Whatever you do whether in deed or word do it all in the name of the Lord Jesus Christ giving thanks to God the Father through Him. If we live as the Lord has told us we will stay saved. Rom.12:1-2, Offer your body a living sacrifice, holy and pleasing unto God for this is your reasonable service to Him. Do not conform to this world but be ye transformed by the renewing of your mind. Don't live by the pattern that the world has set but by God's laws and ways. Then you will know what the perfect will of God is for your life. You will know what's pleasing to Him. We cannot make ourselves holy for it's only through the Holy Spirit.

Other things we must do. Rom.12:9-23, Love must be sincere for God and others as well. We are to love Him with all of our hearts, minds, soul and strength. Love and cling to what is good and hate what is evil. Don't grow weary in well doing. Don't be burnt out but keep yourselves spiritual and serve the Lord always. Be joyful in hope, patience, in afflictions, faithful in prayer and serve the Lord always. Bless those who persecute you and say all manner of evil against you for My name sake. Rejoice with them that rejoice and mourn with them that mourn, live in harmony with each other. Don't repay evil for evil. Do what is right in God's sight and in the eyes of everyone. If at all possible live in peace with everyone. Don' take revenge for revenge is mine says the Lord, I will repay. If your enemy is hungry feed him or her and if they are thirsty give them water to drink. Don't be overcome with evil but overcome evil with good. The grace of the Lord is with you and He will carry you through. He's the One who can and will for He's the keeper of your salvation and of mine. I Cor.16:13-14, Watch, stand fast in the faith, be strong, and keep your eyes open to see what's going on around you. Hold tight to your convictions of faith and give it all that you have. Don't ever give in to doubt for to doubt is sin. Always remember, whosoever endured to the end the same shall be saved. You have to finish this walk with God to receive all that He has for you in the end.

Living by the Law you must keep all

James 2:10-12, Whosoever shall keep the whole law and yet offends in one point is guilty of all. For He that said, you must not commit adultery said also, do not kill. Now if you do not commit adultery and yet you kill you have become a transgressor of the law. There is no way we can keep the whole law. We don't live under the law but we live under grace. When Jesus came He fulfilled the law. We don't have to give blood sacrifices or blood offerings anymore for the forgiveness of our sins for Jesus died for our sins. Using blood sacrifices and offerings was in the Old Testament and in the old letter. Jesus changed that when he died on the cross at Calvary for you and me. The only sacrifice we can give Him is ourselves. That's why we have to die to self daily and live for Him. He bought us with a great price and that price was His life, His blood both now and forever.

James 4:12, There is one law giver who is able to save or destroy and that's God the Almighty Father Himself. God gave the guidelines to Moses for us to follow, when He told him to write the Ten Commandments. They are still in force for it shows us how to live for it is a school master for right and wrongs in our life. We are to do away with all of the wrongs and make everything right in Jesus Christ. Rom.3:19-22, Now we know that whatever the law says it says to those under the law. And every mouth shall be stopped and all the world may become guilty before God. For because of the law we became guilty before God. Therefore no one will become righteous in His sight by observing the law. Because of the law we became conscious of sin. As I said, it was given for a school master to learn right from wrong. The commandments are to never be done away with, for they were given to Moses by God the Father. We now live by faith and not by the law for we could never keep them all and if we break one then we are guilty of breaking them all. God's grace is sufficient and the just shall live by faith. God has shown us a better way of being right in His sight, not by law but by faith in Jesus Christ. We are made right in God's sight when we trust in Jesus Christ to take away our sins. Verse 28 and 31, We are made right with God through faith and not just obeying the law. We can only fulfill the law if we have faith in God. When we live by faith we will want to keep all of God's laws and His commandments. Our desire will be to please Him in all things. We still have many denominations and many are still trying to live by the law alone and it can't be done. Some are still looking for the Messiah to come and fulfill the law but we know Jesus has already come and lived on this earth, died and rose again on the third day and then was ascended up to Heaven and now is sitting on the right hand of the Father interceding for you and me. We know He's coming back soon in the rapture to get His children and take us out of this evil generation where we will be with Him forever.

God made a better way for us when He gave His only Son Jesus Christ to die on the cross at Calvary. He is our freedom and way to live righteous. We can't live a righteous and holy life in ourselves without Him. For our righteousness is as filthy rags. We live and hope in His righteousness. If it were possible to be saved by keeping the law then Jesus would not have had to die the terrible death that He died. His death would have been in vain if that were the case but it's not. We know that it's not possible to be saved any other way than through Jesus Christ our Lord and Savior. If the blood of Jesus has not been applied to you then you are still lost. You cannot be saved and your sins forgiven in any other way except through Jesus Christ. You are cleansed by His blood and by His blood only. You must have faith and accept Him as your Savior and Lord of your life to be saved, and then you have to be obedient and walk in Him daily. There is no other God before Him or never will be. He is king of all kings and Lord of all lords. He is the creator of all things and He is the life. Jesus is the Word and there's life in the Word.

Are all the laws wrong? Certainly not, for God gave them to Moses to show the people their sins to know right from wrong. They were given to him until the seed that was promised was to come on this earth. That seed was Jesus Christ. Rom.3:24, The law was the school master to bring us to Christ that we may be justified by faith. The ten commandments teaches us right from wrong but just keeping the commandments won't save you for you must be born again and washed in the blood of Jesus Christ. I Tim.1:9, The law is not made for the righteous but for the ungodly and sinners, for the unholy, profane, murderers of father and mothers and for manslaughters. When we come to Christ He gives us the wisdom and knowledge of what's right and wrong and He convicts us of our sins and forgives when we ask Him. Thank God that He gave us a conscience that will bother us if we commit sins and wrongs. God gives us wisdom, knowledge and understanding of what's right and what's wrong. To know to do good and to do it not is sin. Heb.10:16-17, The law of God is written in our hearts and minds. The law of God is in our hearts and none of His steps shall slide. We are to keep Him in our hearts always and do His will. He will never beak any of the promises that He has promised to all that follow Him. When you came to Him you promised to follow Him and do His will all the days of your life so you need to keep that promise. A promise is a vow between two people and is not to be broken. David said, I delight to do your will O God for your law is in my heart. God's will for His children is this and it will never change. Rom.12:1-2, I beseech you therefore brethren by the mercies of God that you present your bodies a living sacrifice, holy and acceptable unto God which is your reasonable service. And be not conformed to this world but be ye transformed by the renewing of your mind that you may prove what is good, acceptable and perfect will of God. God never asked anything unreasonable for us but He said this was a reasonable service. It is just as easy to live holy as it is to live worldly. You are married to Christ and you love Him even better than you love your husband if you have been born again. You wouldn't do anything to hurt your husband so you should never do anything to hurt Jesus Christ your spiritual husband. There's blessings and rewards in living holy and righteous here on this earth and then eternal life with Him. There is nothing in this world that's better than this. I cannot see for the life of me, why anyone wouldn't want to live this kind of life. It's a wonderful life here and a perfect place to go to after this life is over.

Gal.3:23-26, Before faith came we were kept under the law, shut up until the faith which should afterwards be revealed. After faith has come we are no longer bound by the law. For we are children of God by faith in Jesus Christ. We are not servants of the law but sons and daughters of God. When the fullness of time has come God sent His Son made of woman, made under the law to redeem them that were under the law that we might receive the adoption of sons. Wherefore you are no longer a servant but a son, and if a son then you are an heir of God through Christ. We are now living under grace and not the law. There is now no more forgiveness in the blood of goats but by the blood of Jesus and faith and obedience to Him. Only God can forgive sins. It's only by His love, grace and mercy. It's not by keeping the ordinances of rituals in the churches or denominations. The law was good and perfect in its day but God gave a better covenant, Jesus Christ His Son. The law is still good but we can't live by them and be saved, because we can't keep them all. If you break one then you are guilty o breaking them all. Just think, if you lie then you have broken the law of committing adultery. So if you are trying to live by the law it's impossible. You cannot get to Heaven just by keeping the law. Thanks to God that He made a better way. If and when we do sin we have an advocate, Jesus Christ who talks to the Father for us and if we ask forgiveness He will forgive and not only that, but He forgets we ever sinned. For He casts our sins as far as the east is from the west never to remember them anymore. Salvation is free to all who will believe and receive it, it is a gift from God. Have faith in God, trust Him with all of your heart, soul, mind and strength and He will receive you and you will become His sons and daughters forever. As long as you stay in Him you are His.

Just remember that God gave the law to Israel. The law is the Old Testament and when Jesus came He is the new and better covenant. He gave His blood once and for all for the forgiveness of our sins. It's only through the blood of Jesus that anyone can be saved. Now we have to die to self daily, walk with Him, serve and be obedient to Him. Death has to come to our life before we can live. It's like a seed that you plant in the ground, that seed has to die before it can live and come up. Then it grows and becomes stronger and good for what it was planted for. We have to die to self in order to grow in the Lord. We have to become like Him. He gave us His all and we need to give Him our all. That's not asking too much. We are not our own anymore for we were bought with a great price. We were bought with the blood of Jesus Christ on the cross of Calvary. Thank God that He didn't stay dead for He was buried but He rose from the grave on the third day and now He lives in our hearts. He's coming back again to take us where He is, to be with Him forever. He's coming back for a church without spot, blemish or wrinkle. No, we're not perfect for we are still in this mortal body but we are striving to be perfect just as He is perfect. Be sure that your sins find you out so you can ask forgiveness and be ready when He comes.

There can be no in between

Rev.3:15-16, Lukewarm, I know your works that you are neither hot or cold. So because you are lukewarm I will spew you out of My mouth. In other words, you make Me sick and you do the things that I hate. You do things half hearted or out of formalism, you are in a backslider's condition because you are indifferent. You do things your way and not Mine. You have to be all the way for Me or none at all. He said that you have to be for Him or against Him for there is no in between. He has to be first place or He won't be any at all. He will not be second place to anyone or anything. There's no such thing as being in between or straddling the fence, as I have heard some say. Hosea 10:2, Hosea said, your heart is divided. This can't be for you have to be all for Him. Luke 12:47, That servant that knows the Lord's will, and does not prepare the himself, neither does according to His will shall be beaten with many stripes. To them that know to do good and doeth it not, to them it is sin. No sin will enter into the Kingdom of Heaven. It's better to not know God than to know Him and then not serve and follow Him. For the Bible says that person will be beaten with more stripes. You will not get by with sin or doing wrong. You will not escape if you know to do good and don't do it. Matt.7:26, All who hears this saying of Mine and does it not shall be likened unto a foolish man who built his house upon the sand. We know the rains came down and the house fell down. Jesus Christ is the Rock and our strong tower and there is no other Spiritual foundation to be built on. He will stand forever and nothing can bring Him down. Acts 28:27, For the heart of the people have waxed gross and their ears are dull of hearing and their eyes have been closed. If they will listen and understand with their heart and should be converted, I would heal them. So many are not listening to what says the Word of the Lord. Many don't even want to listen and be converted. They have become half hearted and dull of hearing. Their eyes have become closed to what God wants them to see. Many believe but won't act upon it. Faith without works is dead as I have brought out many times in this book and the one before this. The devil believes and trembles because he knows he's wrong and on his way to hell. So just believing won't save you for you can't have faith with works.

Some people procrastinate

They say we have plenty of time. We'll do it another time when it is more convenient. Acts 24:25, Felix trembled and answered, go your way at this time and when the time is convenient I will call for you. He thought that he would have more time later. People are like that today. Tomorrow is not promised to anyone. Today is the day of salvation for it may be your last chance to get saved. I can't stress enough , don't put off until tomorrow what you can and must do today. Death can come and snatch you right out of here and you won't be ready in the Lord. Luke 9:61, Another one said, Lord, I will follow you but let me bid farewell to the ones in my house. Luke 14:18-20, they began to make excuses. One said, I bought a piece of land and I have to go check it out. Another one said, I bought a yoke of oxen and I have to go and verify them. Another one said, I just got married and I can't come. Jesus had invited them all to this great meal but they made excuses that they couldn't go. He is making another great supper and He's invited all to go but some won't make it because they are making all kinds of excuses not to accept His invitation. They don't have time now, or they are having too much fun doing their own thing. They think they have plenty of time. People make all kinds of excuses but they have no reasons. They will miss this great supper that the Lord is preparing for His children. And they will miss Heaven because of excuses. You can't get saved anytime you want to, for the Holy Spirit has to draw you, please don't procrastinate.

Some are carried away with false doctrines

There are many who will listen and believe anything they hear because they don't know the true Word of the Lord. There are many false doctrines being taught and many believe them. Epe.4:14, Don't be children being tossed to and fro and carried away with every wind of doctrine by the teaching of men and cunning craftiness whereby they lie in wait to deceive. Immature believers are easily swayed from the truth of God. They are unsure what is true and what is false. That's why you need to study the Word of God to find the truth and learn discernment and to be rooted and grounded in the love of God. Make sure you go to a good Bible teaching church or group that can and will help you grow in the knowledge of Jesus Christ. Live in, and by faith in God. Heb.13:7-9, Don't be carried away with all kinds of strange teachings. Consider the ways and outcome of those prophets of old and imitate their faith and beliefs. Jesus Christ is the same yesterday, today and forever and His teachings never change. They are truth and the only truths. His Word stands forever and it never fails. Make sure you learn the truth and live by them. The truth will set you free. There is only one right way for there is no in between. The only way is through Jesus Christ the Son of God. There was a lady in one of the churches we attended that was always so confused, because she went to different denominational churches and most of them would teach things different. She didn't know what to believe. I ministered to her and told her she needed to study the Word of God and seek Him and He would give her wisdom, understanding and knowledge to know the real truth of His Word. She was born again and had been for many years. She was listening to false teachings and she would listen to every wind of doctrine. I often wondered what happened to her for we were called out to another ministry, I know she passed away. I'm sure she made it in for she believed and was serving God as far as I know but her life was miserable. The truth shall set you free and there's life in the Word.

Get wisdom and learn

What's a proverb? Webster dictionary says this. An often stated observation regarding something from common experience or saying. A parable, intending to teach the truth or precepts. Jesus teaches the truth through parables. Prov.1:1-7, There are proverbs of Solomon. The purpose of these are to teach people wisdom and discipline, good conduct and doing what's right, just and fair. To give prudence, which is foresight and common sense to the simple. To the young man knowledge and discretion or purpose. A wise man will hear and will increase learning and a man of understanding shall attain wise counsels or guidance to understand a proverb and the parable or interpretation of the wise. The fear of the Lord is the beginning of knowledge but fools despise wisdom and understanding. The book of Proverbs is full of topics that affect our daily living. We can only make sense of life when we make the Lord our foundation for wisdom. We learn truths about friendships, money, immorality, wayward wife, adultery, hatred, pride, gossip, dishonesty, envy, strife and many other things in life that we deal with. If you need to learn or know something, go to the Word of God, the Bible, for it covers everything you need to know. Prov.2:6 and 12, The Lord gives wisdom and from His mouth comes knowledge and understanding. Wisdom will save you from the ways of the wicked. God said not to forget His teachings but keep His commands and to ponder them in our hearts. Prov.4:7, Wisdom is supreme, therefore get wisdom, though it cost everything that you have, get understanding. It cost you your life, your flock and your soul but it will get you eternal life in Christ. Wisdom is a discerning heart, a heart to be like Christ. Whosoever finds wisdom finds life and shall have favor of the Lord. If you want to receive honor, grace and joy, you need to pursue wisdom no matter what it cost you. The fear of the Lord is the beginning of wisdom and knowledge of the Holy Spirit is understanding. If you are wise your wisdom will reward you. If you have the Lord in your life then you have the Holy Spirit too and He will lead and guide you into all truth. Prov.19:8 and 11, He who gets wisdom loves his own soul and he who cherishes understanding prospers. A man's wisdom gives him patience. Oh, how we need more of that. We need to pay more attention to the wise and apply what they teach us to our hearts. We need to make wisdom and understanding the basic for all that is planned and done in our lives then we will make fewer mistakes. We can never go wrong in being wise in the Lord. Prov.26:12, Don't be wise in your own eyes for there is more hope for a fool than for you. Be wise in the Lord and you will bring joy to God's heart.

There are benefits of wisdom

Prov.2:1-16, Solomon said, listen to me and treasure my instructions. Listen to wisdom and concentrate on understanding. Cry out for insight and understanding. Search for them as you would for lost money or hidden treasure, and then you will understand what it means to fear the Lord and you will gain knowledge of God. The Lord grants wisdom. From His mouth comes knowledge and understanding. He grants treasure of good sense to the godly. He is their shield, protecting those who walk with integrity. He guards the path of justice and protects those who are faithful to Him. Then you will know how to find the right course of action every time. For wisdom will enter your heart and knowledge will fill you with joy. Wise planning will watch over you. Understanding will keep you safe. Wisdom will save you from evil people and from those whose speech and talk is corrupt and evil. Wisdom will keep you from adultery and the impure woman. We can see how important it is to have wisdom, knowledge and understanding. If you would just listen and heed to what the Lord says you would save yourselves from a lot of troubles in this life. He's given you the instructions on how to live a good and wholesome life in Him. All you have to do is follow His instructions. Verses 20 and 21, Follow the steps of a good man or woman and stay on the path of righteousness. For only the righteous will live in the land of eternity. Prov.3:5-6, Trust in the Lord with all your heart and lean not upon your own understanding and He will direct your path. Seek His will in all you do and He will direst your path. This is wisdom and understanding for man's wisdom will fail you but God never will. It may work for a little while but it's not lasting for sooner or later something will happen to man's wisdom. Trust God with all of your heart and lean on Him and He will prove to you what He will do. These two verses kept me strong in 2002 when my husband, Leon was so ill. I was trying to understand why all of this was happening to him. The Lord showed me that I didn't need to understand just lean on Him and trust Him and He would see us through and He did. It's not easy to do that sometimes but without faith and trust in God we will fail. No matter how big your problem may be God can take care of it. It may not be in the time you think He should but just put it into His hands knowing that He will work it all out for your good. We grow through our trials and troubles. Just remember that the wisdom of God is pure, safe, secure and undefiled. Happy is the person who finds wisdom and gains understanding. Prov.13:16, The profit of wisdom is better than silver and her wages are better than gold. Wisdom is more precious than rubies. Nothing you can do compares with the wisdom. It will guide you down delightful paths and all its ways are satisfying. Wisdom is a tree of life to those who embrace it and hold it tightly. Nothing is more important than having wisdom for it can save your life. A person who has wisdom has knowledge of their sins and they come to Jesus and repent. With wisdom you will follow Him all the days of your life. You will be obedient and faithful to Him. You will want discipline and corrections to keep you on the right path. You will want to please Him in everything you do, everywhere you go and everything you say. This kind of wisdom comes down from above, from the Heavenly Father. It's everlasting and we can't live a life for God without this kind of wisdom. Ps.111:10, Reverence for the Lord is the foundation of true believers. The rewards of wisdom come to all who obey Him. We have to praise and honor God always. James 1:5-6, If any of you lack wisdom let them ask of God that gives to all people liberally and finding no fault and it shall be given them. Ask in faith without wavering or doubting. All you have to do is ask God for wisdom and He will give it to you with no questions asked, if you are asking with a sincere heart. He knows your heart and your every thought. You have to have wisdom to learn and to learn you must have knowledge. You have to have knowledge to understand. They all go hand in hand. It's like having faith without works. You must have works with your faith for it to work. So these three, wisdom, knowledge and understanding they all go hand in hand. These will carry you through this life into eternity with Jesus Christ. Hold on and don't let go.

Some knowledge withheld from us

Acts 1:4-7, And being assembled together, Jesus told His disciples not to leave but wait for the promise of the Father which said, You have heard of Me. He was talking about the Comforter, the Holy Spirit. But there is another promise coming. The coming of the Lord Jesus Christ. They asked the Lord, will you at this time restore the kingdom of Israel? He said to them, it is not for you to know this time or the season which the Father has put in His own power. Jesus didn't give them the knowledge in which they asked of Him. There is no way that He could have written everything in a book because there is no book big enough to hold it all. Neither could we understand it all in our time. Deut.29:29, The secret things belong to the Lord our God. But those things which are revealed to us and to our children forever that we may do the works of the Bible. God has secrets that are not revealed to us yet. He has told us everything that we need to know to live this life He wants us to live. John 1:18, No one has seen God at anytime, the only begotten Son which is in the bosom of the Father, He has declared Him. Moses just saw the back side of Him when he wrote the Ten Commandments. Knowledge is withheld from man for several reasons. One was because it was perilous. Gen.2:17, But of the tree of knowledge of good and evil you shall not eat of for the day that you eat you shall surely die. At this point they could not handle it. Adam and Eve disobeyed God and ate of it and they died spiritually right away just as God had told them. God didn't want them to have the knowledge that's why He told them not to eat of that tree. God always knows best for everyone.

Unable to understand or to handle the truth

John 13:7, Jesus said unto him, what I do you do not know but you shall know later. Peter was asking Jesus, why do you wash my feet? Jesus knew that one of His disciples was going to portray Him and

He knew all that was going to happen but He didn't tell His disciples for He knew that they could not handle it. Some things Jesus has to keep from us still today because flesh is weak. John 16:12, I have many things to tell you but you cannot bear them now. Jesus knows our weakness and when we are able to accept things and carry them through. That's why we have to grow in the Lord so He can increase our knowledge in Him. When we first come to Him we are babes and have to start out on the milk of the Word of God. You don't give a baby meat when it is first born but you start them on milk something that they can digest. So the same with Christians, we have to grow in the Lord and then He can reveal more to us. There are some things that we'll never know until we get to Heaven and talk to Him personally. He keeps some knowledge from us because He knows we have limitations. I Cor.13:12, For now we see through a glass darkly but then face to face. Now I know in part but then shall I know even as I am known. We don't see things clearly not for it's like peeking through a cloud, fog or mist. But it won't be long before we will see everything clearly as God sees us. We will know Him as He knows us. Praise God, I can hardly wait. It's so exciting to know we will see our Savior face to face and be able to give Him a big hug in person. To have Him put His loving arms around me just gives me the chills. Oh what a day that will be, what a time, what a time.

We have gradual revelation of the divine plan

Epe.3:5, Which in ages was not found known unto the sons of men so it's now revealed unto His holy angels unto the prophets by the Spirit. Paul was saying, as you read what I have written you'll be able to see for yourselves into the mystery of Jesus Christ. None of our ancestors understood this. Only in our time has it been made clear by God's Spirit through His holy prophets. In Israel and some of the foreign countries things are being found that proves lots of the Bible and what the prophets have said. Like, Noah's Ark, some of it has been found. There have been scrolls found. There has been lost books of the Bible found. These are gradual revelations and knowledge proven to people. Still some will not believe God or turn to Him. For the believers we need no proof for we have faith that everything God said is the truth.

We stand on His Word. I believe that some knowledge is withheld to give opportunities for faith. I John 3:2, beloved, now are we the sons of God and it does not appear what we shall be but we know that when He shall appear we shall be like Him for we shall see Him as He is. We are the children and that's only the beginning . When we were born again that was the beginning of a new life in Jesus Christ. This was our new birth, our spiritual birth. We who are born twice will die once. If you are born once then you will die twice. Let me explain this. If you are not a child of God and you should die then at the judgment day you will be raise up to be judged and then be cast into the lake of fire for the second death. If you are a child of God when you die you will be rise up to eternal life to live forever. You can escape this second death by accepting Jesus Christ as your Savior and Lord then live for Him until the end of your life here. There will be some Christians that will never die if they are ready when Jesus comes in the rapture of the church. They will be caught up in the clouds to meet Jesus in the air there to be with Him forever. Only the Father in Heaven knows when Jesus is coming back. Not even to Jesus knows that. But He is coming and I believe soon for all signs are pointing in that direction. I believe He's waiting so that as many as want to be saved will be saved. He has such love for everyone that He doesn't want anyone to be lost. He is so faithful, long suffering and patient.

If you're not saved and your name isn't written in the Lamb's book of life then you need to give your heart and life to Jesus Christ right now. He's waiting at your heart's door waiting for you to invite Him in. He won't force His way in for you have to invite Him in. Don't be foolish thinking that you have plenty of time for you don't know that at all. Don't let anyone trick you or deceive you or give you any false words or doctrine. Get wisdom, knowledge and understanding and make your decision to follow Christ all of the way. You don't know when death will be at your door so get ready to meet the Lord. Don't let Him say at the judgment, sorry I never knew you, depart from Me you worker of iniquity and be thrown into the lake of fire for the second death. This is the most important decision you will ever have to make. Choose to serve the Lord today and have eternal life.

CHAPTER FOUR

Who Loves Life and Wants to See Good Days?

CHAPTER 4

Who Loves Life and Want to See Good Days?

Ps.34:11-14, Come My children listen to Me, I will teach you the fear of the Lord. You who love life and want to see good days you will have to keep your tongue form evil and your lips from speaking lies. Turn from your evil ways and do good, seek peace and pursue it. These things you have to do. First, you have to come to Me. Give Me first place in your life above all things. Have fellowship with Me and have a relationship with Me. I am your Father, your provider, salvation, healer, your peace and keeper and I love you. You have to listen to Me for I will teach you the fear of the Lord. Listen and hear what I say to you. You have to heed to what I say and do it with all of your might. Be obedient to Me in all things and at all times. Verse 12 tells us what we can have if we do what God says. God always keeps His promises. We can have what He has promised His children. If you want to prosper in this life then you have to do it His way and not yours. He said He would give you the desires of your heart if you will serve Him and give Him first place in your heart and life. If you love life and want to live many good days then you have to follow His commands.

Keep your tongue from evil and your lips from speaking lies. This means to stop gossiping and down grading people, especially your

Christian brothers and sisters in the Lord. Don't speak vain words and get into a conversation where there is evil and ugly talking, jesting and unholy speaking. If you can't say something good then you shouldn't say anything at all. My dad always told me that there was some good in everyone no matter how bad they were. Be careful what comes out of your mouth for you can't take it back. You can ask forgiveness but words are something that can never be recovered. Words really hurt. I always said that I would rather be slapped than to be hurt with words. It's easier to get over a slap than bad words that has been said to you. Words affect others so be careful what you say. You should always speak uplifting and encouraging words. Let good come out of your mouth and lips. Make sure you don't lie. Never agree with another who is not telling the truth or a gossiper or who is causing division among others. Stand for what is right no matter the cost.

Fear the Lord you saints for those who fear him lack nothing. Those who seek Him lack no good thing. Taste and see if the Lord is good, blessed is the one who takes refuge in Him. God is saying, in Me you have everything you need. Fear here is love for God. He said if you seek Me you will find Me and I will see to it that you have need of nothing. He's talking to the saints, those who are following Him. Those who are born again and are serving Him are His children and the saints. Trust Him for He will prove that He is good. He said to taste of Me and see that I am good. Those who look to Him are radiant, their faces are never covered with shame. You can tell who loves the Lord and is serving Him by the look on their faces. They are happy and have joy down in their soul. They are filled with the praises of the Lord. They are not ashamed of Him and they love to talk about Him as well as to talk to Him. Even in our troubles we can have joy because Jesus lives in us. Verse 19, A righteous person may have many troubles but the Lord delivers them out of all of them. God will make a way for us that we can bear whatever we have to go through for He is our strength. There is no one else that can get us out of trouble like the Lord Himself. That's how much He loves His children. After all the Lord has done for us and is still doing we should always praise and worship Him. Ps.34:1-3, I will extol the Lord at all times. His praise shall continually be in my mouth. I will lift Him up always and praise Him. My soul shall boast in the Lord, let the afflicted hear and rejoice. My flesh may be afflicted but my soul will rejoice in the Lord. Glorify the Lord with me, let us exalt His name together. David is saying here, everyone glorify the Lord with me and lets all lift up His name for He alone is worthy to be glorified and exalted. For He is the only true and living God.

God had everything for His children if you will just serve Him. He wants your whole heart and life and not just part of it. He wants you to serve Him full time and not just some of the time. He's not a part time God and you can't be a part time follower of Him. If you are His then you will want to serve Him all of the time. You will want to spend your time with Him. So if you love life and want to see many good days then you have to go His way and do what He wants you to do all of the time. You will never regret it or want anything any different than to walk with God. Only with Him will you see good days and have a long and fulfilling life. Then when this life is over you will have eternal life with Him and all of the saints of God. Keep praising Him for He is worthy to be praised. God is good all of the time.

Health and long life promised

Prov.3:7-8, Fear the Lord and depart from evil and it shall be health to your navel and marrow to your bones. We have to do something first to be able to achieve the blessings of God. First of all, we have to trust Him with all of your heart, Second, We have to lean on His understanding and not ourselves. Thirdly, we have to testify of Him. Fourth, we have to let Him lead us all of the way. Fifth, we have to fear Him, this means to love Him. Sixth, we can't be conceited and wise in our own eyes. Seventh, we have to shun evil and do good. These are the things we have to do to have good health and a long life as He has promised His children, to all who love and serve Him. Most all of God's promises require something from us. For length of days shall be added unto you. Verse 1 says, Don't forget My law and let your heart keep My commandments. You just can't live just any ole way and expect to get the promises of God. There is a price to pay on our part. With promises come requirements from you and me. God keeps His word and we need to be faithful and obedient you Him. It's His will that we prosper and be in good health just as our soul prospers. From the very beginning this was so. Ex.15:26, God told the Israelites, if you diligently hearken unto the voice of the Lord your God and do what is right in His sight and keep His commandments and all of His laws then I will not put any of these diseases which I have brought upon the Egyptians. For I am the Lord your God that heals you. Deut.7:15, The Lord will take away all of sicknesses and won't put any evil diseases of Egypt. Prov.4:20-22, Listen to my Words and hear. Don't let them depart from your eyes of from your heart. For they are life to your navel and marrow to your bones. God heals in many ways, not always in the ways that we expect or the time but He knows best for all of His children.

Take Joni for instance. Even though God didn't heal her completely and restore her back to what she was, she started to praising the Lord and things changed for her in her heart. This was a turning point in her life and she started to see hope for the first time after her accident. God had given her a purpose to live just as she was. Now she has blessed so many people and given others a reason to live. Because of her faithfulness God has made a way for her. We have to trust God in everything. God has a purpose for everything He does. We don't understand many times why God doesn't heal but we don't know it all. It has to be done His way and not ours. Sometimes God can use us better when we have a disability. Look at Paul, he prayed and prayed for God to remove the thorn in his flesh but God told him that His grace was sufficient. Paul didn't stop but he continued to spread the gospel and live a holy life that was pleasing to God. When we are weak then God is strong for He is our strength. We have to learn to be content in whatever stage we're in and keep on working for the Lord. God does things in a way that He can get the glory and praise.

Remember Job? Even though we don't understand why God doesn't always heal, we can trust Him knowing that He brings something out of sufferings. It is through sufferings that we draw near to God. We pray more, we thank Him more and we walk closer to Him when we go through problems and sicknesses. Praise will sustain us through theses things as well as the good times. The presence of God comes through the praises and worship to God. Job came through of the turmoil that God allowed and in the end he had more than ever before. He stayed faithful to God and continued to walk with Him. Job said, even though the devil might slay me I will still walk with God. He said he would not turn back from serving God. Sometimes we have to be tested and tried to see if we are going to be faithful and still follow God in our troubles. God knows whether we will or not but we have to prove it to ourselves and God. It's easy to serve the Lord when everything is going good. Of course, some will put Him on a shelf, so to speak, until they need Him again. When everything is going good sometimes people don't seem to think that they don't need God and they don't talk to Him as much as they should and they even stay away from church and from fellowship with other Christians. I don't understand this but it does happen to many. They seem to forget how good God has been to them. My husband preached a message about putting God on a shelf until they needed Him for something. That's really sad for God loves everyone so much. These same people will wonder why things are going so bad for them and they're not being blessed. God wants you to love and serve Him through the good as well as the bad. If you want His blessings you have to walk with Him and do His will.

James 5:13-16, Pray for the sufferings, sing with the cheerful. Pray for the sick and call upon the elders of the church and anoint them with oil in the name of Jesus. The prayer of faith will save the sick and raise them up. If there is sin with in them they will be forgiven. Confess your sins one to another and pray for each other that you may be healed. The effectual prayer of a righteous person avails much. Put it all into God's hands and do things His way for He is never too late nor makes any mistakes. God knows our future and He knows what it takes for us to stay true to Him and endure to the end. If it takes sickness or problems to keep us in line with Him it will be worth it in the end. It's better for God to correct and chastise now than later and lose out. It's better to pay the price now than to have to pay the price later and be thrown in the lake of fire, hell.

I Kings 3:14, The Lord told Solomon in a dream. If you walk in My ways and keep My commandments as your father David did then I will lengthen your days. Ps.91:16, With long life I will satisfy him and show him My salvation. God is talking about those who walk a godly life in Him. Prov.10:27, The fear of the Lord prolongs the days of your life. I Pet.3:10, Those who love life and see good days, let them refrain their tongues from evil and their lips from speaking guile. Watch and be careful what you say. To enjoy long life these things you must do. Abraham was promised a long life and he died at an old age. Moses died at the age of 120 and God blessed him with a young body, still strong and still had good eye sight. I was just reading in the local paper just yesterday about this lady who is 105 and seem to be going pretty strong, for she takes part in getting the elderly together and doing activities together. She gave all the praise and glory to God for her long life. She said she accepted Him in her life at an early age.

In the ways of righteousness there is life. If we abide in the Words of God we can have a long life here and we know we will have eternal life in the Kingdom of Heaven. How are you living? Are you living the way that God has taught you to live? Are you living in righteousness and holiness? Do you even want long life here? The Bible teaches as we have seen that if you live life and live in righteousness then you can have a long life here as well as life eternal later. This is what God wants for all of His children. We know there are many who seem to be living a good and righteous life but die at a younger age but only God knows why. He sees and knows everything and He knows whether a person will turn back if they continue to live, for He sees ahead and we can't. It's better to die younger if you are ready to go than to live a long life here and backslide and turn from serving God. We need never to question God for He knows what He's doing for He is love. Our days are all numbered and we know we can shorten them. Many have taken their lives when it wasn't in God's plans to die early. You may be thinking, why didn't God stop them? I'm sure He has stopped many but God will let you do what you want to do. He said, you have to choose whom you will serve for He doesn't make that choice for you. We can choose life or death. There's life is in His Word. Choose Jesus Christ as your Lord and live a good long life here and the eternal life with Him. No matter how long a person may live it should be for Jesus Christ, for that's a far better life here and now and then eternal life in the end. Why not live in the fullness of life here and enjoy all of the blessings that God has for you. In the next topic you're going to find out what level you're living in. God wants you to be prosperous and be in good health but in order for this to happen your soul has to prosper.

The Bag, Barrel and Basket level

The bag

What kind of life here do you want? You can have what you choose and then work for it. There are different levels but it cost you something. Hag.1:6, You have sown much and bring in little, you eat but you don't have enough, you drink but you're not filled with drink. You clothe yourself but there is no warmth. You that earn wages you earn to be put into a bag with holes in it. He is saying you are wasteful with everything you have. You are not being wise with anything. How many people and even Christians do you see like that? They work hard but they spend their money on useless things. They never save anything for a time of shortage or hard time. They are very wasteful and spend their money for the wrong things. They are never satisfied with what they have. They try to please flesh and what makes them happy at that moment. Isa.55:2, Why do you spend money on things that is not bread? And you labor for that which does not satisfy? He's not talking just about the bread you eat but the everlasting bread, Jesus Christ. Your bag will never become full without Him in your heart and life. Just a little bag is not sufficient for life. You need more than just a bag to survive in this life we live in today. John 6:27, labor not for the meat that perishes but for that meat that does not perish and it endures unto everlasting life which the Son can give you for God has sent Him. When you don't seek for that true bread of life, Jesus Christ and you don't work for this meat that does not perish then you profit nothing. It's like laboring hard and putting money into bags that has holes in it. Worldly labor will soon pass away. It's only what you do for Christ that will last forever. What you do for Christ will cause you to prosper materially and spiritually. If you are depending on your money to get you through then you'll not make it. Money will let you down but Jesus Christ will never let you down for He will be with you always in the good and the bad times. He will see you through for He said He would and you can depend on Him.

Ecc.2:11, The preacher said, I looked on all the hard work I had done with my hands and behold it was all vanity and vexation of the spirit and there was no profit under the sun. Everything was meaningless he was saying. It was like chasing the wind and nothing was gained. Christ is the only one that can satisfy your soul. The preacher said he was vexed in his spirit, he was angry with himself apparently for wasting his time and his effort. If it's all for self that you have done then it's all vanity says the preacher. There's surely nothing wrong with working for we all have to work. The Bible teaches that if a person won't work then they shouldn't eat. But what the Word of God is saying is, without God in your life it's all going to nothing. This is but a short life here but when you put Jesus in your heart and life whatever you do will be for eternity. This life is a life for preparing for the next life. You're either preparing for Heaven or for hell for these are the only two places after this life is over. What kind of preparations are you making? What you do in this life will determine where you will be going after this life. You know when you are going on a vacation you have to prepare, most everything you do you have make preparations, so the same way for preparing for the next life, Heaven.

The Barrel

Ask yourself where you stand with giving and receiving. It's better to give than receive.
I Kings 17:8-16, The story of the widow woman and her son you will find here. Elijah had a Word from God to go to Zidon. He said you will find a widow woman there to sustain you. He was saying she

will take care of you while you are there. So he went as the Lord had told him. Elijah asked for a drink of water, and as she was going to get it he asked for a morsel of bread that was in her hand. She told him that she only had enough bread for her and her son and they were going to eat and then die. She said, I have only a handful of meal and a little oil in a cruise and I am gathering two sticks so I can cook it and then we'll eat. Me and my son. Elijah told her what the Lord had said. The barrel shall not waste neither shall the cruise of oil fail until the day the Lord send rain upon the earth. She went and did what Elijah had said. Then she, her son and Elijah ate for many days. The barrel of meal nor the cruise of oil wasted not, or ran out. Her barrel was empty but because of her obedience to the prophet of the Lord it became full and stayed full. It was filled by the Lord Himself. The barrel signifies having enough. Lots of Christians have just enough for just themselves and their family and no more, just enough to get by. Matt. 10:8, Freely give and you will freely receive. If you want to receive you have to give. You that give sparingly will reap sparingly. With the same measure that you mete out it will be measured back to you. Prov.29:27, They that gives to the poor shall lack nothing. Are you giving your tithes? Are you giving to the poor and needy? Are you sowing sparingly? Whatever you give that's how much you can expect back. If your barrel isn't full and running over then you need to check yourself to see why. The Bible tells us that if we give according to His Word we will lack nothing. We will have everything that we need and have enough to give others also. The first Christians sold everything they had and gave to the poor. What are you doing with what you have? It's our Christian duty to take care of our brothers and sisters in the Lord as well as others also. When we give to the poor and needy we are lending to the Lord. If you will do it God's way then you will have God's way. Trust, try and prove Him and see if He won't do what He said He's do.

The Basket

The basket is where we get the over flowing blessings of God. Matt.14:15-21, Lets look at the five loaves of bread and the two fish. There was a great multitude of people there and Jesus was healing the sick. It became late and the disciples told Jesus to send the people away to the city so they could buy food to eat because they only had five loaves of bread and two fish. Jesus said no, for they don't have to leave. He said, bring Me the bread and the fish. So the multitude of people sat down on the grass. Jesus took the five loaves and the two fish and looked up to Heaven and blessed them, brake and gave the loaves to His disciples and gave to the people and they all did eat. When they were all full they took up the remaining that was left over and filled twelve baskets full. There were about five thousand men besides women and children. The moral of this story is, give what you have and in return the Lord will give back a super abundance. Give and it shall be given you, good measure pressed down and running over shall men give unto your bosom. For with the some measure that you mete out will be measured back to you. Jesus is saying, your basket should be running over. You will be very prosperous in your finances and in your soul. You will have much more than you need for yourselves so you can help others who are less fortunate. There's something else that we have to do also to be blessed with much.

Mal.3:10-11, Bring all the tithes into the storehouse so that there may be meat in My house and prove Me now here says the Lord of hosts if I will not open the windows of Heaven and pour out you a blessing that there is no room enough to receive it. I will rebuke the devourer for your sakes and he shall not destroy the fruits of your grounds neither shall your vine cast her fruit before time in the field says the Lord of hosts. God wants to bless His children with super abundance, spiritually and financially. It's up to you how much you will be blessed. If you will give your tithes and offerings of money, time and yourselves He will bless you with plenty for you and you can then give to others. What He says He will do and if you want Him to bless you in the way He wants to then you have to do what He says. You have to prepare for the blessings of the Lord. He said to try Him and see if He wouldn't do what He said. Get out of the bag level where you don't even have enough for your needs. Get out of the barrel level where you only have enough for yourself and nothing to give others. It's time to get into the basket level. This is where you have plenty for your self and to help others too. This is where the Lord will pour out you blessings that you won't have room to receive. Don't you want to experience this position? What a blessing to do for others for it's more blessed to give than to receive. Where do you stand, the bag, the barrel or the basket? If you're not in the basket level then you should check yourself to see why. You can believe one thing, it's not God's fault for He has no respect of people. He loves everyone the same and He wants all of His children to have the best. The tenth of whatever you make belongs to Him and if you're not giving it to Him then you are robbing Him and thieves will not enter into the Kingdom of Heaven. The blessings of God come with what you give after the tithes. That's why He said to bring your tithes and offerings into the storehouse so He can bless you. If you want an overflow of blessings then you have to give more than your tithes. First of all, He wants you, your whole self. If you don't give yourself to Him first then the rest will not get you into Heaven. You have to be washed in the blood of Jesus and live for Him. You cannot pay your way into Heaven like some people think. Once you give of yourself to Him then you have to do it His way in everything. Once you give of yourself then the rest comes easier for you are His now. Amen

Personal resolutions

Ps.101:1-3, I will sing of Your love and justice to You O Lord, I will sing praises. I will be careful to lead a blameless life when You come for me. I will walk in my house with a blameless heart. I will set before my eyes no vile thing. The deeds of faithless men I hate, they will not cling to me. Verse 7, No one who practice deceit will dwell in my house, no one who speaks falsely will stand in my presence. Joshua 24:14, But for me and my house we will serve the Lord. This is what my husband and I have declared. For us, we will serve the Lord all the days of our lives and whosoever comes to our house will abide by the rules of the Lord. We will not allow dirty and vulgar things on our TV or even tapes, or radio. God is going to hold you accountable in what you allow to go on in your home if you are professing to be His child. You don't just show yourself as a Christian outside of your home but also in your home as well. God is watching you everywhere you are and He knows everything about you. We are to stay true and faithful.

These things mentioned here we should declare and be our resolutions for all Christians everywhere. We should declare them everyday of our lives and let the devil hear us. We as Christians have to be different from the world and the unsaved. If your life isn't different then you best check yourself to see if you are really saved and a child of the Lord Jesus Christ. Just professing with your mouth is not good enough for you have to live it daily. A lot of people talk it but they don't live it. It's not what you say that going to get you into Heaven but it's how you live. It's not how loud you say amen and it's not the church that you are in that's going to save you. It's what's inside your heart that God records each day. So if you want your life worth while and hear Him say well done my child, remember it's how you live not just what you say.

Our personal 10 commandments

1 - We will sing His praises.
2 - We will lead a blameless life
3 - We will walk in our home with a blameless heart.
4 -We will not look at any vile thing.
5 - We will hate all vile and evil
6 - We will hate all the deeds of faithless people. (Not the people but their evil deeds)
7 - We will not be around evil and faithless people.
8 - We will not allow any deceitful one to live in our home.
9 - We will not allow anyone who lies to stand in our presence.
10 - For me and my house we will serve the Lord.

If we make these our ten commandments we would be better Christians and would be closer to God. You have to choose whom you're going to serve. Joshua 24:14 tells us whom he and his household is going to serve. David in Psalm made a personal resolution just as Joshua did. We have to make one also. Our hearts has to be fixed on

Jesus Christ and our minds made up to serve God with all of our heart, mind, soul and strength. You can't serve God half hearted or part time. He's an all time and an on time God and we have to be all time and on time child of His serving and worshipping Him always. These men of God were models for us today. They made conscious decisions to be faithful and obedient to the Lord and to keep their hearts pure. The heart is the center of the human spirit from which springs emotions, thoughts, motivations and actions. Prov.4:23, It is the well spring of life. Be true and faithful to Him in the good and the bad times, always.

David understands how important it is to be careful in the way he directs his life, because from his heart felt vows will flow his behavior in private, at home and in the community. After making his resolutions he asked the Lord if He will go with him. He asked the Lord, when will you come to me? He knew he had no power to keep his resolutions apart from the presence of the Lord, and neither do we. Only in Him do we have the resource to accomplish our goals and be all that He has in mind for us to be.

Matt.6:24, We will serve God or mammon for we can't serve both. We will serve one or the other. We know that mammon in the Bible is money. Lots of people and even some Christians put their money first and what it can buy. Anything that you put before God is an idol. It could even be your spouse or your children or even your family. Matt.4:10, God is going to be first or none, He's going to be Lord of all lords or He's not going to be Lord at all. He's a jealous God and He won't be cheated on or be unfaithful to by anyone and let you get by with it. You have to serve Him and Him only. You have to serve Him with your whole being. You can't serve Him with your whole heart and then allow your hands to be used for evil or your eyes and ears to be used for vain things. What is causing you not to serve God as you should? Who is keeping you from walking with Him daily? Rom.8:35, Who shall separate you from the love of God? Shall tribulations, distresses, persecutions, famine, nakedness, peril or sword? Verse 27, No, we are more than conquerors through Jesus

Is God's Name and His Presence in your home?

II Chr.20:9, If and when evil comes upon you as the sword, judgment, pestilence or famine, we stand before this house and in your presence and cry unto you in our affliction then you will hear. This will happen because God is in this house. Verse 15, The battle's not yours but God's. He said, be not dismayed or be afraid. God is the God of all battles if you are following Him. The Lord will fight your battles and you will hold your peace. Rev.3:21, To them that overcomes will I grant to sit with Me. Your house is desolate without Christ and there is no peace there. The Comforter, which is the Holy Spirit said, peace I leave with you and peace I give you. Matt.23:38-39, Behold your house is left unto you desolate and empty. Jesus will depart from your door and from your presence. This is talking about your temple, your body which is the temple of the Lord as well as your physical house that you live in. Please don't let this ever happen to you. Make sure He's living in your heart and in your home where you dwell. He won't live in a messed up temple where there's sin going on for it has to be clean, holy and righteous unto Him.

Our Spiritual house, our soul

II Cor.5:1-2, For we know that if our earthly house of this tabernacle were dissolved we have a building of God, an house not made with hands eternal in Heaven. For this we groan earnestly desiring to be clothed upon with our house which is from Heaven. In order to have our souls right with God we have to have our earthly house right with Him. We can't just live any ole way and Him be pleased with us, and keep our spiritual house dirty and expect God to live in us. This means we have to keep our hearts and minds on Him and the things that are pleasing to Him at all times. You have to be filled with Him all of the time, you have to walk and talk with Him. You have to have a personal relationship with Him and fellowship with Him. Make this a daily resolution to Him to be faithful in all things to Him. He has to be number one in your life. He will not be second place to anyone or anything. Your soul will live eternally somewhere so make Heaven your eternal home with Jesus Christ and all of the saints of God.

God repays good for good

Epe.6:8, Knowing that whatsoever good thing anyone does the same shall be received of the Lord whether it be bond or free. God will render back good for what good you do to others. You can never out give Him for He is good all of the time. Col.3:23-24, And whatsoever you do, do it heartily as to the Lord and not to men. Knowing that of the Lord you will receive the reward of His inheritance for all who serve Him. What you render out to others the Lord will repay you with and even more. He never said that it had to be money but whatever and however it will be from the Lord. Whatever you do make sure you do it as unto the Lord and you will receive a blessing from Him. Some think that money is the only way to get back but I'm here to tell you that money can never buy the blessings that God above gives. Luke 6:35, Love your enemies and do good, lend hoping for nothing in return and your rewards will be great. Give and it shall be given to you for it is more blessed to give than to receive. Whatever you give you give to God. Never repay evil with evil but repay evil that others do unto you with good. That's how the world will see that you are different from the evil ones for you love with a godly love. We have to love everyone and we have to give and help everyone. There are a lot of souls to get saved because of you sharing your love to them and meeting their needs. Let everyone see Jesus in you no matter the cost.

Gal.6:2, As we have opportunity let us do good unto all especially unto them that are of the household of faith. Make sure you give and never mistreat your brothers and sisters in Christ. Do whatever you can to help them and hold them up when they are weak in the faith. The Bible teaches that we are their keeper. We are to hold them up in prayer and minister unto them. Give and it shall be given unto you, pressed down and running over shall men give unto your bosom. For with the same measure that you mete out shall be measured back to you. Love your enemies and do good to those that hate or persecute you for My name sake said Jesus Christ. Bless them that curse you and say all manner of evil against you and despitefully use you. Remember this, Good work will give you good pay from the Master regardless whether you are bond or free, whether you are a slave or in prison. There is no respect of persons in the Lord. Do your very best work from your heart for God knowing you will get paid in full when you come into your inheritance and in this life as well. Keep in mind that Jesus Christ is your Lord, Master and Savior and He sees everything you do, say and everywhere you go. He even knows your every thought and motive.

God will repay punishment in the end

Rom.2:5-6, But after the hardness and impenitent of their heart treasures up unto themselves wrath against the day of wrath and revelation of the righteous judgment of God. Who will render unto every person according to their deeds. God will repay you for bad works. Being a Christian doesn't excuse you and cover up for your bad deeds done or your bad works. You're not going to get by with anything. In the end you will be judged for your works. For those who insist on having their way now and rejecting Christ and taking the path of unrighteousness and laziness it will be eternal death in hell. For those who are saved and are living and working for God it will be Heaven. Col.3:25, They that does wrong shall receive for the wrong which they have done. Jer.17:10, I The Lord searches the heart, I try the reins to give everyone according to their ways to the fruits of their doings. Matt.16:27, The Son of man shall come in glory of His Father with His angels and shall then shall He reward everyone according to their works. Rom.2:6, Who will render everyone according to their deeds. Whether good or bad everyone will be rendered accordingly.

What kind of works or fruits are you doing? Whatsoever you sow you will reap. You will reap seeds you sow here on earth as well as after the judgment. Whatever a farmer plants that's what comes up. So the same is with your life and works here. If you sow good seeds according to the Word of God then you will reap blessings but if you sow bad seeds then you will reap curses. The Bible tells us to till the soil and land and sow good seeds so we can reap a good harvest. What is it going to be with you, blessing or curses? Good rewards or bad judgments, Heaven or hell? It's your choice for no one can do that for you. I pray you will make the choice to go with God and follow His ways and footsteps all of the way. The payoff will be the greatest of everything. You will never have to make anymore choices for you will be made perfect just like Jesus. There will be no more sorrow, troubles, sickness, hurts, evil, sin and death for all will be peace, joy and happiness and you will be with Jesus Christ forever. Jesus is the one who died and paid the price for your sins and mine. He shed His blood for all but many will not accept Him and what He did at Calvary. Then they will have to go into everlasting punishment for their sin of rejecting Jesus Christ as their Lord and Savior.

We are to labor to approve ourselves to Christ

II Cor.5:1-10, Paul in assured hope of immortal glory labors to approve himself to Christ and we have to do the same. Jesus laid the ground work and the way for Paul and Paul did the same for you and me. We are in a body of flesh but our souls has been saved because we have accepted Jesus Christ as our Savior and Lord and we are walking in His ways and footsteps. When our bodies have been deceased our souls will still be alive for your soul will never die. It is headed for our eternal Heavenly home to be with Jesus. One day this body will put on a robe of righteousness forever. We now have infirmities in the flesh and we have troubles and trials that's why we long for our eternal home in Heaven where we'll have a new body. The best thing about Heaven is that we'll be with Jesus the one who gave His life for us so we can have a new body and eternal home of complete happiness. God made our bodies and He gave us the Holy Spirit that leads and guides us all of the way. Because of this we long for our Heavenly home. Therefore we are always confident knowing that while we are at home in this body we are absent from the Lord. Wherefore we labor that whether present or absent we may be accepted of Him. For we must all appear before the judgment seat of Christ to receive the things done in their body whether good or bad. Verse 15, Jesus died for all that they which live should not live unto themselves but unto Him which died for them and rose again so that they may live also. Verses 17-21, Therefore if anyone is in Christ Jesus they are a new person. Behold old things are passed away and all things are become new. All things are of God who reconciled us to Himself by Jesus Christ and have given us the ministry of reconciliation. Be ye reconciled to God. Jesus was our sin bearer and now we are made the righteousness of God in Him. 6:4, So now you are to approve yourselves as the ministers of God. All of God's children have a ministry, you have a work to do and God expects you to do your best for Him for He had done His best for you. I Cor.6:19-20, Know ye not that your body is the temple of the Holy Spirit which is in you, which you have heard of God and you are not your own. In order for the Holy Spirit to live in you must keep your temple clean, holy and righteous. For you were bought with a price therefore glorify God in your body and in your spirit which are God's. We are not our own for we were bought with a price, a great price, the blood of Jesus God's own begotten Son. We now belong to God, body, soul and spirit. We can't do as we please but we have to please God. He has a plan for His children and we need to obey that plan.

I Cor.2:10, God had revealed unto us by His Holy Spirit. For His Spirit searches all things even the deeper things of God. God knows everything about you. You can't hide anything from Him. He makes known the things to us that He wants us to know. As we grow in Him then He teaches us more. You have to get off of the milk and get into the meat so you can understand and have the knowledge of how great He is and the things that He wants to do through you. You can't stay in the baby stage and expect to have the wisdom, knowledge and understanding of God. You have to grow just as a child grows in order to learn. Gal.2:20, I am crucified with Christ nevertheless I live but Christ lives in me and the life I now live in the flesh I live by faith of the Son who loved me and gave Himself for me. The children of God shall live by faith. Our old self is dead and now we allow Christ to live in and through us. We are to die to self daily.

Epe.3:17-19, Paul said, I pray that Christ will be more and more at home in your hearts as you trust Him. May your roots grow deep into the soil of God's marvelous love. And may you have the power to understand how deep His love is. May you experience the love of Christ though it is so great you will never fully understand it. Then you will be filled with the fullness of life and power that comes from God. Paul is saying here, Jesus is to make Himself at home in your hearts more and more. He will feel comfortable and welcome in your home, your temple. Your love will grow deeper and deeper for Him and you will have more power to understand and show a deeper love for Him. We can never explain the depth of God's love for there is nothing that compare with God's love. The more you trust Him the closer you will get to Him. He will never leave you but you can leave Him. Draw near to God and He will draw near to you. Rom.12:1-2, I beseech you brethren by the mercies of God that you present your bodies a living sacrifice, holy and acceptable unto God which is your reasonable service, so that you may prove what is good and acceptable and perfect will of God. Paul said, I plead and beg you to live a holy life unto God. God wants our bodies to be a holy sacrifice to Him He won't accept anything else. This is our reasonable service to Him. He never asks anything hard or unreasonable for us to do. If we love Him we will want to serve Him and be obedient to Him. We'll want to live a holy and sinless life. I Pet.4:2, Peter said, no longer will you want to live your time in the flesh and lust of men but to the will of God.

Matt.16:24, Jesus said, if you come after Me then take up your cross and follow Me. He's saying, die to yourself daily, deny what the flesh wants and come follow Me. Gal.5:24, Those who are in Christ have crucified themselves of all the affections and lusts. You don't lust after the things that are wrong and worldly anymore. They're not important or any fun anymore because you have your eyes, minds, ears and hearts on the things of Jesus Christ. This is showing not only Jesus Christ of your living sacrifice but to the world that you are different from the sinful and evil people of the world. Our bodies are a living sacrifice unto the Lord. Pet.1:16, Be ye holy for I am holy. I John 2:15, Love not the world or the things in the world. If anyone loves the world the love of the Father is not in them. You can stand on these Words for Jesus Christ said them himself. God is a jealous God and He will not share His bride with anyone else. If you are a child of God then you are His bride and you need to be faithful and obedient to Him just as He is faithful to you. You should never do anything to hurt your Lord and Savior, Jesus Christ for He is your

Spiritual husband. You may fool others and yourself but you can't fool God because He knows your heart and your every move and being. Just as you are faithful to your earthly husband then you are to be more faithful to Jesus Christ.

Ps.27:4, David said, one thing I have desired of the Lord, I will seek after Him. I want to dwell in the house of the Lord all the days of my life to behold His beauty and to inquire of His temple. David said that he was going to seek after the things of the Lord. He wasn't going to let go of that for it was most important to him. He wanted to make sure that he was going to dwell in the house of the Lord forever with Jesus His Lord. He was looking forward in seeing the beauty of the Lord and all He had for him. He was saying, I have a lot to ask Him about His temple and of other things too. This should be every Christian's desire as well. I know there are many things I want to ask the Lord when I see Him face to face. On the other hand I may be so happy and filled with joy that nothing else matters but seeing Him and being in Heaven. What we think in our mortal minds here will all be different then. We see through a glass darkly now but then face to face with our Savior Jesus Christ. What we think matters here will be of no concern then I'm sure because we'll be changed from this mortal body to a new immortal body to be like Him. Praise the Lord.

What is your desire? Are you working to please God? Is your body clean and holy? Do you have a desire to be closer to Him? Do you want a closer relationship with Him? Who and what do you love the most? He won't accept anything but first place in your heart and life. He said to seek Him first and Heaven and all of these other things will be added unto you. He said to try Me and see if I won't do what I said I would do. He's waiting for your answer. Don't wait too long for He is coming back soon for His bride and only those who have their wedding garments on are going to be ready to go with Him in the rapture that's going to take place in the clouds. He's coming for those who are waiting and looking for Him. If you're not ready I'm sure you're not looking for Him or even want Him to come. Jesus said, Come while it's today for today is the day of salvation. Don't put off until tomorrow what you can do today for tomorrow may never come. Right now is all you have for you are not promised tomorrow and yesterday is gone forever. You can have life abundantly here and eternal life with Him if you will give Him your heart and life then serve Him with all of your heart, mind, soul and strength. What is your answer? Give up and let Jesus take hold of your life and He'll make a way for you, whatever your need is He will meet.

Ps.15, David asked the Lord, who shall abide in your Tabernacle? Who shall dwell in your Holy hills? The answer was and still is this, they that walks uprightly and works righteousness and speaks the truth in their hearts. They that backbites not with their tongue nor speaks evil of their neighbors not takes up a reproach against their neighbors. In whose eyes a vile person is condemned but He honors them that fear the Lord. They that swears to their own hurts and changes not, they that puts not their money to usury nor takes reward against the innocent, they that does these things shall never be moved. Ps.24:3-4, David asked again, who shall ascend unto the hills of the Lord? Or who shall stand in His Holy place? The answer was this and still the same. They that have clean hands and a pure heart who have not lifted up their soul unto vanity now sworn deceitfully. Ps.23:6, Surely goodness and mercy shall follow me all the days of my life and I will dwell in the house of the Lord forever. This is the assurance from God for His bride, the church, those who are walking in His footsteps everyday. Don't let Him catch you unaware and then you be left here to have to go through the great tribulation. That's going to be a time that has never been before and will never be again. You think you're having troubles now, you have never seen trouble like it will be after the church is called out in the rapture. I like Paul, plead and beg you to accept Jesus now and live for Him. It's such a wonderful life serving Him. It won't be a perfect but there is love, peace, joy, happiness and mercy when you follow Him. He will be with you always and help you through every problem you may have in this life. He will be your best friend as well as your Savior. He loves you and He is waiting for you to come to Him and ask Him into your heart and life. He will forgive you of all your sins and wash you clean and then He will forget all of your past sins and life. No one else can do that for you. No one will ever love you like He does. He said, trust, try and prove Me and see if I won't do the things I said I would do. God is a good God all of the time.

CHAPTER FIVE

What Is A Disciple?

CHAPTER 5

What Is A Disciple?

A disciple is one who follows the opinion and teachings of another. They are a follower. You can be a disciple of many things and people. But we're going to be talking about only one kind of disciple, one who follows the teachings of Jesus Christ. He doesn't have an opinion for what He teaches is the truth of God the Father. HE IS THE TRUTH. If you have accepted Jesus in your heart and life then you are His disciple. Are you a disciple of Jesus Christ?

Luke 14:26-27, If anyone comes to Me and hate not their father, mother, wife, children, brothers, sisters and even their own life cannot be My disciple. And whosoever does not bear their own cross and come after Me cannot be My disciple. He's not talking about literal hatred but Jesus is saying, He has to be first place in your life above all others. If you put Him first place then all else will fall into place. Matt.6:33, Seek ye first the Kingdom of Heaven and all its righteousness and all other things will be added unto you. It's not about us but it's all about Him. We have to deny self and follow Him to be His disciple. Jesus never said it would be easy but it's rewarding. There have been many times that my family was having a get together and I couldn't be with them because I was called into a ministry to work for the Lord so I had to put Him first. Many times they just couldn't understand and even got upset with me. Many times I wanted so much to be with them but I had to do what I was called to do. It's not been easy many, many times but it's been rewarding. I pray they have understood and have the respect of me for serving the Lord and giving Him my life. I know I missed out on a lot of things with my family but God has tremendously blessed me and I don't regret a mile that I have walked with Him. There have been other times that I wanted to do something else but I had to be faithful to God in my calling. This life is going to pass quickly and the only thing that's going to last is what we do for the Lord. I've had a good life in the Lord and I do love my family but the Lord has to come first.

Matt.16:24, Jesus said to His disciples, if anyone would come after me let them deny themselves and take up their cross and follow Me. If you live after the flesh you will die but if you live by the Spirit and mortify the deeds and the lusts of the flesh you shall live. You can't please God if you please the flesh. They that are in Christ have crucified the flesh of all the lusts of the flesh. The flesh is weak but the Spirit is strong in the Lord. Don't listen to your flesh but listen to the Spirit of God and you will overcome the desires of the flesh. If you listen to your flesh it will get you into lots of sin and trouble. Peter said, we have left all to follow Christ. These disciples left their families and everything to follow Christ, they were true followers of Him. Jesus said, whosoever does not forsake all that you have cannot be My disciple. Luke 18:29-30, There is an award for following Jesus. He said you shall receive manifold blessings in this present world and the world to come, life everlasting. All who have left houses, parents, children, brothers and sisters and wife for the Kingdom and God's sake can have many blessings now and later too. There is no better life than to walk with the Lord all of the way. We will stumble at times but He will pick us up and put us on the right road. The disciples made mistakes too because they were human as we are. God knew their hearts and their desires were to follow Him. The disciples went through a lot of trials and sufferings because they follow Jesus. They even lost their lives for the sake of Christ. They would not deny Him even in death. Peter denied Him three times before He was crucified because of fear for His life but he repented and Jesus forgave him because He knew his heart and he had been true to Him through his life.

Phil.3:8, Paul said, I count everything but loss for the excellency of the knowledge of Jesus Christ my Lord for whom I have suffered loss of all things and count them but dung that I may win Christ. Dung is a matter discharged from an animal's canal. So this is what he was saying about anything and all else but what was done for Christ. It is all worthless Paul was saying. Only what you do for Christ and the Kingdom of God will last and profit you. All things will pass away and last only a little but what you do for Christ is eternal. The world and everything in it will be burned up in the end and a new Heaven and earth will be made and only the children of God will live in the new world. Whatever you do, do it all in the name of Jesus Christ. Matt.25, tells us what we do for others we do it to Him. When we visit the sick or the ones in prisons we do it unto Him. When we give to the hungry and thirsty and the needy we do it as unto Him. This is a part of being a disciple of Jesus. Paul said, look not after the things for yourself but also on the things of others. We have to be concerned and care for others especially our brothers and sisters in Christ.

Matt.16:25, Whosoever will seek their life shall lose it and whosoever will lose their life for My sake will save it. To save your life in the end you have to follow Jesus Christ to the very end. They that endure to the end the same will be saved. You have to let the Holy Spirit lead and guide you in the right way in all things to be His disciple. You have to surrender your whole life and not just part of it. You are either for Him or against Him for you can't serve two masters. God will not settle for part time followers. Rom.6:11, Reckon you, yourselves to be dead indeed to all sin but alive unto God through Jesus Christ our Lord. You who belong to Christ have crucified your flesh of the affections of sinful things and lusts. You now love the things of God and what's pleasing to Him. You have to be submissive to the will of God and your whole heart is required. You can have no other god before Him for He is Lord of all lords and King of all kings.

Ps.40:8, David said and we should also, I delight to do Thy will O God, yes the law is within my heart. Teach me to do your will for you are my God, lead me into the land of righteousness. Do you know that we are Jesus brothers and sisters? Matt.12:50, Whosoever shall do the will of My Father which is in Heaven the same is My brother, sister and mother. He's our everything that's why we can sing, He's all we need for when we have Him we have everything. I sing a song, He's everything to me, and I really mean it from my heart. We don't do things for eye service or men pleasers but as servants of Jesus Christ doing the will of God from the heart. Always pray and ask God what His will is for you and to have His will be done in you. James 4:15, Don't say you will do this or that but say if it's the Lord's will you will do this or that. The reason so many Christians get themselves in a mess or in trouble is because they don't seek God's will for them. They just do what they feel they want to do and it doesn't have to be sin but you need to always ask God for His decision or approval. God will never lead you astray or in the wrong direction for He wants the best for His children. They that do the will of the Father will live forever. He wants our hearts and our eyes to observe His ways. Many get into great financial and money problems because they don't consult God and ask what's best for them.

Rom.12:1, I beseech or beg you my brethren by the mercies of God to present your bodies a living sacrifice, holy and acceptable unto God which is your reasonable service. He said, our bodies meaning our entire body not just part of it. We are to present our eyes, ears, hands, feet, mouth, mind, strength and our entire heart completely to Him. I Thessalonians 5:23, And the very God of peace sanctify you wholly and I pray God your whole spirit, soul and body be preserved blameless unto the coming of our Lord Jesus Christ. You can see here that God wants your whole life to serve Him. You can't serve Him one day and then not the next day. God is not a part time God so we can't be a part time follower. Jesus said, you are either for Me or you are against Me. Remember, a disciple is a follower. What or whom are you following? If you are following Jesus Christ then you are to walk and talk like Him, go about doing good. The very first commandment is, There shall have no other god before Me. He is the one and only true God. Don't let anything or anyone cause you not to serve or follow Christ. Don't put most of your time in something else and then give Him what's left over. Many put television, sports and family, reading other books, other outings and even work before God. Then they are too tired to get into the Word of God or go to His house to praise and worship Him. Now there's nothing wrong with any of these things, but if you put any of them before God then you make it wrong. Do the things of the Lord first and then what time you have left do the other things. Be careful of whom you follow, make sure it's Jesus Christ. Some follow the preacher or pastor but you can't put your eyes on men or women for they will fail you many times. The one in the pulpit is not the one you follow but you follow Jesus for He will never fail you or leave you. Be a disciple of Jesus Christ and live forever. Amen

Believers, true church of God

Acts 2:42-47, The Christians and the saints devoted themselves to the apostle's teaching of Peter and to the fellowship of the breaking of bread and to prayer. Everyone was filled with awe, or fear, and many wonders and miraculous signs were done by the apostles. All the believers were together and had everything in common, for they were in one accord. They sold all of their possessions and gave to the poor and needy. They met everyday with each other in the temple court. They broke bread, and ate together along with their meat with gladness and singleness of heart. They had sincere hearts toward God and each other. They praised God and enjoyed the favor of all the people and the Lord added unto them daily those that were saved. These people worshipped God and was in the temple everyday together eating and praising God. Jesus broke bread with His disciples. Luke 24:30, And it came to pass as Jesus sat at meat with them that He took the bread and broke it and gave it to them to eat.. Verse 44, They were all in one accord. Rom.12:5, So we being many members are one body in Christ and everyone members of one another.

What is a believer? What does it mean to be in the saint's fellowship? A believer is one who has put their faith and trust in

Jesus Christ. One who has a conviction of the truth and stands on it. One who has a certainty and assurance of what you believe and then follow it. A believer of Jesus Christ is one who has been born again and now is living and trusting in Him. Their whole life depends totally upon Him. Believers are empowered by the Holy Spirit and called to operate in the name of Jesus. A saint is one who follows Jesus Christ and proves it to others by doing what He has taught them to do. They live their life for Him and they are not of the world nor have their sights on anything in this world. The most important thing in this world is Jesus Christ and doing His will. Ps.119:63, David said, I am the companion of all those that fear the Lord or love the Lord and those that keep the commandments or laws of God. He was saying, I keep myself among those who love the Lord and not those of the world who are not of the household of faith. He is saying, I have separated myself from all else except those that follow the Lord. Mal.3:16, They that fear or loved the Lord spoke often to one another and the Lord hearkened and heard them and a book of remembrance was written before Him for them that thought upon His name. God keeps a record of what we do. He loves it when the believers and saints of God come together and fellowship and worships Him. I John 1:7, If we walk in the light as He is in the light we have fellowship one with another and the blood of Jesus Christ His Son cleanses us from all of our sins. Ps.92:13-14, Those that be planted in the house of the Lord shall flourish in the courts of our God. They shall bring forth fruit in old age and they shall be fat and flourishing.

Guidelines for the believers

Gal.5:22-23, The fruit of the Spirit is love, joy, peace, long suffering, mercy, grace, gentleness, goodness, faith, meekness and temperance. Epe.5:9. The fruit of the Spirit is in all goodness, righteousness and truth. These are the qualities that believers should always live by. There is one fruit of the Spirit but many qualities. Living by these qualities we can know who are believers and saints of God. We have to love everyone and we are to show mercy and grace to them. Jesus said that if you want mercy then you have to show mercy. We can have the peace and joy of the Lord even when things are not going well with us for the joy of the Lord is our strength. We have to be long suffering for one another and be gentle with each other and we have to be good to one another. We are not to fly off the hinges or get angry with others but have temperance one to another. Be meek and gentle with each other instead of being judgmental. And of course, we have to have faith in God in everything. If we follow these guidelines then we will be followers of Jesus Christ. Just saying you believe isn't good enough for you have to be obedient and follow His guidelines. You have to be a doer and not just a hearer only. I Cor.10:17, For we being many are one bread and one body for we all are partakers of that on bread, Jesus Christ. I Cor.12:12-13, For as the body is one and has many members and all the members of that one body being many are one body so also is Christ. For by one Spirit are we all baptized into one body whether we be Jews or Gentiles, whether we be bond or free and have all been made to drink into one Spirit. I Cor.1:10, Now I beseech or beg you brethren by the name of our Lord Jesus Christ that you all speak the same thing that there be no division among you but be perfectly joined together in the same mind and in the same judgment. There should never be a division among God's children. If we would stay in one accord we would see much more of the working of the Holy Spirit and miracles of God working among us when we meet together. Look what happened in the upper room when the one hundred and twenty were all in one accord. They were all filled with the power of God and spoke in other tongues. Oh how I'd love to see more of the power of God fall when we all get together with God's wonderful people. II Cor.13:11, Be perfect be of good comfort, be in one mind, live in peace and the God of love and peace shall be with you. Do you want God's love and peace to be with you? Then you will have to live in peace with everyone, be in comfort with yourself and others and stop worrying and fretting and put your trust in God and He said peace shall be with you, for God is love and peace. Epe.4:3, Endeavoring to keep the unity of the Spirit in the bond of peace. You need to want and try to keep peace with everyone and stay in the same spirit with one another. Stay in the Spirit of God. Phil.1:27, Let your conversation only be as it be comes the gospel of Christ, stand fast in one spirit, one mind striving together for the faith of the gospel. Be in one mind having compassion one to another, love the brethren and be humble. Live in harmony with each other and love one another.

True Ministers of God

I Thessalonians 2:4, As we were allowed or called of God to be put in trust with the gospel even so we speak, not as pleasing men or women but God, which tries our hearts. Paul said, we beseech you brethren or beg and urge you by the Lord Jesus Christ, that you have received of us how you ought to walk and please God, more and more. We are to do good and share with other Christian brothers and sisters for this pleases God. 1 Cor.1:9, God is faithful by whom we were called unto the fellowship of His Son Jesus Christ our Lord. John said, that which we have seen and heard declare to you our fellowship is truly with the Father and His Son Jesus Christ. There's nothing that God loves better than for His children to have a good relationship and to fellowship with Him. He loves for you and me to talk to Him always. The way we do that is to pray to Him. When you stay that close to Him then you will walk with Him also. All are ministers of God in some way. All are not preachers or teachers but all are to pray and seek Him for others as well as for yourselves. There are many deeds that need to be met by God's children. Many need visits, food, and shelter, transportation to and from places. Many just need some encouragement and to be brought joy into their lives. There are some that just a telephone call will minister to them. Many in the nursing homes never have visitors or anyone to care for them. All of these things call for ministering to.

Family of God

These words describe the family of God. Dependant, connected, related and loved. These words describe the community of the first Christians. The first century Christians shared their resources, and willingly invested in their hard earned money in the lives of others who didn't have anything and who were in need. They met in the temple regularly to feed on the Heavenly bread, the Word of God.

They gathered in homes to break bread and enjoyed fellowship with each other. Their lives were intertwined and connected with each other. What has changed all of that in our day? Why is it that Christians aren't doing the same today? Did God change that? I don't believe so because He never changes. of course, I don't recall any scripture saying to sell what you have to give away to others but it does say that we are to take care of the hungry, thirsty, widows, fatherless and those who are in need. If all of the churches are doing what they are supposed to do then why are there so many living on the streets? This is not only for the churches but all of the Christians as well. What are we doing to help and do the things that God has told us to do? God is going to hold us accountable for not meeting the needs when we see them, I believe. I know, there are some who you can't help because they like the way they are living and don't even want to change if you even tried to helped them. My husband and I have helped a lot of people and they just wasted it all away. It takes wisdom and knowledge from above to do the right thing. There are some who accepts Christ from others meeting their needs and we have seen that too. What a great blessing that is. We are our brothers and sisters keeper the Word tells us. We need each other just as those early Christians did. They drew life from each other and shared with each other with joy and through sorrows. They were real family, the family of God. Epe.4:4-5, There is one body and one Spirit, even as you are called in one hope when you were called. One Lord, one faith, one baptism, one God and Father of all who is over all and in all.

Jesus is knocking

Rev.3:20, Behold I stand at the door and knock if anyone hear My voice and opens the door I will come in to them and I will sup with them and they with Me. God has done all of the work for us and all we have to do is accept His Word, which is Jesus Christ His Son, confess our sins and ask Jesus Christ in our heart and life. Then we have to love Him above all others and all else. We have to be obedient and serve Him all the days of our life. Christians are believers in God and they are the true family of God. I'm so glad to be a part of the family of God. Aren't you? If you aren't then you need to accept

Jesus today and then you will be a part of the family of God too. It's wonderful to have Spiritual brothers and sisters in the Lord. But best of all it's good to have God the Father as your Father. Your earthly father loves and cares for his children but there's nothing like the love and care of the Heavenly Father to His children. Lets do everything we can to please the Father. Let's do it His way and go back to our first love. John said in Revelation that some had lost their first love for Jesus Christ and they have become lukewarm and God said that makes Him sick. He said He would spew you out of His mouth for you have to be either hot or cold for you can't be lukewarm. There is only one right way and that's God's way. Jesus Christ has designed the way so let's walk in it, and then we will truly be the true church of God. There are many denominations but there's only one church, and that's the true Christ of God.

A call to be faithful to God

Jude 1:2-12, Jude sounds a passionate warning to believers who's faith is under attack from immoral and rebellious elements within the church. The warning is directed to those who have become arrogant in regards to the Spiritual realm. We are to conduct ourselves with humility. Our responsibility is to submit to the authority of God Himself and not to use His authority by taking it on ourselves. This is to all who are called to live in the love of God the Father and care of Jesus Christ. We are to receive more and more of God's mercy, peace and love. Jude is urging the children of God to defend the truth of the gospel news, the gospel of Jesus Christ. God entrusted this with His saints of old and to His holy people. We're to keep the truth still and spread it to everyone all over the world just as they did of old. Don't be deceived by false teachers that has come in or crept into the world and churches today. Make sure you know the true Word of God so you will know when someone is teaching false doctrines or the wrong thing. The way that you can do that is to study the Word of God, the Bible and God will reveal the truth to you. Some teach that you can live immoral lives because He has forgiven you of your sins. Be reminded that even though God rescued the Israelites out of Egypt that He later destroyed them who did not remain faithful and obedient to Him. The angels even had to leave their homes because they didn't keep their positions and authority in God. They fell and God has them bound and reserved in darkness for the Day of Judgment. Sodom and Gomorrah were destroyed because of their sexual sins and perversion. They were destroyed by fire because of their unbelief and sins. Likewise these filthy dreamers defiled the flesh, despised the dominion and spoke of dignities. They speak evil of those which they do not know but what they know naturally as brute beasts, in those things they corrupt themselves. Woe unto them for they have gone the way of Cain and have run greedily after the error of Balaam for reward and perished in the gainsaying or denying the truth. They are like clouds carrying no water and carried away with wind their trees and withered away without fruit, twice dead and plucked up by the roots. Jude is saying here that they are false teachers not understanding what they are talking about and are corrupting themselves. How terrible for them for they went the way of a killer and a liar for it was Cain who killed his brother and then lied about it. These kinds of people will do anything for money and gain but will perish in their rebellion. Jude calls them hypocrites. They are shepherds just feeding themselves and are nothing but air bags without any good fruit. They die twice because they have been uprooted from their roots. These kind of people will die once here and then be raised up at the judgment day be judged and thrown into the lake of fire for the second death. Rom.6:23, For the wages of sin is death. You cannot get by with sin for no sin will enter into the kingdom of Heaven. Prov.21:16, They that wander out of the way of understanding shall remain in the congregation of the dead. You have to abide in Christ and endure to the end and then the same shall be saved. 1Tim.5:6, They that live in pleasure are dead while they live. Jude is talking about the pleasures of sin. Heb.9:27, For it's appointed unto men to die once but after that the judgment. So you see false teachers and all who deny Jesus Christ, all the rebellious and disobedient people are dead now while they are living for they are without God in their life. Then they will die at the time appointed by God and then they will be raised up at the great white throne judgment and be judged and thrown into the lake of fire along with the devil and his angels for the second death and be doomed forever.

The only life one can have is in Jesus Christ for He is the Word. Why anyone wants to waste their life here and then have to go to hell I just can't figure it out. Let me urge you to turn to Jesus Christ while you have time. Get into a church that teaches and preaches the full gospel of Jesus Christ. God will forgive you of all your sins if you will just ask Him into your heart and life and then you follow Him.

Verses 14-15-19, As far back as Enoch, the seventh from Adam have prophesied saying, the Lord is coming with His ten thousand saints to execute judgment upon all to convince all that are ungodly and their ungodly deeds which they have committed, along with all of their insults that they have spoken of against Him. Generation after generation has been warned about rejecting Christ Jesus and living evil. There's no reason or excuse for not knowing the truth. There are still many Islands of many people that have not been reached yet as the missionaries have been telling. But for all else, there will be no excuse when they stand before Jesus Christ to be judged. Please take warning from all of these prophets of old and from the true teaching and preaching today of Jesus Christ and turn from your ungodly living and turn to Him before it's too late. Jude lists some of the evil in the churches as well as some other places also. There are murmurs, complainers walking after their own flesh and their mouth speaks great swelling words, these are boaster. They boast about themselves and flatter others for their own advantage to get what they want or to get favors from them in return. There are grumblers and complainers, fault finders and they confuse others. There are mockers in the last days that walk after their own ungodly lusts. There are those who separate themselves sensual because they don't have the Spirit of God dwelling in them. We need to remember what the apostles of Jesus Christ said. Verse 19, In the last days there will be scoffers who would follow their own ungodly desires. These are the one who divide and cause division among the church. They follow their own instincts and do not have the Spirit of God in them. Don't let these kinds of people contaminate you and lead you astray or cause you to be weak in the faith and fall. Do not follow them for you will fall into the ditch with them. The Bible tells us that if the blind lead the blind then both will fall into the ditch.

Our Spiritual foundation is in Jesus Christ

Verses 20-25, Our spiritual foundation is in Jesus Christ, our hope and service unto Him. Continue to hold your lives on this foundation with holy faith and continue to pray always. This is our hope and security if we are going to persevere in Him. We have to grow spiritually and pray always in the Spirit. Keep yourselves holy and righteous in the love of God looking for mercy of our Lord Jesus Christ unto eternal life. We are to have compassion, mercy and sympathy for others. We have to be soul winners and help the weak in faith. Verse 23, Save others with fear, which is love, pulling them out of the fire of hell, hating even the garments spotted by the flesh… We have to hate sin but love the sinner. We have to live our lives in a way that God's love can bless us as we wait for His coming and for eternal life that our Lord Jesus in His mercy has promised. Never grow weary in your Christian walk, for in due time you will reap if you faint not. Be sure to bring others to the saving knowledge of Jesus Christ and don't be contaminated by their sin or fall to their level. Never compromise with sin or any anything that contradicts with the Word of God. We should never argue with others over the Word of God. We are to show them the truth and walk in it and if they reject it then the Bible say to shake the dust off your feet and walk away, for the blood won't be required on your hands if they don't make it into the Kingdom of Heaven. We can't save anyone but we must try to lead them to Christ and tell them the plan of salvation. Not everyone will listen but the angels rejoice over one that comes to Christ and we can too. Win all you can while it is still day for the night is coming when our work will be done.

We cannot keep our salvation, only God can

Verses 24-24, Now unto Him that is able to keep you from falling and to present you faultless before the presence of His glory with exceeding joy, to the only wise God our Savior be glory, majesty, dominion and power both now and forevermore. We give God all the glory and honor for our salvation through Jesus Christ His Son. Yes, glory, majesty, power and all authority belongs to Him from the beginning, now and forevermore... Just think, we will live with Him forever if we persevere and endure to the end in Him. We have to continue to walk with Him, be obedient and faithful to Him and keep our faith in Him to the end. We can never praise and thank Him enough for all He's done for us and in keeping us. He will never leave or forsake His children and we can be assured of this. Again I will say, Jesus said to trust, try and prove Me and see if I won't do what I said I'd do. Praise God for His keeping power for we don't have that kind of power. Jesus gives us a lot of power through the Holy Ghost but not the keeping power of our salvation. Just like we can't make our bodies holy it's only through the Holy Spirit. We can try with everything we have within us but we cannot be perfect living in this flesh. God is so awesome and His love is unexplainable to us, His children. There is never a time that we shouldn't praise Him for who He is and what He does. He is our keeper of our soul. We need to do all we can to keep our bodies clean and in order.

One thing

Everyday we have options on how we will spend our time and what we will focus our minds and hearts on. Desires are one thing we think about. Ps.51:6, Behold you desire truth in the inward parts and in the hidden part You shall make me know wisdom. David is talking about God here. He is saying, my desire to know more truth is down deep inside of me and he knows that God is going to make him know wisdom. In Prov.13:19 it says this, the desire accomplished is sweet to the soul. How much do we feed our souls? The Bible teaches us that we shall prosper and be in good health just as our soul prospers. When you look around and see so many sick Christians it makes you wonder, what is going on? Then you see so many Christians living in poverty. What's going on with this scene? I believe every Word of the Lord and if He said it then it will happen. Our souls must be in order and we need to check it out. God said we can prosper and be in good health just as our soul prospers. Our desires must not be in line with God's desires if our souls are not prospering. Something is wrong and we know that it's not God. We need to check ourselves out to see what is missing that we can't stay in good health and prosper. Now, we have to look at it in another way as well. It was God's will from the very beginning of the creation that when He made man and woman they were perfect and there was no sin or temptations. God made everything good and perfect. Adam and Eve allowed sin to come in and changed all of that. This was to be Heaven on earth and God wouldn't have had to make another plan to make another Heaven. It was His will that all would be in good health and be prosperous then and He has not changed that. For God made it that way in the very beginning for He has always wanted the best for His children. Not everything bad that comes upon you is because you have failed but because when Adam and Eve sinned it brought sin and sickness into this world. Christians are tested many times to see if we are going to stand the test and come out stronger. Many saints of God have died with sickness and they walked with God. Please don't get me wrong for all sickness and problems are not brought on by your failures but by the failures of Adam and Eve in the very beginning. We really need to take inventory of our soul and our entire being to be able to maybe improve our health and our prosperity. Search me O God and see if there be any thing in my life that should not be there and if I am lacking anything that should be there. Show me Lord if there's any evil in my heart and soul and convict me of it. Wash me and cleanse me and make me holy. This should be every Christian's prayer. God said we can have the desires of our heart when we delight ourselves in Him and commit our ways unto Him then He would bring it to pass. (ps.34:4-5) What do you spend the most of your time on? Decisions reveal what we value the most in life. Now I know there are things like going to work, taking the children to school that is a must for it's important but what about the rest of the day? There are many things in a day's time that we can choose to do with our time. Are you leaving God for the last and giving Him what is left over? He doesn't want your leftovers when He can go somewhere else and get the very best. Luke 10:41:42, Jesus tells His friend Martha, there are many things that demand our attention, energy and certainly many things are important BUT only one thing is needed and Mary has what is better and it will not be taken away from her.

Verse 41, Jesus said one thing is needed and Mary has chosen that. The thing that is needed is a vital constant fellowship with the Lord. Mary's thoughts and desires were on Jesus. When we keep our minds and hearts on Him then He will take care of all other things. Jesus knows there are things you must do early in the morning and He honors that. But you can set your clock an hour early and have time with Him before your day starts in other things. It will make a much better day for you. God wants your first fruits not what's left over. Early morning with God is the best part of my day and I yearn for it everyday. There has been times when emergencies came up and shifted things around and it seemed everything went wrong on that day. I love to study God's Word and I like doing it early in the morning. You're fresher and your mind seems to grasp the things of God quicker and it's so powerful. There's truly life in the Word of God. When God said He wanted your first fruit He wasn't just talking about your money, your tithes but He was talking about your time, talent, desires and your plans. Never forget that He has to be number one in your life in everything. When He is number one in your life then He will cause everything else to come together and be in place and in order for you. He will not let you down. I have seen it happen many times. When I have given God the first part of the day it seemed I got more done in the rest of the day and it was so much smoother for me. Ps.27:4, David said, one thing I ask of the Lord that this is what I seek, that I may dwell in the house of the Lord all the days of my life to gaze on the beauty of the Lord and to seek Him in His temple. He wanted to be in the presence of the Lord all of the time. He said, more than anything else in the world he longed to be conscious of God's presence. This was his greatest desire, He wanted to worship God and to be led by His power and by His perfect wisdom. Such a goal will be "ONE THING" that gives our life meaning. This one thing should be our prayer and goal, when we wake up in the morning to seek God and seek what He wants for our life this day. He may want something greater than what you may want for the day. He wants the very best for His children.

One thing's going to happen to all

Ecl.3:19-20, All die humans and animals alike and all go to one place. All are of the dust and all will turn back to dust. We have no power over death. It will be the last thing conquered by Jesus Christ. It's appointed unto men and women once to die and after this the judgment, we know that Jesus is coming in the rapture to get His children and take them with Him to Heaven. We believe that will happen soon but no one knows the day or the hour. Some have predicted Jesus to come on May 11 of 2011 and some say 2012, but you can't fall into that trap, for the Bible tells us that no one knows the day or the hour when He is coming, not even the angels in Heaven. That's why you need to know the Word of God so you will recognize the false prophets. Jesus could come at anytime for we can see that by the signs of the times. Jesus said, when you see these things at hand then you can know the time of His coming is near. Wars upon wars, all nations divided against each other, earthquakes in diver places, change in the weather, strange things happening in the heavens and other things as well. Our world is in a real mess and the only one who can ever make it right is Jesus Christ. Get yourselves ready for He can come at anytime now to get His children and take them out of this sinful and evil world. He's going to take His children out by the rapture of the Church. The ones that go through the rapture will never die but everyone else will die sooner or later. We aren't promised tomorrow or ever the rest of this day so you should be ready to go when God calls you. After death there will be no more chances for one to get saved. You plan here while you are living where you will spend eternity, Heaven or hell. You make the choice for no one else can do that for you. There are many decisions that we can make for others but this one has to be made by each individual themselves. If you end up in hell you can't blame anyone but yourself. Please make the right decision today, right now.

One thing we lack

Mark 10:21, Jesus was talking to the young rich man. One thing you lack, go and sell what you have and give to the poor and you will have treasures in Heaven then come follow Me. Of course, he didn't follow Jesus because he was rich and he desired to worship his money and riches more than to worship Jesus. He wasn't going to give up the one thing that was needed for him to make it into the Kingdom of Heaven. There are a lot of people today that worship their money and their riches more than anything or anyone in this world. Their money is going to perish one day with them and then what will they have? He let that one thing keep him from following Jesus and going to Heaven. Life here is such a short one but Heaven is eternal. This man had kept all of the commandments from his youth he told Jesus. He was interested in getting saved for he asked Jesus, what must I do to get save and have eternal life? Jesus told him what to do but he loved his money and riches too much. He wouldn't give it all up for Jesus and that's how it is with many people today. They want to hold on to some things but that can't happen. Jesus wants your all, He wants your entire body, soul and spirit. He will give you back more than you can ever expect if you will just trust Him. It's all about Him, trust and have faith in Him. God don't want His children to be broke and without money but He want to see if you will trust Him to give you more. He gave us His all so why won't you give Him your all?

One thing known

John 9:25, He answered and said, whether he be a sinner or not I don't know. One thing I know that where I was blind I now can see. The blind man didn't know about being a sinner but he knew that he was blind and now he can see. He knew this one thing. Phil.3:13, Brethren I count myself to have apprehended or taken hold of, or know it all. But this one thing I do, forgetting those things which are behind and reaching forth unto those things which are before. Paul is saying here that it doesn't matter what things are behind for he's going to reach for better things ahead of him. The Bible says that he that looks back at the plow is not worthy of the Kingdom of God. You want to forget the bad things in the past and press on to higher grounds with the Lord Jesus Christ. II Pet.3:8, But beloved be not ignorant of this one thing, that one day is like a thousand years and a thousand years as one day. God's time table is different from ours on this earth. While we have the time let's press on to the high calling of God and win this race for one thing I know, He Is Coming Soon. Be ready for He will come in a twinkling of an eye. You won't have time to get ready so prepare now.

One thing to do

I Tim.4:13-16, Until I come give attendance to reading, exhortation and to doctrine. Neglect not the gift that is in you and take heed unto yourself and unto the doctrine, continue in them for so doing this you shall both save yourself and those that hear you. Neglect not the gift that is in you which was given to you by the prophecy with the laying on of hands of the presbytery. Meditate on these things, give yourself wholly to them, that your profiting may appear to all. Take heed to yourself and unto the doctrine, continue in them for in doing this you shall both save yourself and them that hear you. You are to stir up the gift that is within you for you are to use the spiritual gift that God has given you. You are responsible to God to use what He has given to you. Keep yourself and to be soul winners for the Lord Jesus Christ. Like I have said before, we all have talents and gifts that God has given and we are to be sure to use them for His glory. There's no time just to sit around and do nothing for the Kingdom is at hand. We only have a certain allotted time to do the work that the Lord has given us and only He knows how long and when. Be faithful in what He has called you to do and do it whole heartily. In I Timothy you can find these words. We are to pray everywhere lifting up holy hands unto the Lord without wrath and doubting. Follow after righteousness, godliness, faith, love, patience and meekness. Keep the commandments without spot and sacred until the appearing of our Lord Jesus Christ. You are to live holy and righteous in Him. Titus 2:7-13, In all things show yourself a pattern of good works in doctrine, showing no corruption, gravity, which is to be earnest and sincerity. These things speak, exhort and rebuke with all authority with sound speech that can't be condemned. Live soberly, righteous and godly in this present world looking for that blessed hope and the glorious appearing of the great God and our Savior Jesus Christ. Make sure to be ready when He comes for you will be going home, your permanent home forever to live with Jesus and all of the saints of God in that land that He has gone to prepare.

Renewed heart

Ps.57:57, My heart is fixed O God, my heart is fixed and I will sing praises. David is saying here that his heart is fixed on God and doing what He wants him to do. Is your heart fixed on the Lord? Jer.24:7, God said, I will give them a heart to know Me, that I am the Lord and they shall be My people and I will be their God for they shall return unto Me with their whole heart. To give our whole heart to God we must do these things. We must be earnest in love for Him. You shall love the Lord with all your heart, soul and with all your might. We have to be obedient and faithful to Him. Blessed are they that keep His testimonies and that seek Him with their whole heart. Ps.119:33, Teach me O Lord the ways of Your statues and I shall keep them unto the end. Give me understanding and I will keep Your laws and will observe them with my whole heart. Make me to go in the path of Thy commandments for in them do I delight. Incline my heart unto Your testimonies. Verse 40, Behold, I have longed after Your precepts so quicken me in Your righteousness. This is what a renewed heart is, one that is after God's own heart and not obeying the flesh. Now we have to trust and lean on Him to lead and guide us all of the way. Prov.3:5-6, Trust in the Lord with your whole heart and lean not upon your own understanding. In all your ways acknowledge Him and He will direct your ways. We have to pray and seek Him for what He wants to do in our lives. He said, seek Me and you will find Me when you search for Me with your whole heart. He said, come unto Me and I will answer. I will be with you in trouble, I will deliver and honor you. God wants to help you but you must call upon him. He wants to talk to you for He is your Father and you're His child. Isa.65:24, And it shall come to pass that before they call upon Me I will answer and while they are speaking I will hear. He knows our needs even before we ask. Many times the answer has come before we ask and we can't even see it or know it. Ask and you shall receive, knock and it shall be opened unto you. John 15, says, Ask anything in My name and it shall be done unto you, if you abide in Me and My Words abide in you. This is the part that most Christians don't see. In order for you to get what you ask for you have to abide in Jesus Christ and His Words to abide in you. That's why lots of prayers aren't answered. To abide in Him you have to live holy without sin for He won't live in a temple all messed up with sin in it. If there's something in your life that shouldn't be there you need to repent and be sorry for your sins and turn from them and turn to Jesus and He will forgive you of all of them and wash you and make you clean with His blood. Joel 2:12-13, Therefore says the Lord, turn to Me with your whole heart with fasting, weeping and mourning. Rend, or tear your heart and not your garments and turn unto the Lord your God for He is gracious, merciful, slow to anger, He's of great kindness and repents Him of the evil. God doesn't want to punish you for He would rather bless you that's why He wants you to come to Him and repent with a sorrowful heart. Get rid of all of the bad stuff in your heart and life and serve Him only. God said, love me with your whole heart, mind, soul and strength, this is the first and great commandment. We are still in the flesh but we have to be spiritual minded. We are to be led by the Holy Spirit and not by our flesh. When you gave your heart to the Lord then you were spiritually resurrected in Him. We're not the same as before for you are a new person in Jesus Christ. Old things are passed away behold all things are become new. We're not to go to the same places anymore as when we were out in sin. We're not to talk the same way anymore, even our thought pattern has changed. We think different for we now want to be what Jesus wants us to be. We are to be careful what our eyes look upon, what our ears are hearing, what our hands are doing and where our feet are taking us. We are to keep our minds and thoughts on Him and being the loving kind person as He is. Rom.8:6, For to be carnally minded is death but to be spiritual minded is life and peace. I Cor.2:16, For who has known the mind of Christ that He may instruct him, we have the mind of Christ. Phil.2:5, Let this mind be in you which was also in Jesus Christ. If we keep our hearts and minds on Jesus Christ we will then have a mind like

Him. We should always desire to be like Him. No, we're not perfect but we are to strive to be perfect as He is perfect. This should be our greatest desire to be like Him. When He comes back He's coming for a people without spot or wrinkle. He has told us how to live and what He expects from His children so there's no excuse for living wrong or not knowing His will for us.

Believers as spiritual persons

Ezek.11:19, I will give them one heart and I will put a new Spirit within you and take away the stony heart out of their flesh and will give them a heart of flesh. II Cor.5:17, Therefore if anyone is in Christ they are a new creature, behold all things become new. Epe.4:24, You have put on a new person whom God has created in righteousness and true holiness. Col.3:10, You have put on the new person who is renewed in knowledge after the image of Him that created you and now you are a new person in Him for you have become spiritual. You are not your own anymore for you were bought with a price at Calvary. Jesus died for you and me and gave His own blood. Everything is different now, your thinking, your actions, your speech, and all of your ways since you chose to serve Jesus Christ. Even though we are still living in this same flesh we can live spiritual. When you became a believer and were born again Jesus Christ lives in you and He makes the difference. You have been spiritually resurrected in Christ. Many say they are believers but are not any different than before, because they only confessed with their mouth and not with their heart. They have a head knowledge but not a heart knowledge. If you are a child of God then you have to act like, talk it and live like it.

Now you are spiritually resurrected

Rom.8:11, But if the Spirit of Him who raised up Jesus from the dead dwells in you, which is God the Father, He will also quicken you who were dead in trespasses and sins. Verse 6, He has raised us up together and made us sit together in heavenly places with Christ Jesus. He has changed us, forgiven us and one day He will give us a new body just like Jesus. If you then are raised with Christ seek those things which are from above where Christ sits on the right hand of the Father. We are to seek the things of God and not the things on the earth which are just material things and one day will fade away or be done away with. The heavenly things will last forever. Heaven and all its glory will last forever. Rom.6:4, Therefore we are buried with Him by baptism into death like Christ was raised from the dead by the glory of the Father, even so we also should walk in newness of life. You should walk as Jesus walked since you are born again and have been baptized in Jesus Name. The old person is crucified with Him and the body of sin might be destroyed that from now on you should not serve sin. There's no reason to sin anymore if you are in Christ Jesus and He is in you. Jesus loves everyone so much that He was willing to give His life on an old rugged cross at Calvary. The worse death that can ever be is to be nailed both hands and feet and then be stabbed in the side while you are alive. That's how much He loves everyone. Thank God He didn't stay dead but He arose on the third day and was received up to Heaven where He is today interceding for you and me. He is living within our hearts and He sent His Holy Spirit to lead, guide and protect His children. There has never been such love as this and never will be as the love of Jesus for you and me. He has forgiven our sins and has cast them away as far as the east is from the west never to remember them anymore. You can't live on yesterday's salvation for today is a new day and you are renewed daily. We are to live the fullest in Christ Jesus always. We are to grow in grace, love and mercy everyday. His mercy endures forever and His love for us never dies. He said that He would never leave or forsake His children. Praise the Lord. In turn, we should never forsake Him either. No matter what comes your way stand up for what is right and holy in Christ Jesus.

Spiritual renewal

Phil.1:6-11, Being confident in this one thing, that He that started a good work in you will perform it until the day of Jesus Christ. God has started a good work in you so do the very best you can and He will perform it and give you the grace you need to continue on with it. He will not lead you to where He will not keep you. Paul prayed that your love may abound more and more in knowledge and in all judgment that you may approve things that are excellent, that is sincere and without offences till the day of Christ, being filled with the fruits of righteousness which are by Jesus Christ unto the praise and glory of God the Father. God wants and desires you to renew your Spirit in Him to be what he began in you and then he will perform what you let Him to do. He wants you to have more knowledge of Him and to love Him more. He wants you to be sincere with Him, love and be loyal to Him just as He is sincere with you and loves you. He wants you to bear the fruits of righteousness which are, love, joy, long sufferings, gentleness, goodness, faith and happiness and peace in the Holy Ghost. You see, God never asked us to do anything that is hard to do. I thank Him that He is still working on me for I see a lot of clean up still to be done in my life. Because you don't go out and do a sin that shows on the outward there are many on the inside that needs to be dealt with. That's why Jesus said to judge no one because we all have something to clean up in our own lives. I'm so glad that He's still working on me. Others may not see or know it but we know ourselves and we need to put away the old person and live the new one with all of these fruits of the Spirit. God help us for we need it. That's why we need to renew our hearts everyday to clean up the mess. Just as we clean our homes we live in, we need to clean our temples that Christ lives in everyday. When we get up in the mornings we need to make sure we put on the whole armor of God for without it we will mess up. Read and study the Bible more and pray always. You need to do lots of fasting as well, for fasting takes out the real bad crud. It also is healing to the body and there's power in prayer and fasting. Jesus said that there are things that won't come out except through prayer and fasting. We need to stop feeding the flesh so much and feed our Spirit to be able to grow in the Lord Jesus. Our spirit gets hungry too and we need to feed it.

We can expect God's performance in us

When we meet the requirements of God we can always expect His performance in us as He has promised. Phil.1:20-21 and 27, According to my earnest expectation and my hope that in nothing I shall be ashamed but that with all boldness as always, so now also Christ shall be magnified in my body whether it be by life or by death. For me to live is Christ and to die is gain. Let your conversation be as it becomes the gospel of Christ, stand fast in one spirit with one mind striving together for the faith of the gospel. We can expect things from God when we meet His requirements. You can hope in Him and be not ashamed of whatever or however He leads you. You can stand with boldness and magnify Him in your body, spirit and soul. You are not yours anymore for you were bought with a price through the death and resurrection of our Lord and Savior Jesus Christ. Your conversations should always be pure and holy as to edify the gospel of Jesus Christ. Strive to be what God wants you to be and be in one spirit with the brethren. Ps.51:10, We should say as David said, create in me a clean heart oh God and renew a right spirit within me. David was a man after God's own heart but he did wrong and he prayed and sought God to renew in him a right spirit. God waits and longs for people to come to Him and ask Him to renew them and ask Him to draw them near to Him. He said if anyone would call upon Him He would hear and answer them. His love is so great for all. He doesn't love their sin but He loves them. I am so glad that God heard me and brought me out of the world and then forgave me of all of my sins. I pray everyday that He would draw me closer to Him for I need Him more everyday. Isa.40:31, They that wait upon the Lord shall renew their strength, they shall mount up with wings of an eagle, they shall run and not be weary, they shall walk and not faint. Our strength is in the Lord. The joy of the Lord is our strength. If you have the Lord living in you then you have joy. His joy can keep you from becoming weary, weak and keep you soaring high in Him. Nothing else can do that for you and me. Some try medicine, alcohol, sex and other things but they only work for a while and then they are back to being worse than they were before they tried all of these things. Only God can do give you the help that you need in everyday needs and what He does is always right. Rom.12:2, Be not conformed to this world but be ye transformed by the renewing of your mind that you may prove what is good and acceptable and perfect will of God. When you renew your mind then your body will line up with the Word of God also. You can know the will of God for your life for you will have the mind of Christ. Things start in the mind of people. So by renewing your mind it will change everything else to become good and acceptable will of God. Whatever the Word of God says you can stand on it for it's the truth. You don't have to question it if it comes from the Word of God. I Cor.4:16, For which cause we faint not but though our outward man perish the inward man is renewed day by day. It's just beyond understanding how God can and does renew the inward person everyday from all of the wrongs we commit each day. That's why we need to pray always that if we have committed any sin that God will forgive us. No one is perfect but we are to strive to be perfect just as Jesus is perfect. Col.3:10, Put on the new person which is renewed in knowledge after the image of Him that created us. Even though our bodies get older and look different and it gets tired at times our spirit inside is growing in the Lord and we are stronger and have more knowledge of Him because He is living in us.

God saved us to serve Him

Titus 3:15, Not by works of righteousness which we have done but according to His mercy He saved us by the washing of regeneration and renewing if the Holy Spirit. This ole person is crucified with Christ that the body of sin might be destroyed that henceforth we should not serve sin. If you live after the flesh you shall die but if you live after the Spirit you shall live. Rom.8:13-14, For as many that are lead by the Spirit of God are the sons and daughters of God. We are to die daily to self, to the flesh. We can't please self and men and please God. Self, our flesh is our worse enemy. Our flesh loves to be pampered and pleased. But we have to die to self to meet God's requirements to stay saved and reap from the benefits He has for us. If you love Him you will keep His commandments and do His will. Nothing else in this world is more important than pleasing God. Our life here will be more profitable, happy and fulfilled with God and then we will have eternal life with all good and nothing bad to face. What more can you ask or want? Gal.5:24, They that are Christ's have crucified the flesh of the affections and lusts. Walk in the Spirit and you shall not fulfill the lusts of the flesh. Paul said, I am crucified with

Christ nevertheless I live yet, not I but Christ lives in me and the life I now live I live by faith of the Son of God who loved me and gave Himself for me. We don't live to please self but to please God. The Holy Spirit will lead and guide you into all truth. He will never lead you astray or ever leave you alone. He's there when no one else is with you. Just remember, all you have to do is call upon Him, ask what you need and expect to receive it. He may not give you everything you want but He said that He would meet your needs according to His riches in glory. It would not be good for us if He gave us everything we wanted.

Your body is the temple of the Lord.

I Cor.3:16, Know ye know that your body is the temple of the Lord and the Spirit of God dwells in you? They that keep His commandments dwell in Him and He in you. When God saved you He came into your heart and soul. You are to keep your temple holy and righteous because He won't live in a sinful temple or messed up body. You can't have both God and the devil living in your temple. God is a jealous God and He will not share you with anyone else. You are His bride and you are to be faithful to Him always. Keep His commandments and be obedient unto Him. James 4:7, Submit yourselves therefore to God, resist the devil and he will flee from you. Draw near to God and He will draw near to you. We have a choice in everything in this world so we can choose to serve God or the devil. You can't serve both. You get rid of the devil by calling on the name of Jesus. There's power in the name of Jesus. There's no other name that the devil is afraid of but Jesus. Make every effort to live a pure, blameless and holy life and be at peace with God. There's only one life to live so live it to the max in God. Everyday is a new day in God so enjoy everyday as it is your last. Don't let the devil have a part of your life and steal your joy and happiness that you can have in Jesus Christ. Live in the fullness of the Holy Ghost. Grow in the special favor and knowledge of our Lord and Savior Jesus Christ. God wants His children to enjoy life here for He said that it was His will that we prosper and be in good health just as our soul prospered. Living a Christian life is wonderful.

Be careful not to fall and backslide

II Pet.3:17, Therefore beloved, seeing you know these things before, beware lest you also being led away with the error of the wicked fall from your own steadfastness. Peter was saying, I am warning you ahead of time dear friends and loved ones so that you can watch out for anyone who can lead you astray and back to the world of sin. Don't be carried away or led astray from God by the wicked people or the unsaved and sinful people or things. I don't want you to fall back into sin again. Each time one falls away the devil gets a tighter hold or grip on them and it's harder to come back to God. Don't let sinners entice you or persuade you to do wrong. Do not enter the paths of sinners and go their way. Rom.6:13, Paul said, do not yield your members of your flesh to unrighteousness but yield yourselves holy to God unto all righteousness. These are all warnings and encouragements from the Word of God. Everything you need is recorded in the Word of God, the Bible. You can stand strong and true to God no matter what else goes on around you. Don't yield yourselves in any way to fall back into sin again.

Put on the whole armor of God

Epe.6:13-18, Take unto you the whole armor of God so you can stand in the evil days. In the next five verses it tells you of the whole armor of God and what they mean. It's important that you put them on everyday, in other words, all of the time. Stay dressed so you can always be ready to fight your enemy. Stay true to God, live righteous, make spiritual preparation, have and keep your faith in God, put on the helmet of salvation, and read the Bible which is the Word of God. Pray always and be watchful. You have to first of all be true to God, obey His commandments in love and do His will. Do what is right in God's eyes not what the world thinks is right. Your plans should always be spiritual plans, plans that are pleasing to Him. When you are doing for others you are doing spiritual things. Trust God in everything and lean on Him. Before you can do any of these things you must be born again by believing in Jesus Christ and accepting Him as your Lord and Savior and then serving Him with all of your heart, mind, soul and strength. Watch for His coming and be ready at all times. Be always alert of the devil who roams around seeking whom he can devour. Always remember, you have the power in Jesus name to overcome the devil and your enemies. You have no power within your self without Jesus. There is power in His name.

Don't look back

Luke 9:62, Jesus said, no man having put his hand to the plow and looking back is fit for the Kingdom of God. You are to keep your eyes on Jesus Christ looking ahead for you can't change a thing in your past and it's only a tool for the devil to use against you. That's why Luke tells you not to look back. None of us are worthy of the Kingdom of God it is all because of the mercy, love and grace of our Lord and Savior Jesus Christ that we are made worthy. We stand in His righteousness and it's by His blood that He shed on Calvary on that ole rugged cross that any of us are saved and on the way to Heaven. Don't ever think that it's by any work that you have done and you surely can't buy your way in.

There's no other way except through Jesus Christ. So keep looking ahead and don't look back to your own way of thinking of what you could have done. The only thing that you will get for looking back is hurt, pain, sorrow and grief. We could all have live closer to God and done more for the Kingdom of God. The thing you need to do now is to follow Him and draw closer to Him. Do all you can to walk close to Him and bring others to Him. God has a plan for each and every one of His children so listen to Him. Everything we need is written in God's Word and it's all for our good and for our pleasure. There's strength, knowledge, wisdom, understanding love, mercy and grace for all of us. Wisdom comes from God above so you need to ask for it. We will see what Paul said about looking forward, pressing on and not looking back.

Phil.3:13-14, Brethren, I count myself to apprehended but this one thing, forgetting those things which are behind and reaching forth for those things which are ahead. I press toward the mark of the high calling of God in Jesus Christ. He said, I can do all things through

Jesus Christ which gives me strength. Verse 19, God shall supply all of your needs according to the riches in glory by Jesus Christ. The peace of God which passes all understanding shall keep your hearts and minds through Jesus Christ. Thank God for His peace that only He can give us. The world and people can't give you peace. Even through the hard times and troubles God can and will give His children peace. This is one time it's good to look back or be reminded is when God has given you peace when you were going through such a hard battle. It encourages you when you are in another problem to know that God can help you and give you peace when you are in a storm. There is peace in the midst of a storm. Whatever you do in deed or word, do all in the name of Jesus giving thanks to God and the Father by Him. Walk worthy of God who has called you unto His Kingdom. We have to walk the straight and narrow path to be worthy of His Kingdom. Whatever you do you have to do it in His name and for His glory and not for any glory for yourself. He has a work for you and me and we are to do it willingly and freely. He didn't call us to do nothing but to do the will of the Father. So spend your time wisely and don't waste any of it. Time is very precious and what you lose can't be brought back.

God forgives all sins

Rom.3:23, For all have sinned and fallen short of the glory of God... We have all come short of the glory of God. There was only one perfect one and that is Jesus Christ. There are those who willfully sin and there are those who are unaware that they are sinning. There are sins of omission that many are guilty of. Many of us should be doing things that we're not doing. But thank God that we have an advocate, Jesus Christ who goes to the Heavenly Father and intercedes for you and me when we fail and do wrong. God loves us and He want to forgive us when we make mistakes. We should never sin willfully for the Bible teaches us that to know to do good and doeth it not is sin. That's what you call willfully sinning when you know what's wrong and then you still do it. You can't have Christ living in you and continue to sin willfully. David prayed, O God search my heart to see if there be any evil way in it or in me, wash me and make me white as snow. That's how we should pray and God will show us if there's any sin in our heart and life. God will and does convict us of our sins because He loves you and me so much. He wants us to be free of sin and to serve Him with our whole heart, mind, soul and strength. When He forgives us then He forgets our 'sins and cast them away as far as the east is from the west never to remember them anymore.

We are free of condemnation

Rom.8:1-3, There is therefore now no condemnation to them which are in Christ Jesus who walk not after the flesh but after the Spirit. We have been made free by the Spirit in the life of Jesus Christ. You are spiritual minded now and not walking after the flesh desires. We are not the same person we were before we were born again in Jesus. So now we have to act different and be different and walk after the Spirit of Christ. We are more than conquerors through Him that loved us. I am persuades that neither death nor life or angels or principalities nor powers or things present or things to come can separate me from the love of God which is in Jesus Christ our Lord. God's love is forever for us and nothing will ever change that. He still loves us when we make mistakes but He doesn't love the sin. Gal.2:12, Paul said, to work out your own salvation with fear and trembling. The Bible says that it's a fearful thing to fall into the hands of the living God. We are free from sin after salvation but we're not free to sin again. The teaching of eternal security just isn't true to those who continues to sin after they have known the Lord Jesus. The Bible teaches that if you continue to sin that God will blot out your name in the Lamb's book of life. Only the names that are written in the Lamb's book of life will enter into the Kingdom of Heaven. It's better to pay the price here on earth than to have to pay for them when you stand before Christ in the judgment. You will pay the penalty for your sins. Jesus Christ paid the price for your sins once and for all and you have to stay saved to enter into the Kingdom of Heaven. He that endures to the end the same will be saved. It's an everyday thing to live for God and keep ourselves from sin. You are to grow in grace and the favor of God through Jesus Christ. We are not perfect but we are to strive to be perfect just as Jesus is perfect. Don't let others or the devil trick you into thinking you can do anything you want or live anyway you want and still be saved, for that's a lie straight from the pits of hell. Get yourself in a church that is teaching the full gospel of Jesus Christ and read and study the Word of God and you will see all of the truths. Don't listen to every wind of doctrines that you hear, make sure it's the Word of God. If you are truly saved then the Holy Spirit will lead and guide you into all truth. Many people never pick up the Bible to read, much less study and when they do go to church they believe everything the preacher or teacher is saying. Jesus said to believe in Him and what He teaches and if you don't read and study the Bible yourself then you may never know what the truth is. You really need always to read your Bible along with whoever is preaching or teaching to make sure they are telling the true words of God. Don't just read when you go to church but everyday. Make this your priority to read, study and pray to God.

Our duties to the weaker believers

Rom.15:1, We who are strong ought to help the weak and not to please ourselves. We have to step out of our comfort zone many times to help others. It's not always easy to do that but that's what God expects of us as His children. We are to be Christ like and He was always going about doing good and helping others. Gal.6:2, Bear one another's burdens and so fulfill the law of Christ. Heb.13:3, Remember them that are bound as bound with them that suffer adversity as being yourselves also in the body. We are to show mercy to those that are suffering whether in the body, spiritually or financially. We are to help them and hold them up. They are bound because of their problems. There are times when it seems that you can't reach God for your problems. When you see this happening to others then you should help them and take them to God. If this happens to you it doesn't mean that you are lost and God isn't hearing you but sometimes you can't see the forest for the trees. Sometimes the pain is so great that you can't focus on anything else. Then it's the responsibility of the believers to stand in the gap for you and help. We as Christians have a big responsibility to God and for our fellow believers. There are many hurting Christians in this world we live in today. Hard times are here and it's hitting many very hard. Many are taking their own lives because of the pressure of their problems. They get to the place that they don't know where to turn that's why we need to be there for them and turn them to God and remind them that He care and He's there for them if they will just call on Him. When Jesus comes in all of His glory He's going to separate the sheep from the goats and will have to say to the goats on the left, I was hungry and you didn't feed Me. I was thirsty and you didn't give Me to drink. I was sick and in prison and you didn't come and visit Me. I was a stranger and you didn't take Me in. I was naked and you didn't clothe Me. These are the lost ones and they thought they were okay and living righteous but they never really accepted Jesus as their Lord and Savior or put Him first place in their heart and life. These will ask Him, when did we see You in such a place as this and He will say to them, inasmuch as you did it unto them you did it unto Me. And these shall go out to everlasting punishment. The ones that were obedient and took on the responsibilities that God had said they should, in taking care of all of these needs will go into eternal life with Him. It will be so awful to live the life here in doing what you think is right and then to miss Heaven because you didn't feed the poor and take care of the needy. This is a serious matter with the Lord and we all need to check ourselves to make sure we're doing all we can to please Him. The Bible says that whatever we render out to others we do it unto Him. Whatever we do in word or deed do all in the name of Jesus Christ. James 1:27, Pure religion and undefiled before God and the Father is this, visit the fatherless, widows in their afflictions and to keep themselves unspotted from the world. We are to be busy about the Lord's business and reach out to all of the hurting especially the household of faith. We are our brothers and sisters keeper. Stay away from the worldly cares and things of this world and keep our eyes and minds on Heavenly things. This doesn't mean that we are so Heavenly minded that we're no earthly good. Put God first and all of these other things will be added unto you.

Exhort one another in the Lord

Heb.3:13-15, Exhort one another daily while it is still called today lest any of you be hardened through the deceitfulness of sin. We are to warn each other everyday and don't put off until tomorrow what you can do today for tomorrow may never come. We are to lift up, encourage and correct those in the wrong. Never forget the warning, today you must listen to His voice. Today is the day of salvation so accept it and live it to the maximum. Look not everyone on their own things but on the things of others. Let this mind be in you which was also in Christ Jesus. Col.1:28-29, We are to preach, warning everyone and teaching everyone in all wisdom that we may present everyone perfect in Christ Jesus. We need to labor striving according to His working which works in me mightily. God wants to do mighty things through you. That's why Paul kept warning us about the things we need to know and do. We should do all we can to keep others on the right path and to keep them out of hell. We do have a great duty as Christians of the most high. Col.4:5-6, Live wisely among those who are not Christians and make the most of every opportunity that you have to show them the love of Jesus Christ and the importance in following Him. Know how to give an answer to everyone who asks of you. We are servants of the Lord and we are to labor fervently for our brothers and sisters in Christ, praying that they will stand perfect and complete in God's will. This means that we are to strive for perfection until we are changed from mortality to immortality either in the rapture when Jesus comes for His bride which is the church, all who are living and abiding in Him, or when we are resurrected from the grave. We have to seek God's will for our lives always and to help others do the same. Our work is never ended as long as we live here on this earth. There is never a retiring time for Christians to stop spreading the Word of God for there's life in the Word.

Our duties as stewards and called ones of God

Acts 20:35, I have shown you all of these things how to labor and support the weak. I Pet.4:10, As everyone has received gifts even so minister the same one to another as good stewards of the manifold grace of God. Matt.10:8, Heal the sick, cleanse the leper, raise the dead, cast out devils for freely you have received so give freely. John 13:15, For I have given you an example that you should do as I have done for you. Jesus Christ is our example and we are to walk as He walked. What a blessing it is and how thankful we should always be for His Word which He has given us to give out to others. The highest blessing we can ever have is to see souls saved and to be able to help the weak in Spirit and the needy helped. When we hear the Word of God and receive it from God and not the words of man, it's mighty. Everyone was inspired of God in the Bible who has written the Bible. It's straight from the throne of God from Him personally. It is all truth so you need to accept it all and be obedient to it. What a blessing to have such a book that tells us everything we need to know on how to live a life after God's own heart. It's a love letter from God to us. It's our road map to Heaven on how to get there. You can't get there any other way but God's way. There are curves, pot holes and bumps but there is no dead end for Christians as long as you are serving God and obeying Him. To know the way you have to read His Word, the Bible. Remember, God gets all of the glory for any and everything we do and there's a soul winning joy that's unlike any other joy. Lets get out and win others to Christ to save them from destruction of their life and soul. We can't save them but we can show them the way to get saved. The time is running out for Jesus is coming soon. As I have said before, work while it is still day for the night is coming when our work will be done. Souls are dying and on their way to hell everyday, every second even. So lets work until Jesus comes or we go by the grave. I Thessalonians 3:11-13, Now God Himself and our Father and Lord Jesus Christ direct our way unto you. And the Lord make you increase and abound in love one toward another and to all people even as we do toward you. To the end He may establish your hearts in holiness before God even our Father at the coming of our Lord Jesus Christ with all of His saints. God directed Paul to tell the Gentiles the way just as He directed him and he's directing us from the Word of God. God always has a people to carry His Word to others. He wants us to stay holy before Him. That's the only way we can stay ready when Jesus comes in all of His glory. You can't have sin in your lives when He comes for you will be left here to face the tribulation period. You do not want to be left here after Jesus takes the church out for it's going to be a time like never before and will never be again. You can read all about that in Revelation.

Exhortation for all believers

I Thessalonians 4:1-4, We beseech you brethren and exhort you by the Lord Jesus Christ that you have received the truth how you ought to walk and please God so you can abound more and more. You know the commandments so keep them. You know how to keep your vessel in sanctification and honor to God. God has called you to live holy and Paul is begging you here to live holy and spotless. He said, you know the commandments so you need to keep them. You also know how to keep your body clean and holy unto God. Your body is the temple of the Lord and you should always keep it sanctified unto Him. Paul never waters down the Word of God and neither should we as ministers of the Lord. We are to tell it like it is for we're going to be held responsible. We are to lift up and correct when needed so others can grow in the wisdom and knowledge of the Lord. All believers are to be ministers of the Word of God. No one is exempted from this calling. This doesn't mean that you are to be preachers or teachers but you are to always tell someone about Jesus Christ and to correct when you see they are in the wrong. By doing this you may same someone from the fires of hell. We are to love each other enough to tell them the truth. Where love abounds there is no hate. I Thessalonians 5:14-24, Paul said we are to exhort all brethren to warn them that are unruly, comfort the feeble minded, support the weak and to be patient with everyone. Don't render evil for evil to no one but render good for evil to all. We are to rejoice evermore. Pray without ceasing and in everything give thanks for this is the will of God in Christ Jesus concerning you. This is the believers Paul is talking to now. Quench not the Holy Spirit, and despise not the prophesying. Prove all things and hold fast what is good. Keep away from all evil and things that are not of God. May your soul, body and spirit be preserved unto the coming of out Lord Jesus Christ. Faithful is He that calls us for He will perform what He said. God is the one who has called us and He is always faithful and will never leave us,

His children. He said that He would go with us all of the way and we can be assured of this. Every promise that He has promised He will keep. We should always keep our promises to Him also and be faithful to Him. We are to test every spirit to make sure that it lines up with the Word of God. Keep the good and throw away the bad. Not every spirit that you may feel is of God but you can know. That's why Paul said to test all of the spirits.

Jesus Christ is our Comforter and Guide

II Thessalonians 2:16-17, Now our Lord Jesus Christ Himself and God even our Father has loved us and has given us everlasting comfort and hope through grace. He will comforts out hearts and establish us in every good word and works. 3:3-5, But the Lord is faithful and will establish you and keep you from evil. We have this confidence in the Lord touching you both do and will do the things that we command you. And the Lord directs your hearts into the love of God and into the patient waiting for Christ. The Lord is faithful to stick by you and to keep you from all evil if you will just follow Him and do His will. You can walk out of the protection of the Lord if you sin and follow your fleshly desires. Just as Paul had confidence in God so can we. We can trust God in everything, little or big for He will never fail us if we stay in Him. He will accomplish what He has started in you. You can have the riches of His love, mercy and grace. Wait patiently for what you ask of Him and don't doubt. Sometimes He doesn't answer right away so you have to wait on Him for He always knows what's best for His children. He knows all that you and I are going through and He will give us peace and the comfort that we need through all of our trials and tests. Paul also said to wait patiently for the coming of the Lord Jesus Christ.

We are to make ourselves examples to others

II Thessalonians 3:9, Not because we have not power but to make ourselves an example unto you to follow us. Paul told the Gentiles to follow him as he followed Christ. We want to walk as Jesus did. Our testimonies should always be good as to lead others to Christ. People are watching to see if you are what you say you are. If you have not made a change from what you were before you were born again then something is not right. Others can see that in you whether you are a true Christ and a follower of Christ or not. Our lives are sometimes the only gospel others see. We can win them to Christ by the love we show and give out, the kindness, patience, comfort, peace, joy, happiness and the interest we show in them. If your life doesn't show these qualities, then what makes you any different from all other sinners and the lost? We are to be the light of the world. Jesus is the light of the world and we are to be like Him. Always be careful not to act better than thou for you can push people away. You have to love them to Christ. Jesus said to separate yourselves from the world, meaning not to go to the places that the worldly people go, talking like the sinners or acting like them. He said that you can't win anyone if you go about doing what the sinners do. If you are rude, unlovable, always complaining about something, bad attitudes and putting others down, then you have a need of change of yourself before you can help others. You need to be careful and watch over yourself, always being grounded and rooted in the Word of God so you will live a life of holiness and righteousness unto God. We are to live this way not only in church and when we are out with others but when we're at home with the family or even when we're alone. Try hard never to offend anyone because a person offended is hard to reach. The Word says to be instant in season and out of season. Meaning, know what to speak at all times. Pray and God will give you just what to say when you need to speak. Don't ever push a person down when they're already down. You are to feel their hurt or pain, cry with them, be humble and patient with them. Just love them and try to understand what they're going through. You don't tell a person who is really sick that you were that way and God healed you at once. There's a time and place for everything and you can find that in Ecclesiastes chapter 3. God does heal many times instantly but there are other times when He doesn't. This would be the wrong time to testify of this. God says to use wisdom and when you need wisdom just ask Him and He will give it to you. I know there's been times in my life that I was in such need that I didn't know where to turn and someone would say the wrong thing to me at that time, and I would only feel worse, For it was then that I felt that God didn't love me as much as He loved that person or persons. I even felt like, what's the use to try if God wouldn't do the same for me as He did for them. We know that God has no respect of persons for He loves everyone the same. So be careful to use the right words in a given situation. You should never tell a person of another that is sick unto death that God doesn't want them to die, for you don't know the will of God for another. God has a plan for everyone and He's the only one who knows when our time of death is coming. I've seen this happen to others and they were devastated and could not understand and it almost cost them their salvation. So be very careful that you say the right words. If you don't know what to say then it's best that you say nothing except, that God will be with them and see them through. If they are Christians then God will do just that for them.

To summarize it all up, we need to show love out of a pure heart, keep a good conscience, and don't let our faith waver. Always be thankful to God for His love, mercy, grace and for keeping us. Give Him the honor and glory forever for He's the only true God. Always pray and lift up holy hands to Him. We were born to serve the Lord and to worship Him. This is our whole duty for He is worthy to be praised. Seek Him and His Kingdom first and all else will be added unto us. Remember, they that endure to the end the same will be saved. You can't serve God for a while and then walk away and think that you can make it into His Kingdom. You can't serve God and the devil too. You have to choose this day whom you will serve. Joshua said, for me and my house we will serve the Lord. That is what my husband, Leon and I have said as well and we are striving with all of our hearts, minds, soul and strength to do this. I know I have said this several times before but I want to make sure the devil to hear me good. What about you? Whom are you serving? Where do you stand with the Lord today? Have you given Him first place in your heart and life? Are you keeping His commandments and being faithful and obedient to Him? It's your decision and your decision alone for no one can make that decision for you. God doesn't make anyone serve Him but He's waiting at your heart's door for you to open the door and invite Him in and He said that He would come in and sup with you and you with Him. He won't open that door for you have to do it. He's waiting patiently saying, come unto me and I will give you rest. The biggest mistake for anyone is to refuse to accept Jesus Christ into their heart and life. You have one life to live and this life you now live you have to choose whom you will serve and where you will spend eternity. Once you leave this life through death there is no other chance to accept Him as your Lord and Savior. Your preparation time is now while you are still living. There are only two places to go after this life is over, Heaven or hell. Both are eternal. Heaven is going to be a wonderful place with all joy, happiness, peace and most of all, being with Jesus the one who made all of this possible for His children. There will be no pain, sickness hurts, problems, troubles, separation, death and no more sin. Hell will be a burning furnace and all of the different qualities from the ones of Heaven. The fire will burn forever and will never be quenched. No one really wants to go there but you choose for yourself where you are going. God loves you and He wants to save you. He gave His only Son to die on the cross and was risen again for you, what more could He do? Why don't you give up and let God. Give up and let Jesus take a hold of you and save you today. My prayer is that everyone that reads this book is on the right path for the Lord. And if you're not, that you will accept Him right now and live for Him and we can all be in Heaven together. I pray this in Jesus Name, Amen

I would love for you to write me and let me know if you gave your heart and life to Jesus Christ. I will start right now rejoicing for the souls saved as I know the angels are also. Praise the name of the Lord.

CHAPTER SIX

The Dominion Of The Mind

CHAPTER 6

The dominion of the mind

Prov.23:7, As a person thinks so are they. Let your heart rule you and not your mind. Our minds can deceive us many times. We need to let our hearts tell our minds what to do and when to act, say and where to go. God lives in our hearts and He will direct our goings and doings. Temptations and sin comes from our minds so it can cause us to stray from the truth and righteousness. The Bible says even our hearts are deceitful so we need to make sure that the Lord is leading in everything. Rom.14:14-23, As one is in the Lord Jesus I am convinced that no food is unclean in itself. But is one regards or thinks that something is unclean, then for them it is unclean. That's one of the reasons that we should never judge another Christian. Some may feel it's wrong in doing something and another feels it's good. God will convict us of any sin in our life. Do not allow what you think to be good be evil spoken of. For the Kingdom of God is righteousness, peace and joy in the Holy Ghost. If anyone serves God in this way it is pleasing to Him and approved by man. Whatever you believe about these things keep it between you and God. Blessed are they that do not condemn themselves for what they think is right and approves of it. If you have any doubt then you are condemned, everything that does not come from faith is sin. Titus 1:15-16, To the pure all things are pure but to those that are corrupt and do not believe, nothing is pure. Both their minds and consciences are corrupt. They claim to know God but their actions and deeds they deny Him. They are hateful, disobedient and unfit for anything good. There is really nothing good outside of Jesus Christ. Just confessing with your mouth is not good enough for the Kingdom of God. Your actions have to show that you believe also. Actions always speak louder than words. Tim.1:5, Now to the end of the commandment is charity, which is love out of a pure heart of a good conscience and of faith unfeigned, which is sincere faith. The beginning and the ending of everything is love. Love is the greatest gift of all. I Pet.1:22, Purify your soul in obeying the truth through the Spirit into sincere love. If you do these things then your mind and conscience will be stayed on the Lord and they will be clean and clear. Let the love of God rule in your minds and hearts as they won't be dominated by evil. We have to keep our hearts and minds stayed on the Lord in order to keep control of them. When we call on the Lord and do the things He says then we're letting the Spirit of God rule. If you don't allow the Spirit to lead you then you're letting the flesh dominate your hearts and minds. Sin first begins in the mind. Prov.4:23, keep your heart with all diligence for out of it are the issues of life. So as you think in your heart so are you. Whatever comes out of your heart are the issues of life. For out of the abundance of the heart the mouth speaks. A good person brings from their heart what is good and an evil person from their heart brings what is evil. We have treasures in our hearts so speak good and pure things. What comes out of a person's mouth makes them unclean if it's evil thinking. The thought of foolishness is sin for it will defile a person. Don't let evil thoughts come into your mind. You may say, I can't help it but, yes you can for you can brush them away as soon as you acknowledge them. Don't let the bad and evil thoughts become actions for they become sin. To be tempted is not sin for it's when you yield to temptation that it is sin.

We should be Spiritual minded. Rom.8:6, For to be carnally minded is death but to be Spiritual minded is life and peace. You can see from the Word of God that it is most important that we keep our minds right. To keep them right we have to keep them on things of Christ. I Cor.2:16, For who has known the mind of Christ? The thoughts of the righteous are right. Let this mind be in you which was also in Christ Jesus. Phil.4:8, Finally my brethren, whatsoever is true, honest, just, lovely and whatsoever are of a good report, if there be any virtue and if there be any praise think on these things. We are to fix our minds and thoughts on whatever is true, honorable and right. Think positive and not negative. Think on the best and not on the worse. Think on the beautiful and not the ugly, things of praise and not things to be cursed. Put into practice all of these good things. Don't let the devil blind your eyes, thoughts and minds. He has blinded many and they have gone astray or either never believed in the first place. The devil will start in your mind. He knows if he can get your mind then he has you also. II Cor.3:14, The Israelites minds are blinded until this day. Until this day there remains the same veil untaken away in the reading of the Old Testament. The veil was taken away when Jesus Christ came. They are still looking for Christ to be born and are living under the old law. We live under grace since Jesus came, died and rose again and He is coming back. Paul was very concerned of Christians falling back and falling away from the truth by the devil. II Cor.11:3, I fear unless by any means as the serpent deceived Eve that he will deceive you and then you are led away from your pure and simple devotions to Christ. Your minds can be deceived and corrupted just as Eve's was. Then she deceived her husband Adam. Be careful for the devil roams around seeking whom he can devour. People with evil and corrupt minds cause a lot of problems and they don't tell the truth. There are lots of killings and wounding because of the evil and corrupt minds and the devil is behind all of it. People with corrupt and evil minds resist the truth and reject the faith in God. Never grow weak, weary, feeble and faint in your mind. Remember, you have the mind of Christ.

God can keep your heart and mind. Phil.4:7, And the peace of God which passes all understanding shall keep your hearts and minds through Jesus Christ. God told us that He would put His laws in our hearts and in your minds and I will write them upon your hearts. We have been told and shown the truth so we need to abide in the truth always. You know right from wrong so there's no excuse for sin. The surrendered mind will give you peace, good conscience and it will dominate your life through Jesus Christ. Rom.12:2, Be not conformed to this world but be ye transformed by the renewing of your mind that you will prove what is good and acceptable and perfect will of God. Don't copy the world's system or customs in behavior but be a new person in Christ by the way you think in your mind. Then you will know what God wants you to do and what pleases Him. II Tim.1:7, God has given us a sound mind and with it He has given us power and love. So with these things we are to discipline ourselves and be all that God wants us to be. He has shown us the way so there's no excuse for not pleasing Him. To be Spiritual mined is life. Be all that He wants you to be for He loves you and me. Let your mind be dominated by Him. The more of Him you have the clearer mind you will have. It is good to keep our minds on the things of the Lord for they are all good things. They lift us up and keep us.

What's on the inside will show on the outside

Acts 13:45, When Jesus saw the multitude they were filled with envy and spoke against Paul concerning the things he was saying. They contradicted and blasphemed him. What they were feeling on the inside came out from their minds and hearts. They didn't believe what Paul was teaching them so they cursed him and that's when Paul turned to the Gentiles. Verse 46, Paul said that it was necessary that we preached to you Jews first but since you don't want to hear it and believe we will turn to the Gentiles. He told the Jews, you have judged yourselves and are not worthy to have eternal life. They did not believe in their hearts and it showed on the outside of them as well as the inside. Proverbs tells that a sound heart is the life of the flesh. Envy is the rottenness of the bones. Let us never be envious of one another nor desire vain glory or provoke one another. These kinds of things show a problem from the inside of a person. In order for you to get into the Kingdom of God you have to believe in Jesus Christ and walk with Him in obedience and faithfulness. You have to live righteous and holy before God always. The Jews just didn't believe that Jesus had come for they were still looking for Him to be born. They were not faithful and were very disobedient to God. If they were turned away from the Promised Land why do you think that people today who claim to be a Christian and are not would be able to enter into the Kingdom of God? They were God's own chosen people but since they would not believe and be obedient to God, God told Paul to go down and preach to the Gentiles. You see, God will have a people that will follow Jesus and be faithful and obedient to Him. Is your heart right with God? Are you worshipping Him from your heart? What's on the inside will come out and show on the outside of you. Mark 7:20-23, Jesus said, it is the thought life that defiles us. For within, out of a person's heart come evil thoughts, sexual lustful pleasure, envy, slander, pride and foolishness. All of these things come from within a person's life. These things make you unacceptable to God. Jesus knows your every thought and your motive, so why do you think evil in your heart? Keep your heart with all diligence for out of it are the issues of life. The heart is the center of life.

Matt.23:25-28, How terrible for you teachers of religious laws and you Pharisees and hypocrites, you are so careful to clean the outside of the cup and leave the inside filthy, full of greed and self indulgence. You are so blind. First clean the inside and then the outside will be clean also. You are whitewashed and beautiful on the outside but filled on the inside with dead bones and impurities. You try to look like upright people outwardly but inside your hearts are filled with hypocrisy and lawlessness. He is saying, you put on a good show to others but you can't fool Me for I see all things you do and say and everywhere you go. I know your thoughts and your motives. You may fool people but you will never fool Me. Some sit in church and look so posed but their hearts and minds are far from God, it is on things on the outside of the church and they are not really serving God and loving Him with a whole heart. There are even some preachers that look and sound so good but their motive is far from the truth. They may even be preaching the truth and some sinners do get saved but if their motives are wrong, it is not pleasing to God. God's Word will not return to Him void. It is His Word and Spirit that convicts and saves. Some are in it for the money and self gain. They will be judged with great condemnation. James 3:1, My brethren, be not many masters or teachers, knowing that you shall receive greater condemnation or judgment. God knows who's real and who's not. He knows whether you are doing it because you have been called of Him or whether you are preaching for gain and for fortune. You will get your reward someday so make sure you're doing what you do for the Lord in Jesus name. Paul didn't preach for money for he worked for his living while he was preaching and teaching. It should be the same today for God has not changed. It's just gotten where people want so much, far more than they really need. They have to have the finest of everything and are never satisfied. Luke 6:45, A good person out of the treasure of their heart brings forth that which is good and the evil person out of the evil treasure of their heart that which is evil. For out of the abundance of the heart the mouth speaks. Whatever is over powering your heart will speak whether it is good or evil. Make sure your heart is renewed, regenerated and cleansed. For if you know there's something in your hearts and minds that's not right with God you need to make it right with Him before it's too late. Clean the inside and the outside will be clean also. God judges us from our heart. He wants the outside to look good but it's the inside that matters the most. You cannot get into Heaven with an unclean or evil heart. There was a time when we were like the unsaved are today for we were lost too. But we came to Jesus and He cleaned us up by His blood and washed all our sins away and He sanctified and justified us just as though we had never sinned. It's all in the name of Jesus that we are what we are today. The Holy Spirit that's living within us is leading and guiding us into all truth. If you are pondering evil thoughts in your mind them you need to come to Jesus, repent and have a change of mind. We have to have self control and bring it all under the blood of Jesus.

Spiritual minded Christians have this kind of mind

Rom.8:6, Mind of life and peace
I Cor.2:16,The mind of Christ
Phil.2:5, The mind which is in Jesus Christ
Ps.48:9, The thoughts of Thy loving kindness
Prov.12:5, The thoughts of righteousness
Rom.12:13, We think soberly as God has dealt to everyone the measure of faith

Phil.4:8, Finally, whatsoever things are true, honest,just, pure, lovely, good report, virtue or praise, think on these things. We are to think on things of righteousness, worth, value and excellence. All these qualities are of God and these are the qualities we as Christians are to always have. All good things are of God.

Be Spiritual clean not contaminated by things

Isa.52:11, Depart, depart from her, touch no unclean thing and be clean you who bear the vessel of God.All who are called by My name is what He is saying. Make sure you keep your body and spirit clean and holy. If you are a Christian and have been washed in the blood of the Lamb then you confess the name of the Lord then you bear the vessel of God, for Jesus lives within you. You must keep it clean for He won't live in a dirty and messed up temple of sin. Col.3:1-3 and 10, 15, 17, Set your affections on things above and not on things of the earth. Seek and look for those things that are above. Your old self is dead and risen with Christ who sits on the right hand of the Father in Heaven. Put on the new person which is renewed in knowledge after the image of Jesus Christ. Let the peace of God rule in your hearts to you who are called and always be thankful to Him that has called you. Whatever you do in word or deed do all in His name, giving thanks to the Father by Jesus Christ. Be sure to give Him the credit for everything good in you. The only thing good in any of us is Jesus Christ. We have to be a separated people from the world. Paul said to come out from among them and be a separated people said the Lord and touch no evil or unclean thing and I will receive you. I will be a Father to you and you shall be My sons and daughters, says the Lord Almighty. You are the children of God if you are following Him. We are to present our bodies a living sacrifice, holy and acceptable unto God. This is our reasonable service unto Him. Be not comformed to this world but be ye transformed by the renewing of your mind that you may prove what is good, acceptable and perfect will of God. God gives grace to every Christian not to think more highly of themselves than they should but to always think soberly. He has dealt to everyone a measure of faith. Let love always be sincere, hate what is evil and cleave to what's good. We are to love one another and honor each other with humility and kindness. Take care of your own business, work hard and don't be lazy. Proverbs tells us that better is a little with righteousness than great riches without honesty. Don't ever lie to get rich for it is vanity tossed to and fro with a deadly trap. Good planning and hard work leads to prosperity. If you get rich by being dishonest it will soon take you down the drain or lead you to hell. Don't walk a crooked path for you will lose in the end. Dishonesty never pays off for you will always lose more than you gain in the end. Rom.12:17-21, Never pay back evil for evil to anyone and provide things honest in the sight of all people. Do your part to live in peace with everyone as much as possible. Paul put it this way because he knew there were going to be some that you just could not have peace with. There are some that nothing can please them and you just can't make peace with them. But we are to do all that we can do to make peace and then we won't be accountable to God for not trying. Do not revenge anyone for the Lord says that revenge belongs to Him and He will repay. Do not be overcome with evil but overcome evil with good. We don't have to be worried or concerned about payback for the evil done to us for God will take care of that. The evil people will get what's coming to them. Never wish anything bad upon them either for we are to love and pray for our enemies. Be careful not to let evil thoughts enter your minds. We will be blessed for being good to others especially our enemies. It's easy to be good to those who are good to you but not as easy to be good to one who causes you problems and hurts. Remember the commandment, do unto others as you would have them do unto you. We are not exempt from that in any situation or anyone.

Submit yourself to God

James 4:7-10, Submit yourself to God, resist the devil and he will flee from you. Draw near to God and He will draw near to you. Cleanse your hands, wash your hands you sinners and purify your hearts you double minded. If we come near to God and serve Him only, then we will escape a lot of problems and troubles that we bring on ourselves. When we're walking close to God then we can resist the devil and he will have to flee from us in Jesus name. Paul said to come and repent, mourn and weep for your sins and all of your wrong doings. You are to be sorry for your sins to the point where you will weep and mourn. Let your laughter of the world be turned into mourning and your joy to heaviness. What you thought was fun and laughter in the world you see now that it was for just a season. Sin and pleasure of the world is for just a season the Word tells us. Once you see your wrong and you are sorry for it and repent then you see it wasn't real happiness like you thought, for now you have the real joy of the Lord and it's lasting. Once you come to Him then He will lift you up. We are to never lift ourselves up or boast in self for we are to be humble. For all that we are after we come to Christ we give Him the glory for anything good that we are. Our righteousness is as filthy rags so now we live in His righteousness. Veses 1-6 tells us what causes fights and quarrels among you. They come from the lusts that's bottled up within a person. Your flesh is fighting against your spirit. You want something but you don't get it, you desire to have, you covet but you can't have because you don't ask God or you ask amiss. You ask for wrong motives so you can spend what you get on pleasure and not for the sake of God or for good. Paul calls us an adulterous generation or people. Friendship with the world is hatred toward God. It makes you an enemy of God to be of the world. God gives us more grace when we go His way. We could not make it without the grace of God. He opposes or resists the proud but gives grace to the humble. We have to humble ourselves before Him. Verses 13-17, Life is uncertain for we don't know wht is going to happen. You say, today or tomorrow we will do this or that, this is man's plans and it is carnal security. Man makes their plans but God carries them out. There is a way that seems right but the end thereof is death. Everyway of a man is righteous in his own eyes but the Lord searches the heart. Prov.27:20, Hell and destruction are never full so the eyes of man are never satisfied. People are dying and going to hell everyday. There's room for more the Bible teaches. But you don't have to go there if you are serving Jesus Christ and following Him. There's room in Heaven for all who want to go and if you want to go you have to make reservations. Jesus died and rose again so all who will believe in Him and follow Him could go. Prov.19:21, Many are the plans of a man's heart but it's the Lord's purpose that prevails.

Many make their plans here on this earth and many are carried out but many fail as well. I believe that God stops many of our plans for our own benefit or we didn't ask Him about them first. Many of our plans would not be good for us and I believe that Jesus intercedes for us to stop them. Praise the Lord for that. God always knows what's best for His children. Never take advice or make plans with the evil. When we do God's will it will never fail and where He leads us He will keep us. If it's His will then our plans will work out. Job 5:8-12, Go to God and present your case or your plans for He does great work too marvelous to understand for He performs miracles without number and He frustrates or confuses the plans of the crafty, cunning or sly so that their efforts will not succeed. They think that they are wise in their own eyes but God sees that and He stops them. God will block sinful, evil acts or plans against His children. He is our fortress and high tower, a place of safety. So draw near to Him and resist the devil and he will flee from you. Submit yourself to God and draw near to Him and you will be safe. If you know to do good do it.

We are to be patient in sufferings and troubles.

James 5:7-12, Be patient therefore my dear brothers and sisters as you wait for the Lord's return. Consider the farmer who waits eagerly for the rains in the fall and in the spring. This is the early and latter rain. You plant most things in these two seasons and you need rain for the crops to make them grow and get the harvest in time. Just as the farmer needs the rains to make their crops grow we need the spiritual rains to grow in the Lord. You need to be filled with the Holy Ghost in order to be patient and to be ready when the Lord comes. Be patient and establish your hearts for the coming of the Lord is near. Don't grumble, complain or hold drudges against each other or you will condemn yourselves. God is our judge and He judges everything for He is standing right at your heart's door. The prophets suffered for the Lord so why shouldn't we? They were doing good and and doing the Lord's work but they still suffered many afflictions and many even died but they were patient. Job is a great example but we see how it all turned out in the end for Him. The Lord's plans for him turned out for his good in the end for God was full of tenderness and mercy.

Suppose Job had not been patient and would have turned his back on God what do you suppose would have happened to him? Paul said, we count them happy that endure to the end. We have a great honor and respect for all of the apostles and disciples that endured to the end with God. It's not easy when you are suffering for the cause of Christ. We have to suffer here because of the sin of Adam and Eve for before them there was no sin for everything was made perfect by God. The Bible teaches us that we must go through many trouble and trials here all of the days of our life if we follow Christ Jesus but He said He would make a way for us through it all and He will never leave or forsake His children. Paul said, above all my brethren, never swear by Heaven or earth or by any other oath but let your yes be yes and your no be no unless you fall into sin and be condemned for it.

We are restoring wandering believers back to God. We are our brothers and sisters keeper and we are to help the fallen ones, the weak and needy brethren. It's our duty to do this because the Lord said so. Verses 19-20, Brothers and sisters, if anyone of you wander from the truth and is brought back in the fold again you can rest assure that the one who brings you back, that person will save that sinner from death and bring about forgiveness of many sins. God will forgive all sins but the blaspheming of the Holy Spirit. None of us are perfect for we all make mistakes and we need to have a brother or sister in the Lord to correct us in the love of the Lord Jesus Christ. We are to love each other enough to lift up and correct so that no one will miss out on Heaven. We are all to be soul winners for the Lord. There are times that we just don't realize we have made a mistake. There is a difference in sinning willfully and making an honest mistake I believe. God hates all sin but if you know to do good and doesn't do it to you it is sin because you know better. This kind of sin should never be in your life. When you correct someone it doesn't mean that you are judging them but out of love you are helping them. God is the only judge. Don't ever do something that will hinder someone else for it may cause someone not to be saved. We have to be careful in everything we say, everywhere we go and everything we do. Let nothing harm your testimony for the Lord Jesus Christ for we are a living testimony for Him and to others. We are to be a living sacrifice and testimony unto Him.

We are to put away all evil

I Pet.2:1, Lay aside all malice, all guile, hypocrisies, envies, evil speaking and all lies. Epe.4:25-32, Put away all lying, be angry and sin not. Don't give place to the devil, steal no more but work for your living. Let no corrupt thing come out of your mouth, no bad conversation or communications be spoken by you. Grieve not the Holy Spirit of God. Let all bitterness, wrath, anger, clamor, malice and evil speaking be put away from you at all times. Forgive one another and be kind one to another. We cannot allow any evil to enter our temple for we are to keep our bodies holy and righteous for the Lord. Epe.5:3-5, Do not commit fornication, covet, do no uncleanness and don't let any foolishness or jesting, which is joking, come out of your mouth. Now I believe the joking here is to tell bad or evil jokes or even to joke at a serious time. I remind you again as I have already stated, in Ecclesiates 3, there's a time for everything. The Ten Commandments cover it all so we can put away the evil from our lives. We are to keep the commandments for it is the school master to show us right from wrong. We know that we now live under grace since Jesus Christ came. Ex 20:3, You shall have no other god before Me, make no graven image or likeness in Heaven or earth. Do not take the name of Jesus in vain. Keep the Sabbath day holy and honor your father and mother. Do not kill, do not commit adultery, do not steal, do no lie and do not covet. We are to stay away from the love of money for it is the root of all evil. Money is not evil but the love of it makes it evil. Love fulfills the law for when Jesus came He was love and He was and is the fulfillment of the law. Rom.13:8-10, When the disciples heard Jesus teach these principles they asked Him, who then can be saved? Jesus said unto them, with man it is impossible but with God all things are possible. For all have sinned and fallen short of the glory of God. We could never save ourselves or do anything to earn salvation for it is the gift of God through faith in Jesus Christ. God forgives all sin when you come to Christ but there's one sin will never be forgiven for and that blaspheming against the Holy Ghost, rejecting Christ as your Savior and Lord. II Pet.3:9, The Lord is not slack in His promises as some count slackness but He is longsuffering to us not willing that any should perish but all come to repentance and have everlasting life. For the grace of God that brings salvations has appeared to all. In John's gospel Jesus said that it was not His will that any should perish but that all would have everlasting life. Jesus came to save the world not to condemn the world. If you don't accept Jesus then you condemn your ownself. Isa. 43:25 and 55:7, I am He that blotted out your transgressions for My own sake and I will remember your sins no more. Let the wicked forsake their ways and the unrighteous their thoughts. Let them return to the Lord and He will have mercy on them, return to God for He will forgive abundantly. God is pleading to all to come to Him and repent. He has such love for everyone that He's willing to forgive all you have done wrongfully. I John 1:19, If we confess our sins He is faithful and just to forgive and to cleanse you from all unrighteousness. We have redeemption through the blood of Jesus, the forgiveness of sins according to the riches of His glory. All you have to do is come to Jesus Christ, accept Him as your Lord and Savior, ask for forgiveness and He will forgive you. But you don't stop there for you have to follow Him, be obedient and faithful to Him to the end. You will find that you don't want any other life but to serve Him with all of your heart forever.

Hard work, attitude and love of God

Hard work will get you close. Attitude will get you there but the love of God will take you over the top. II Thessalonians 5:12-13, We beseech you brethren to know them that labor among you and over you in the Lord and we admonish you to esteem them very highly in love for their work's sake. Paul is talking about spiritual workers. We know that we cannot work ourselves into the Kingdom of Heaven. It's not the work that will get you there but we all have a job to do after we're saved. Our work is to follow us for it is important to work. God didn't call anyone just to sit and do nothing. James tells us that faith without works id dead. Titus 3:5, It's not by works of righteousness that we have done that He saved us but's it's according to His mercy by the washing of regeneration and renewing of the Holy Spirit. We could never work our way in but we have to be washed in the blood of Jesus Christ first of all and then walk in Him enduring to the end. Epe.2:9, Our salvation is not of works lest anyone should boast it is the gift of God. If we are truly saved our works will follow us. You can't do much work for the Lord if your heart is not in it and it won't pay off in the end. If you have not given your heart and life to the Lord then whatever you do will be in vain. You have to have faith and works working together to be rewarded for one without the other is dead. Hard work may get you close but it won't get you into the Promised Land of God.

Attitude will get you there

An attitude is your disposition, mood, belief, out look, state of mind and determination. You can have all of these qualities and it will get you there but there's something else missing and we will see that later. Mark 1:15, You must repent and believe then follow Jesus. If you can believe all things are possible. Lord I believe but help Thou my unbelief. You have to believe that Jesus Is the Son of God. I Thessalonians 4:14, You have to believe that Jesus died and rose again and is coming back again. Those that have died in the Lord are asleep in Him and will come back with Him. If you believe then you will live says John. I John 4:1, Don't believe every spirit but try every spirit to see if it's of God because there are a lot of false prophets gone out in the world. We must believe all things that are written in the Word, the Bible. David talks about us having a merry heart and how it makes a cheerful face. That's part of our attitude, our smiles and laughter of joy that we have in God. The joy of the Lord is our strength. So if you have the Lord then you should always show joy and it will always show. God said, I will put My Spirit in you and you will live. Our attitudes should always be filled with meekness and sympathy, love and mercy.

The love of God will take you over the top

Love of God will surely take you over the top. John 4:24, You must worship Him in Spirit and in truth. Rom.7:6, You must serve Him in newness of your spirit. We're working now and we have a good attitude so we have to have love. Our minds are made up and our hearts are fixed to love and serve God with all of our hearts, minds, souls and strength so now we're going to worship and praise Him for the rest of our days. Gal.22:23, Now we must have the fruit of the Spirit and they are, love, joy, peace, longsuffering, gentleness, goodness, faith, meekness and temperance. By doing all of these things it will take us over the top. Does this mean that we will never make another mistake? No, because we are not yet perfect but we are striving to be. As long as we are in this flesh we will make mistakes but we have to pray always that God will forgive us and He will. David praised and worshipped God but he made many mistakes and God said that he was the apple of His eye. God knows your heart just like He knew David's heart. David wanted more than anything else to please God and serve Him. If that's your desire then God sees it. David told God that He was his Lord and his strength and he told Him that his heart was fixed on serving Him. He told God how much he loved His law and he meditated on it all day long. Ps.119:97 and 159-160, I love Thy preceipts, God's Word for it is my meditations all day long. Thy Word is true from the beginning and every one of Your righteous judgments endures forever. Do you love God's Word? Do you long to read and study it everyday as David did? Is it the most important book that you read? When you begin to love the Lord as David did it will change your entire life. The Bible will become the most important, most treasured master piece that you have. God's Word and prayer are the most vital part of your life. We're living in the last days and it's important that we stay in the Word of God and pray always. We have to keep ourselves in the love of God to get over the top. If we love God with all of our heart, mind, soul and strength we will be obedient in these things listed in the Word of God and it's for all Christians.

We have to hate evil and love what is good then love our neighbor as ourself. Always abide in love for one another. We have to serve one another in love and let brotherly love continue in you. Remember, there's no fear in love for love casts out all fear. We love God because He first loved us and gave His only begotten Son for us. We're not to just love our brothers and sisters in Christ but we are to love our enemies and all those that persecute us and say all kind of evil aginst us. This is not always easy to do for it's easy to love those who love you. If we do these things then we will go over the top because God is with us and He will carry us through the hard places in our lives. We have to hang in there to the end with Jesus Christ. You can't just start and then fall away and expect to get to the top and enter into the Kingdom of Heaven. Remember, we have to walk by faith for without faith no one can please God. The just shall live by faith. The just ones are the Christians, those following Jesus. Love covers a multitude of sin and love will hold us all together. John 13:1, Jesus loved His own to the end and He loved them to the fullest degree and He still does today for He never changes. Jesus died for all and loved to the end. We also have to love Him to the end. **L...LOVING...O...OTHERS...V... VALUABLE...E...EVIDENCE**

Believers are living epistles

II Cor.3:2-3, You are our epistles written in our hearts known and read of all men. You are delared to be epistles of Christ ministered by us written not with ink but with the Spirit of the living God. Not in tablets of stone but in fleshly tables of the heart. Verse 17, Now the Lord is that Spirit and where the Spirit is there is liberty. We are free to be epistles of Jesus Christ. Verses 5-6, Not that we are sufficient within ourselves but sufficiency is of God. Never think that you are anything but it is God in you. We are all some people will ever read, for they don't read the Word of God so they watch our lives. God has made us ministers of the New Testament, not of the letter but of the Spirit, for the letter kills but the Spirit gives life. Verse 11, For if that which was done away with was glorious, much more that remains is more glorious. God didn't do away with the Ten Commandments but when Jesus Christ came we have a new covenant. He is our new covenant now. So the covenant that we have now is more glorious. II Cor.4:6-7, For God who commanded the light to shine out of darkness has shined in our hearts to give light of the knowledge of the power that it may be God in the face of Jesus. For we have this treasure in earthly vessels that the Excellency of the power may be of God and not of us. We have no power of ourselves for it is the power of God working in and through us. We can do all things through Jesus Christ who gives us strength. Make sure your life is what it should be in Christ because we are living epistles for Him. Jesus did His work when He was on earth and now we need to do what the Lord has called us to do. We are to live holy and righteous and let the light of Jesus shine through us all of the time.

Even through troubles and trials we are to still be epistles.II Cor.4:10-16, Always bearing about in the body the dying of the Lord Jesus Christ that the life of Him might be manifested in our own body. We are to never forget His death on the cross at Calvary over two thousand yeares ago. Whatever we go through in this life the life of Jesus should be manifested in our mortal flesh. God will carry us through and make a way when we go through problems or even failures. We should never faint or quit, even though our outward person perishes or gets tired the inward person is renewed day by day by the Holy Spirit. We are still living in the flesh and we do get tired, discouraged and troubles many times but God renews our strength. All we have to do is ask God and He will help us to be renewed. Matt.5:14, Jesus said, we are the light of the world, a city set on a hill that cannot be hid. We were once in darkness but now you are in the Lord so walk as children of the light. Whatever we did when we were out in sin when we came to Jesus He forgave us and never will He remember them anymore. O what a mighty God and Father is He. We are living epistles for Jesus always. We are to be blameless and shine as lights in darknes in this dark and sinful world that we live in. We are to try to reach all the lost that we possible can. Matt.5:16, Let your lights shine before others that they may see your good works and glorify your Father which is in Heaven. We are the light of the world. No one when they light a candle do they put it under a bushel or hides it but they set it on a candle stick so that they that enters can see a light. If you hide the light then you are in the darkness and you can't see. So let the light of Jesus shine through you wherever you go. John came for a witness, to be a witness of the light that through him all would believe. He was not that light but was sent to bear witness of that light. Jesus was and still is that light for He is the light of the world. We are His instruments that He uses. We should always pray, Lord make me an instrument to be used by You. Make me a vessel of honor for You Lord. Paul was sent to be a light to the Gentiles. Rom.13:12, Paul said, the night is far spent and the day is at hand so let us put on the armor of light. We have to walk the walk and talk the talk. We have to do all we can to testify of Jesus Christ for the time is running out for many to get saved. Let others see the joy, peace and happiness in you. God who commanded the light to shine out of darkness has shone in our hearts to give light of the knowledge of the glory of God in the face of Jesus Christ. We are to endure to the end as epistles of God. Just think, there will be no darkness in Heaven for Jesus will be the light. Rev.22 tells us about that. There shall be no night there and we'll need no candles neither the light of the sun for the Lord Jesus Christ gives light and they shall reign forever.

Mortify the flesh

Rom.13:12-14, The night is far spent and the day is at hand, let us cast off the works of darkness and put on the armor of light. Let us walk in honesty as in the day not in rioting and drunkenness, immoral living, worldly things, strife and envying. Put ye on the Lord Jesus Christ and make not provisions for the flesh to fulfill the lusts of the flesh.We are to die to self daily and do nothing that will make our brothers or sisters in the Lord to stumble or fall. Don't ever offend the weak in faith. Acts 14:21-23, It is good not to eat any flesh, drink wine or anything thereby that will make them stumble. Some things may not be wrong for you but if others believe something is wrong then it would be wrong for them. Happy is the one that condemns not thyself for what they allow or believe. They that doubt are damned if they eat because they eat not of faith for whatever is not of faith is sin. If you know something will be offensive to someone else then don't do it for this could be a stumbling block to them. You have to die to self and overcome the flesh. Don't think of only yourself but of others also and what's best for them. Whatever you eat or drink or whatever you do, do it all for the glory of God. Paul said in verse 33 that he tried to please everyone in everything he did that they may be saved. That is our main goal is to see all saved that can be. Our minds should always be on soul winning. Matt.16:24-27, Jesus said, If anyone will come after Me let them deny themselves and take up their cross and follow Me. Whoever will not bear their cross and come after me cannot be My disciple. If you live after the flesh then you will die but if through the Spirit do mortify the deeds of the flesh you shall live. We that are strong should help the weak, bear their infirmities and not please ourselves. They that are in Christ have crucified the flesh with the affections and lusts. You have died to self and are living by the Holy Spirit for He is leading you now. Paul said that he kept his body under subjection of Jesus Christ so that he would not become a castaway. You cannot please self and please God too. Put on Jesus Christ and make no provisions for the flesh. Live in the will of God and seek Him for what He wants you to do. Have a good relationship with Him, talk with Him regularly for you can lose yourself in Him. Stay in tune with Him always by reading the Word of God and through prayer to Him. Do not forsake the assembling of yourselves together in the house of God as a matter as some do. We need each other and that's why we should fellowship one with another in Christ. God works through His people and many times He has a Word for you through others.

Consistant life in Christ

Phil.1:27, Whatever may happen conduct yourselves in a manner worthy of the gospel of Christ. Whether I come to you or hear about you in my absence I will know that you stand firm in one Spirit contending as one man for the faith of the gospel. No matter what you're going through keep yourselves honorable and obedient to God. Never do anything to offend the gospel of Jesus Christ. Stand firm in the truth of the Word of God. Make sure that your behavior is Christ like. Let others see Jesus in you through your problems and trials in your life. It's easy to serve God when all is going good but how do you present yourselves when things are not going good for you? Paul told the church how to present themselves always whether in good times or bad. This still applies to us today. People are always watching to see how you act so we need always to show Christ in our lives. I Thessalonians 4:11-12, Make it your ambition or desire to work with your hands just as we have told you, so that your daily life will win the respect of oursiders and so that you will not be dependant on anyone. The Christian's life is a journey. We are growing, maturing and learning to walk more intimately with the Savior Jesus Christ. Our greatest desire should be to grow into a deeper relationship with Christ and a deeper life in faith. This means we have more wisdom and understanding of the obedience of the Word and a fresher and deeper encounter with the Holy Spirit. We have a deeper experience in worship and prayer. We also have a closer relationship with the people of God and a deeper commitment to the service of God and a purer life of holiness. It is God's will for us to live a sanctified and holy life. Don't be dependant on anyone but lean on the Lord and work with your hands so that others will respect you. I Tim.3:7, Have a good reputation with others especially with outsider so that you will not fall into disgrace and into the devil's trap. This is the qualification for ministers or overseers, but we should all have the same qualification. Don't ever do anything to shame God or bring disgrace to His Word. Always be careful and alert to do what's right in God's sight. James 3:13-17, Who is wise and understanding among you? Let them show it by their good life and deeds done in humility that comes from wisdom from above. That kind of wisdom comes from God. David said, if you lack wisdom then pray and ask God for it. The wisdom that comes from Heaven is first pure, peace, love, consistent, submissive, good fruit, impartial and sincere. A wise Christian will have this kind of wisdom and with wisdom you will have understanding.

II Pet.3:8-12, Live in harmony with each other, be sympathetic, love as brothers and sisters, be compassionate and humble. Whosoever will love life and see good days must keep their tongue from evil and his lips from deceitful speech. They must turn from evil and do good, seek peace and pursue it. The eyes of the Lord are on the righteous and His ears are attentive to their prayers. This is the life in Christ for this is the way He lived and walked and so should we live and walk as He did. Our conduct should always be like His. You know if you will try to look for peace you will find it and it will cause others to find it also. Good qualities do rub off on others many times. We have always known that bad qualities will rub off, that's why Paul said that bad company will corrupt good morals. Well, good company can also cause bad company to change for the better. I Pet.2:12, Live such good lives around the pagans that though they accuse you of doing wrong that they may see your good works and deeds and then glorify God on the day that He visits us. (when Jesus comes to judge the world) Always be careful of what you say, what you do and where you go. Always have a great testimony for the Lord to others. We don't know when Jesus is coming but we know that He is and we believe it will be soon but you need to always stay ready. It could be today, tonight or tomorrow for we just don't know. The Bible says that He will come as a thief in the night, in the twinkling of ans eye so be ready and looking for Him. The Bible says also that He is coming for those who are looking for Him. Are you looking for Him? We are to make every effort to be found spotless, blameless and at peace with Him. Have you made your peace with Him? Be sure to check your life each day and always make sure you are ready for His coming. Phil.2:14-15, Do everything without complaining or arguing so that you may become blameless and pure children of God. Grumbling and complaining is an outward indication of an inward problem. You know I have said before that what's on the inside will come out, it will sooner or later show itself. We are to rejoice in the Lord always and again I say, rejoice.

Rise to the level of your solution

How do we do this? We do it through the praise and worship to God. You may be saying, how can we praise God when we're going through such big problems? Jesus Christ is the key to freedom, peace and happiness don't ever let yourself sink to the level of your problems. You need to praise and worship God no matter what's going on in your life. You don't praise Him for the problem but you praise Him for the way He's going to bring you through your problems. Worship and praise brings power for there's power in the Holy Ghost and we need that. We have no power within ourselves but there's power in the name of Jesus. It's easy to praise God when all is going good and all of your desires are being met. But, what if God says no or wait awhile, what then? Do you still praise and worship Him then? Don't let your mind or spirit sink down into your problem but rise into the Spirit by praising God and things will turn out better and different. You need to start praising God at the beginning of your problems, troubles, sickness and sorrows knowing that He will make a way and carry you through whatever it is that you have to go through. You need to look more at the problem solver than at your problems in order to rise above the level of your problem. Remember, the problem is much smaller than the problem solver, Jesus Christ. Ps.55:22, David said, I cast my burdens on You Lord knowing you will sustain me and I will not be shaken. II Cor.5:7, We walk by faith and not by sight. We need to trust God in everything. Just because you don't see a change in things that you pray for doesn't mean that it's not going to happen. God will answer when the time is right. He's never too late for He's always on time and He never makes a mistake. Don't give up because you don't see anything happening right away, have faith in God and wait patiently for what you ask. Don't go by your feelings or what you see. The Bible teaches that the just shall walk and live by faith and without faith you cannot please God. Don't doubt or worry for they both are sin and if you do these things you are not leaning and trusting fully in God. James 2:1-3, A person who doubts receives nothing. Keep your heart, mind and eyes focused on God and not your troubles. He will answer according to His will and His time, just trust Him for He knows whats best for you. There are times when He will answer immediately, some times He will say to wait awhile and sometimes He will say no. The main thing is to praise and worship Him while you wait. This will bring you peace and strength in the Holy Ghost. Never tell God how to answer your prayers for He knows what best always. It's not wrong to tell Him what you want or what you need but pray that His will be done. Jesus prayed that way in the Garden of Gethsemane when He prayed to God that if it was His will to remove the cup of suffering from Him. So we need to pray that His will be done in us as well.

James 1:2-3, Count it all joy when you're going through testing and trials because the trial of your faith brings patience. God allows us to go through things to make us stronger. This is how we can rise above the level of our solutions. Our ending is better than the beginning. The more trials you go through the closer to God you'll get if you're a child of God. Your faith will grow stronger because you're learning to lean and trust in Him more. Jesus has told us in His Word that if we follow Him that we will have troubles and trials all the days of our life but He also told us that He would never leave or forsake us and He would make a way of escape that would lighten our load. He will give you the strenght you need to make it through. I Pet.6:9, He said that He would refine us as gold tried in the fire and we would be more valuable than gold. Verse 5, We are kept by the power of God so rise to the lever of your solution.

10 things to do when you're in a battle or trouble

1 - Stop everything and worship and praise God.
2 - Thank Him for already defeating your enemy.
3 - Thank Him for fighting your battle for you.
4 - Ask God if there's anything that you need to do that you're not doing.
5 - Fast and pray.
6 - Declare your dependance on Him.
7 - Recognize that the battle's not yours but His.
8 - Position yourself in the right place with God.
9 - Refuse to have fear, worry and doubt.
10 - Quiet your soul in worship and watch God move and take care of you.

Epe.6:13, Put on the whole armor of God so that you can stand against the wiles of the devil. After you've done all to stand, just stand. II Cor.10:4, The weapons that Christians fight against are not carnal but mighty through God to the pulling down of strong holds.

It takes divine power to tear down strongholds of the devil and evil. Such power as, prayer and fasting, the sword of the Spirit, which is the Word of God, shield of faith, helmit of salvation, breastplate of righteousness, belt of truth and feet shod with the preparation of the gospel of Jesus Christ. These are the garments that we should dress in each morning before we start the day so we can stand against the evil of the devil in these evil and dark days. We're living in hard times and the devil is out to get everyone that he can. He's out to steal, kill and destroy so you have to be on the watch for him. He can only do what you allow him to do so that why it's so important to put on the whole armor of God everyday. There's power in the weapons of God to fight against the evil. Rom.8:37, We are more than conquerors through Him that loves us and that is Jesus Christ. We can do nothing on our own but all things are possible through Him. Ps.18:17, David said, He rescued me from my powerful enemy, and my foes were too strong for me. Verses 29-30, He also said, with Your help I can advance against a troop and I can scale over a wall. He was saying, I can fight against a troop and I can jump over a wall with God on his side and helping me. For my God's way is perfect and the Word of God is flawless. He is a shield for all who will take refuge in Him.

II Chr.20 tells about Jehosphat's battle. He stood in Soloman's temple and prayed before all of the people and said, O Lord, God of our fathers aren't You the God of Heaven? Aren't You the ruler over all the kingdoms of the heathen? Aren't You our God that drove out all the heathens from Israel and gave the land to the seed of Abraham forever? When evil comes our way whether famine, pestilence, sword or judgment we stand before You and in Your presence and cry unto You in our afflictions and you will hear and help us. Our eyes are upon You because we don't know what to do. The Lord said, be not afraid nor dismayed for the battle is not yours but God's. You do not need to fight just stand still and see the salvation of the Lord. For the Lord will be with you so be not afraid. And Jehosphat bowed his head with his face to the ground and all the people of Judah and Jeruaslem fell before the Lord and worshipped Him. Believe in the Lord so you can be established and so you shall prophesy. He appointed people to sing for the Lord and praise Him in the beauty of holines as they went out before the army. Praise the Lord for His mercy endures forever. As they sang and worshipped the Lord the Lord began to work in their favor. He slew all of their enemies. They had complete victory and they rejoiced. The reign of Jehosphat was quiet for the Lord his God gave him rest. When we turn it all over to God He will fight our battles for us just like He did back then for He doesn't respect one over the other. He's the same today, yesterday and forever for He never changes. be earnest when you call upon Him and trust Him completely and stay out of His way. Sometimes we can get in God's way and hinder Him. Pray earnestly to Him and believe what you pray for. Jehosphat didn't grumble and complain for he knew that God was a God of miracles and he knew he was going to get one. God gave him complete rest through it all for he had peace knowing that God was in control. Why can't you and I be the same way when troubles come? We know the answer and we have to do what it takes, turn it all over to God and watch Him work it all out.

We have spiritual battles as well as physical ones and we can't make it without wearing the whole armor of God.We are soldiers in the army of the Lord and He is our Captain, our defense, protector and our keeper. We're always going to face some kind of problems as long as we live here on this earth. God will see us through if we trust Him and lean on Him. We are to live holy and righteous and do what's right in His sight for Him to fight our battles. II Cor.10:4-6, For the weapons of our warfare are not carnal but mighty through God to the pulling down of strongholds. Casting down imaginations and every high thing that exalts itself against the knowledge of God and bringing into captivity every thought to the obedience of Christ, having a readiness to revenge all disobedience when your obedience is fulfilled. Don't be puffed up with pride and exalt yourself. Keep your spiritual sanity of mind and be obedient at all times to Christ Jesus and ready to serve Him at all times. Be instant in season and out of season to minister and testify of Him. Always inforce church discipline and never let evil imaginations enter into your mind and spirit. Be sure to keep the spiritual armor of God on to endure this life in order to enter into life eternal with Jesus Christ and all the saints of God. Ps.18:17, David said, The Lord delivered me from my strong enemy. What and who is your enemy? It could be people, sickness, troubles, poverty, financial problems or many other things. David said that He delivered me because He delighted in me. He said he ran through a troop and leaped over a wall all because of God who helped him. A troop is a large groop of soldiers and we know the wall was high. It doesn't matter how big your problems are or how small they may be God can still take care of them. He said He is our defense and deliverer. David knew that he could not have gotten the victory if God had not helped him and we can't either. God is love and He is power. God's ways are perfect and sure. God's Word is tried and is a buckler, which is a divine protector, to all who will trust Him. It's God who protects me and gives me strength and He makes my way perfect. We could never make our way perfect for we fail many times and get on the wrong way. David said that God had given him great deliverances, set him on high places and has shown mercy to me and not only me but His seed forever. I will give thanks to Him forever and sing praises to the Lord Thy great name. Ps.18:3, I will call upon the Lord who is worthy to be praised, so shall I be saved from my enemies. Put all of your trust in Him and totally depend on Him. Always remember He's fighting for you. David said, the battle is not mine but God's. We should realize this in all of our situations. Let the peace of God comfort your heart and spirit and give you understanding. Phil. 4:7, The peace of God that passes all other understanding shall keep your hearts and minds through Jesus Christ our Lord. To be spiritual minded is life and peace. Our defense is of God which saves the upright in heart. I will praise God according to His righteousness and will sing praises to the name of the Lord most high.

Don't tell God how big your problem is but tell your problem how big God is. If God sends it to you He will bring you through it. God will not lead you where He won't or can't keep you. There is nothing that you go through that God doesn't know about it first. He knew about it even before the problem was sighted by you. He will make a way for you but you have to trust Him.

At what level are you in the Holy Spirit?

1 - Intimacy with Him
2 - Partnership with Him
3 - Leadership of Him
4 - Fellowship with Him
5 - Total dependence on Him

Lets see what level you're experiencing the Holy Spirit's work in your life. We never want to limit Him because He wants to do everything that Jesus has promised for you. Even before Jesus death He promised the disciples that He was going away but He was going to send the Comforter. John 16:7 and Acts 1:8, For if I do not go away the Comforter will not come to you, but if I go I will send Him to you. Jesus told them, you shall receive power after the Holy Spirit is come upon you and you shall be witnesses unto Me both in Judah and in Jerusalem, in Samaria and unto the uttermost part of the earth.

Intimacy

I Cor.6;19, Know ye not that your body is the temple of the Holy Ghost which is in you, which you have of God and you are not your own.For you were bought with a price therefore glorify God in your body and in your spirit which are God's. God put His Spirit in us for this cause, we are to walk in His statue, walk in His commandments and laws and keep His Word. If you are one of His then He is living within you. We are in Him and He in us. If you don't have His Spirit living in you then you are none of His. I Cor.3:16, know ye not that your body is the temple of the Lord and that the Spirit of God lives in you. God saved you from death and your enemies and you are to serve Him and listen to the Holy Spirit that leads you without fear and holiness and righteousness before Him all of the days of your life. You are to cleanse yourself from all unrighteousness and filthiness of the flesh and spirit in perfect holiness in the fear of the Lord. Jesus said to be holy for He is holy. Follow peace with all holiness for without no one will see the Lord. Make sure all of your conversations are holy and godly. Following the Word of God should be and has to be the most important matter in your life as a Christian. God has to be number one above all others and all else.

Partnership

We are to be partners with the Lord Jesus Christ. A partner is a person to whom another is married or a part of. Partnership is the state of sharing interest or effort in. We as Christians are partners with Jesus Christ for we are His bride and He's the Bridegroom. So we have a partnership in Heaven for we are heirs to the Kingdom of God. When we came to Him and ask forgiveness and ask him into our hearts and lives then He forgave us of all sins and He accepted us unto Himself so that made us partners with Him. He will never sell us out, leave or forsake His children or His bride. We can sell out to Him if we do not follow Him and be obedient to Him. If you turn back to the world and to your old life then you will have walked away from Him. He said that if you were of the world then you were none of His. Jesus left the comforter, the Holy Spirit to lead, guide, direct and keep His children. You can see in the Bible that the Spirit left Saul because he sinned. He will not live in a temple are messed up with sin.

Leadership of the Holy Spirit

John 16:13, When the Spirit of truth is come He will lead and guide you into all truth. He will also show you of things to come. Rom.8:14, For as many that are lead by the Spirit of God they are the children of God. The Spirit gives life. The Spirit quickens the flesh and the Words spoken to you are life. The same Spirit that raised Jesus up from the dead is the same Spirit that lives in you and gives you life. The Holy Spirit convicts you of sins and wrongs. He will never lead you astray. It is up to you to follow where He leads. If you go your way then you are failing to let Him lead you. The way of men leads is to death but the way God leads is life and life eternal. Someone has to lead so let the Holy Spirit lead you all of the way and you will be sure to make it into the Kingdom of Heaven.

Fellowship with Him

I John 4:3, Hereby know ye that we dwell in Him and He in us because He has given us His Spirit. David said, I have set the Lord always before me because He's at my right hand and I shall not be moved. He said, it is good for me to draw near to God for I have put my trust in Him so that I can declare all of His works. We need to draw near to God with a true and a pure heart. The HolySpirit wants to have fellowship with us. In order to have a good fellowship with Him we have to pray always and talk to Him. You have to be close to Him and let Him know that He's the most important person in your life. In order to have fellowship you have to have a good relationship with Him. You have to know Him and not just know about Him. You have to believe and trust Him in all things. Matt.18;20, Where two or three are gathered together in My name I will be in the midst of them. Jesus said, do what I have commanded you and I will be with you always even to the end of the world. There is no fellowship like the fellowship of the Holy Spirit. He will never let you down or forsake you as long as you are following Him. God called you into the fellowship of His Son Jesus Christ our Lord. He invites everyone to come to Him, believe, accept Him and follow Him and have fellowship with Him. He said to open the door and He will come in and sup with you, meaning that He will come in and fellowship with you for He will eat with you and He will feed you. He desires your fellowship so why not?

Total dependence on the Holy Spirit

Rom.8;26-28, The Holy Spirit helps you out in your weakness for He interceded for you. We don't know how or what to pray for many times but we can totally depend on the Holy Spirit to pray for us for He knows what we need. He makes intercession for His children with groaning which cannot be uttered. He makes intercessions for the saints according to the will of God. And we know that all things work together for the good to those who are the called according to His purpose. The Holy Spirit is an ever present help in time of trouble and in good times too. We cannot do God's work in our own power. Zec.4:6, It's not by power or by might but by My Spirit says the Lord Almighty. We have to have the power of God working in us for we don't have the power with our flesh. Luke 1:35-37, The Holy Spirit shall come upon you and the power of the highest will over shadow you. For with God nothing is impossible. We can do all things through Christ Jesus who gives us the strength. These five things we are to always do. We have to have an intimacy with the Holy Spirit, be partners with Him and we are to let Him have leadership of our life. We are to have fellowship with Him and we are to be totally dependent on Him. Mark 16:17-18, When we are totally dependent on Him then we have the power to lay hands on the sick and they will recover. We can cast out demons in Jesus name. We will speak with new tongues. Are thesre signs following you? Jesus said they would, if you have been saved, baptized in water and baptized in the Holy Ghost. He said by faith we can do these things all in the name of Jesus. This was the last time that He spoke with His disciples before He was ascended into Heaven. He was receive in Heaven and is sitting at the right hand of the Father interceding for you and me. We are His disciples too if we are following Him so we can do the same things that His disciple did back then. Remember, you have to be totally dependent on Him always. Keep your faith and trust in God for all things for there's life in God's Word. Always pray and ask the Holy Spirit what you should do in any situation. He will show you a sign or put into your spirit and mind what to do for He will never mislead you.

CHAPTER SEVEN

Who Are You When No One Is Watching?

CHAPTER 7

Who Are You When No One Is Watching?

This is a true test of character.Babylon thought they were alright when no one was watching. They forgot one thing, God always see you even when others doesn't. God sees everything, for He even sees your thoughts and motives. You can hide from others but never from God for nothing in creation is ever hid from Him. Heb.12:13, Everything is uncovered and laid bare before the eyes of Him whom we must give an account to. God's eyes can be disturbing or comforting. To the believer it's comforting to know He's watching over you but to the sinner it is disturbing for them to know He's watching everything they do especially if they have ever known about the Lord. There are many sinners that know right from wrong but don't follow the right. With sincere confession there is always forgiveness for sinners. You who are Christians be sure that you never sin willfully because God will turn from you if you continue to sin when you know better. This is what you call backsliding. You can fall away from God and be lost. Ps.19:12, You can pray like David did, forgive my hidden sins and faults for that's the way to freedom. We all make mistakes many times and maybe not realize it and that's the reason we should always pray and ask God for forgiveness of any wrong that we've commited. The Bible teaches that all have sinned and fallen short of the glory of God. There are none righteous, no not one. We stand in God's righteousness for our righteousness is as filthy as rags. Isa.47:10-15, God told Babylon, you have trusted in your wickedness and have said, no one sees you but your wisdom and knowledge mislead you. Disaster will come upon you and you will not know how to control it or cast it away. Keep on with your magic spells and your sorceries. Keep on with your astrologers and star gazing that have made all the predictions in your life and see if they can save you from the things that is coming upon you. They are like stubble for the fire will burn them up. They can't even save themselves from the power of the flame. All they can do for you is predict things for you, they are just empty words. There is not one that can save you for only God can save and keep you. Verse 1, God told Babylon to go sit in the dust for they had fallen to the lowest. Verse 3, Your nakedness will be exposed and your shame uncovered for I will take vengeance and spare no one. Many are called by God's name and are playing with the fires of hell because they are not following Him and doing His will.

Many are dealing with witchcraft and that is from the devil himself. The things like magic, sorceries, astrologers, star gazing, fortune telling and other things that are all evil.Horoscopes are horror and scopes of the devil. There are many Christians that look at there horoscope everyday, for this is one of the first things that they do early in the morning. Some even make their plans according to what it says. They're looking for something to come to pass from them instead of looking to God for their blessing and to lead and guide them for each day. There may be some time times they will come to pass just to encourage you to continue looking at them again and again. It's just enough to deceive you into believing something that's not of God. That's the way the devil works. God sees all of this and He's not pleased with His children. He warns of this in His Word. Isa.43:10, God said, there is no other god before Me, now or will there be anyother after Me, now or ever. You are to serve Him and Him only for He is the truth. Ex.20:5, God is a jealous God. You shall not bear down to false gods, idols or any graven image and serve them. I am your God and I am a jeaalous God. Many say, I'm not worshipping them or neither do I serve them. If it's not of God then you should leave them alone. Anything that you put before God is an idol. God wants our first fruits not what's left over. This means your first part of the day, your self especially, your heart, mind, soul and strength. Go to Him first and He will make your day. Let Him plan your day for you for He knows what you need and what your heart's desire is. He said if you draw near to me and follow Me I will give you the desires of your heart. II Cor.6:17, Wherefore, come out from among them and be a separated people says the Lord and touch not the unclean thing and I will receive you. He is saying; don't be of the world and of the devil's evil doings. You can't be of the world and be of God too. Jesus said, if you are of the world then you are none of Mine. Depart from the evil and don't even touch the unclean things. Col.2:21, Touch not, taste not and handle not. In other words, stay away from all evil, anything that is not of God leave it alone. The devil is so conniving that he will make you think that there's nothing wrong in just reading the horoscopes and looking at some of his evil things but that's one of his lies. You look at them and then it goes to your mind and that's where sin in conceived, in the mind. Then you put it into actions. The devil is a liar, deceiver, destroyer and a killer. He came to deceive, steal, kill and destroy. God has told all of us to stay away from him and his doings. Isa.8:19, God told the people of Israel, don't seek familiar spirits and wizards but seek the God of the living and of truth, which is the Father of all things the only God, the Heavenly Father.

Gal.5:19-21, Now the works of the flesh are these, idolatry and witchcraft. As I have told you before and I tell you again, they that do these things will not inherit the Kingdom of God. It would be a terrible thing to miss Heaven just because you read and believe your horoscope. The horoscope is witchcraft along with other things as well. I Sam.15:23, Rebellion is a sin unto witchcraft and stubbornness is iniquity and idolatry. Did you know that? That's why you should always be obedient to God and do what He says. Just think, rebellion and stubbornness will keep you out of Heaven. They're not my words but they are God's Words. No witchcraft or idolaters will enter in the Kingdom of God. Please listen to His message and do what He says. This means that being stubborn toward God, your spouse and to your parents is the sin of witchcraft. Wives, the Bibles says that we are to be submissive to our husbands and if we are stubborn and rebellious toward him than we are in trouble with God. This doesn't leave the husband out either because if he's stubborn and rebellious toward his wife it is sin also. God didn't tell the husband that he had to be submissive to his wife but he was to love her and treat her like Christ loves and treats the church or His bride. If you will study you will get these deep things of the Word of God. I love God's Word and I rejoice when He shows me the deeps things of His Word. I never want or intend to write anything but what the Word says. I never want to tell or write anything that the Word of God doesn't back up. The book of Revelation tells us not to add or take away from the Words that are in this book, the Bible. If we add then God will add plagues to us and if we take away then He will take away our names out of the book of life. So you can see it's a dangerous thing to do either one.

You are a slave to whatever controls you

II Pet.2:19, For you are a slave to whatever controls you. Whatever masters you then you are in bondage to it for you are addicted to or enslaved to it. People let things get a tight grip on them and then before they know it they have a hold on them and it rules them. Prov.5:22-23, The evil deeds of a wicked man ensnares and the cord of his sins hold him fast. He will die for lack of discipline being led astray by his own great folly. The Lord sees clearly what a person does, examining every path that they take. An evil person is held captive by their own sins. They are ropes that capture and hold them. They die for lact of self control and they will be lost because of their incredible folly. Acts 8:23, For I can see that you are full of bitterness and held captive by sin. Some make all kinds of excuses for doing what they do. Some use drugs, alcohol, sex and some even overeat, some won't even eat at all because of oppression or depression from things that have controlled them. Some even hold others accountable for their actions. There are many make TV their master, some allow their work to be their master. It doesn't have to be something bad or evil that you're doing but if you put it before God then it's become your master or your slave. Everyone has a choice to do good or evil. You don't have to be a slave to anything or anyone. Jesus Christ made a perfect plan for you and me. He's a loving God and He wants to lead and guide us in through this life in everything we do. You can be free in Him and have perfect peace in Him. Only Jesus can give you this. John 8:34-35, Jesus answered them, Verily, verily I say unto you whosoever commits sin is the servant of sin. He was saying I assure you that everyone who sin is a slave to sin. Now a slave has no place in the family but a son belongs forever. God is saying, if you are a sinner then you are none of Mine, but if you're a child of Mine then you are a child forever as long as you follow Jesus Christ. There's a time and a place for everything. There's a time to work, a time to play, a time to cry, a time to laugh and a time to rest. Just make sure that you give God His time first. He will not be second place to anyone or anything. He wants and loves for His children to enjoy life to the fullest as long as it pleases Him and you're doing nothing of the world and of the devil. He said that He came to give us life and life more abundantly. He does want us to be happy Christians and we Christians are the happiest when we are serving Him and doing His will. Rom.6:16, Be sure you realize that whatever or whoever you yield yourselves to becomes your master. You can choose which leads to life in the obedience to God and receive His approval and live or you can choose death and follow the devil's ways. Do not let sin control the way you live or give in to its lustful desires. Don't let any part of your body or life become a tool of wickedness to be used for sinning, instead give yourselves completely to God.

You can recover yourself out of bondage

II Tim.2:26, That they may recover themselves out of the snares, net, bondage or slave of the devil who have been taken captives by him at his will. If you will come to your senses then turn from your ways and come to the Lord, He will help you to escape the snares of the devil that has taken and captured you and the Lord will set you free. Even to Paul struggled with sin and bondage. Rom.7:14-24, Paul said that the law is good. The trouble is not with the law but with me, for sin is my master. He said, I don't understand myself at all, for what I want to do I don't do it and what I shouldn't do I want to do for I do the things that I hate. I love God's law with all of my heart but there's another law within me and is at war in my mind. This law wins the fight and makes me a slave to sin that's within me. Oh what a miserable person I am. Who will set me free of this miserable life that has dominated me by sin? Paul is saying, I am a slave to some kind of sin. He didn't say what it was but he knew he was miserable within even though he loved God and His laws and he wanted to do what was right in God's sight. The answer is in the next verse. Thank God that the answer is in Jesus Christ our Lord and Savior. Paul was saying, you see how it is? In my heart and mind I want to serve God and obey Him but because of my sinful nature I am a slave to sin. In Paul's mind he was a slave to God. That's why we have to keep flesh under control and under the subjection to the Holy Spirit. We have to be led by the Spirit not by our flesh. Thank God for His patience and longsuffering, love, mercy and His grace. Rom.2:4, Don't ever despise the goodness, forbearance and long sufferings of God which leads us to repentance. Don't ever forget how kind, tolerant and patience that God has been with you. He loves you and me so much that He's been waiting for you to turn from your ways and turn to Him. He has given you plenty of time to turn from your sins. He wants to lead everyone from sin and come to Him. God is good and upright and He will teach sinners in the way. Epe.1:7, We have redemption in the blood of Jesus Christ and the forgiveness of sins according to His riches. You can only be saved through Jesus Christ and cleansed by His blood that He shed on the cross at Calvary. I John 1:9, If we confess our sins He is faithful and just to forgive our sins and to cleanse us from all unrighteousness. In the way of righteousness is life and in the pathway thereof there is no death.

II Pet.3;9, The Lord is not slack concerning His promise as some men count slackness to us, not willing that any should perish but that all should come to repentance. Once you come to Him the old life is dead and the new you have a new Master, Jesus Christ. Consider yourself dead to sin and now able to live for the glory of God through Jesus Christ. Rom.6:14-23, Sin is no longer you master and you are no longer a slave to sin and you are no longer subject to the law which enslaved you, instead you are free by God's grace. Remember this, you are not saved to be free to sin but you are free from sin. You are now a slave to righteousness unto holiness. When you were a slave to sin you were free from righteousness for you were in sin and away from God. Now you are free from sin and become a servant to God and you have your fruit unto holiness and the end everlasting life. For the wages of sin is death but the gift of God is eternal life through Jesus Christ our Lord, Savior and Master. Now you are lead by the Holy Spirit and not your flesh. Spiritual life brings freedom of all past sins. Rom.8:1, There is therefore no condemnation to them which are in Christ Jesus who walk not after the flesh but after the Spirit. God doesn't remember your past sins or life. He said that He cast them into the deepest sea as far as the east is from the west never to remember them anymore. That's the love, mercy and grace of our Lord and Savior Jesus Christ. That's how much He loves you and me. Thank God for His love, mercy and His grace.

I want to personally thank Him for His longsuffering, His patience, love and forgiveness to me and for all He's done for me. I don't deserve His goodness, mercy or grace but I know that's because of His love for me. It is a gift of God for I could have never earned, bought or worked for it. His goodness and mercy endures forever. Amen

I was saved when I was 9 years old and was called of Him to do a work for Him at the age of 11 but I did not heed to His calling or was I obedient to him. I choose the wrong way for my life and I have had to suffer for it for many years. Not only did I suffer but it caused my children to suffer also. No, I was never a bad person and I didn't do the bad things like drugs, alcohol, sex, murder, neither was I a mean person but I didn't follow the Lord as I should and as I could have. I wasn't always obedient to my parents and I know that I hurt them many times and I so regret that. I went to church all of my life and did a lot of good works but I failed God. As I look back it makes me so grateful to God for waiting on me and giving me so many chances for my failures to make them right. We can never change anything but we can improve them all. There were times when God would make a way for me where there seem to be no way and then I would make more bad choices and mess up again. I know the Bible tell us never to look back at the plow, for if we do, we are not fit for the Kingdom of Heaven. I only look back and praise God for what He has done for me. I can feel what Paul was saying about himself. I always wanted to serve God for I loved Him so much and have always read and studied the Word of God for I love His Word. I am reminded of the desire of my heart that I always prayed for after so many years and God answered that prayer and He gave me my heart's desire. It's hard to understand how good God is after I had failed Him so much to do this for me. Most of my life I struggled to serve God because of my wrong choosing of decisions. For many years I blamed someone else but it was my bad choosing that put me where I was. We don't like to accept the blame for ourselves but we have to look at the truth. Now, it's like new rain or dew in the morning. It's so sweet and it gets sweeter every day to walk and talk with Him. That desire and prayer was met when God brought my great husband Leon in my life almost 27 years ago. When God did this my life has been fulfilled. I have first of all my Savior Jesus Christ and a wonderful husband of God. He is such a man of God and loves Him with all of his heart, mind, soul and strength. His love and care for me cannot be compared with any other outside of Jesus Christ. We made a vow to each other before we were even married that we would always be number two to each other that God was first place in our hearts and lives and then our children and so on down. He's been a good father to our children and we have all in common. No one could have matched us like God did. Do we have a perfect marriage? No, for there is no perfect marriage here on this earth. We strive to make it perfect everyday just like we strive to be perfect in the Lord. Marriage is to be respected by each spouse to each other for the first marriage was made of God and it is to be kept holy unto Him. You see when I speak of your desires being met I know it can happen because it happened to me. Never give up but wait on the Lord for when you get things right in your own life He will fulfill your desires. My greatest desire now is to help others see their needs and come to the Lord and for them to give their lives to him and live a happy life. I want to see all of our children back in and serving God. No matter what your problem is it can change if you want it to, with God's help. God never forgot my heart's desire and He gave it to me. The reason it took so long was my fault by not yielding completely to Him. I love life and want to live as long as I can for I enjoy the things of the Lord and then I will have eternal life after this life with Jesus and all of the saints that have gone on before.

Sonship of believers, children of God

I John 3:1-3, Behold what manner of love the Father has bestowed upon us that we shall be called the sons of God. Therefore the world knows us not because they don't know Him. We are now the children of God. We don't know what we shall be like but we know this, when He shall appear we shall be like Him for we shall see Him as He is. Everyone that has this hope has purified themselves even as He is pure. We are to strive everyday and every night to be like Him. Walk and talk like Him and even think like Him. The Word of God says that we have the mind of Christ. He lives in our hearts and guides us in His footsteps. All who receive the grace of God through Jesus Christ are adopted as His children. He pours out a flood of Heavenly love and acceptance upon us. Rom.8:16, The Spirit Himself testifies with our spirit that we are the children of God. There is no greater confirmation that we can have than the Holy Spirit sealing the truth to our hearts. We see in John 3:1 that God and the Holy Spirit agree as always that we are the children of God, if we believe and follow Him.

Difference in God's children and the devil's children

I John 3:4-10, Everyone who sin breaks the law for sin is the transgressor of the law. All sin opposes the law of God. Jesus came to take away our sins for there is no sin in Him. If we continue in Him then we won't sin either, willfully. No one who lives in Him will keep on sinning. Whosoever continues to sin has not seen Him or neither do they know Him. Meaning, if you know Him then you won't sin willfully. He that knows to do good and doesn't do it to them it is sin. Don't let anyone deceive you for whosoever does what is right is righteous just as He is righteous for it is Jesus in you that make you righteous. He that commits sin is of the devil for the devil sinned from the beginning that's why he was kicked out of Heaven. Jesus the

Son of God came to destroy the devil and his works. Whosoever is born of God does not sin for His seed remains in Him and He cannot sin because He was born of God. This is Jesus Christ for He was the Son of God and He cannot sin and He never has. Verse 10 tells us how we can know who the children of God are and who the children of the devil are. Anyone who does not love his brother or does not obey God the Father and His commandments or doesn't love other Christians does not belong to God. Jesus said also, if the love of the world is in you then you are no child of His. He said, he that is in the world is none of Mine. I John 2:3, 15 and 17, We can know and be sure that we belong to God by obeying the commandments. We can't just keep part of the commandments but all of them. The Bible says that if we break one of them then we are guilty of breaking them all. Love not the world nor the things of the world. If anyone loves the world then the love of the Father is not in them. The world passes away and the lust thereof but they that do the will of the Father abide forever. When you come to Christ He forgives you of all your sins and never remembers them anymore. Those sins are forever gone but you must stay sinless. If and when you do commit a wrong you have an advocate to the Father, Jesus Christ who you can go to and ask forgiveness and He will forgive you. Don't be caught up in sin when He comes, for you won't have time to change and ask forgiveness for it will be too late. He will come in a twinkling of an eye. Don't be deceived, for anything that is not of God is sin. The time is getting late for it's almost the seventh hour and Jesus is coming soon. Be ready and watching for Him for He said that He was coming for those who are waiting and watching for Him.

What kind of an example are you?

I Thessalonians 1:7, So you were examples to all who believed in Macedonia and Archaia. Paul was talking about the Christian believers here. They were so excited about what the Apostles had taught them that they wanted to be examples and testify. What kind of examples are you in your neighborhood, in your church, in your work area, in your home and everywhere you go? What do your children see in you? Are you leaving a good legacy behind? Are you living a life that you would be proud for them to live and follow? Verse 6, Are you followers of us and the Lord having received the Word in much afflictions with joy and of the Holy Ghost. Paul was a good example after he received the Lord as his Savior in his heart and in his life. Are you following the right person, Jesus Christ? Are you setting a good example for others to follow? Even through all of the afflictions, pain and troubles that Paul went through he still retained his joy in the Holy Ghost and stood strong in the Lord. There may have been times that he was not happy but he kept his joy of the Lord down deep in his heart and soul. He showed this joy to others and ir rubbed off. To follow means to mimic or to copy. Whether you realize it or not people will mimic you so make sure what you do is good and pleasing to God. Paul's good example is still reaching others today. Does your community see Jesus in you? If they were to ask what kind of person you are what would their reply be? Are you a good neighbor? Do you even know them? Anyone is your neighbor that needs you, but I am talking about the ones who live beside or near you. What does your church see in you? Do they see and feel God in you? Are you a worker in your local church or are you just a pew warmer? Are you a happy Christian and do they see the joy of the Lord in you? Verses 2-3, Paul told the church these words. We give God thanks for you always, making mention of you in our prayers, remembering your faith and labor of love and patience of hope in our Lord Jesus Christ in the sight of God and our Father. Does this fit you? More than anyone or anything else does God see a good example in you? Does your work of faith, love and patience of hope please Him? We are to please Him and not ourselves. Others are watching you everywhere you go and everything you do so make sure that you present yourselves a good example and testimony to them. Our families are sure to be watching and many criticize and judge so make sure that they can only say and see God in you. How are you acting in stressful times and times of troubles? Can they learn something good from your actions that will help them in the same situations or are they confused with your actions compared with what you confessed with your mouth? The Bible tells us that many are the confessions of the mouth but the heart is far from them. Whatever is in the heart will come out through the mouth. What about temper, impatience, false accusations to spouses or children? Many spouses show a happy relationship with each other in front of others but at home one or the other is false accusing the others and can have no communication with each other without a fuss. God sees it all for you may fool people but you will never fool God. Just saying that you are a Christian is not good enough, you have to be a doer as well. Just going to church will not get you into the Kingdom of Heaven. I heard a preacher the other night, and I quote. There are a lot of people go to church all of their life but will end up in hell because they're not living the way God has told them to live. They are still partly in the world and doing the things of the world. This can't be for you have to serve God and God alone. The book of Revelation Jesus Christ says, because you are lukewarm I will spew you out of My mouth. Jesus said, you make me sick. What He says He will do and you can believe that and stand on it. You have to be all for Me, He is saying or none at all. You are either for Me or against Me. There is no other God or any in between for there's only one way and that's through Jesus Christ. He wants all of you for He said to love Him with all of your heart, mind, soul and strength. Matt.5:13, You are the salt of the earth, salt is good and you have to have it. Salt preserves many foods and keeps them from spoiling and going bad. Mark 9:50, Have salt in yourselves and have peace with one another. When a Christian loses their salt they become good for nothing. Those that don't present themselves a holy and living sacrifice unto God's grace shall be made dying sacrifices to His justice. And since they will not give honor to Him they will not be salted with the salt of the divine grace of God. If you live for Him then He will preserve you and keep you from evil and going the wrong way. Lean on Him, trust Him and follow Him all of the way wherever He leads you. Make sure that you set a good example, for good influence is inspiring to others. To have good food it has to be seasoned with salt so is the same with your life. You have to be salted with the love of Jesus and walking with Him to be a good influence and example. Jesus said that His children are the salt of the earth.

I Thessalonians 1:8, Paul was giving thanks to the church, the Christians for sounding out the Word of the Lord these places and everywhere that they went. Their faith in God was spreaded about and everywhere they went they witnessed about the Lord Jesus Christ. They went about doing good and being good examples of the Lord. Being good influences and examples pleases God. Heb.13:20-21, Now the God of peace that raised Jesus from the dead, the Great Shepherd of the sheep through the blood of the everlasting covenant make you perfect in every good works to do His will, working in you what is pleasing in His sight through Jesus Christ to whom be glory forever, Amen. I Tim.2:1-3, Paul exhorts all to live this life of being good examples for the Lord. He said, I exhort first of all supplications, prayer, intercessions and giving thanks to be made for all people. All that are in authority to lead a peaceful and quiet life in godliness and honesty for this is good in the sight of God. Acts 10:31, God sees our good works for He sees all things. Just good works won't save us for we have to have faith with works. First you have to have faith in Jesus Christ and accept Him into your heart and life and follow Him all the way. I Pet.1:22, Seeing you have purified your souls in obeying the truth through the Spirit unto unfeigned, natural love of the brethren see that you love one another with a pure heart fervently, with a burning love He is saying. This means you have a deep everlasting love for one another and are a good influence to all. This is what pleases God. Only if you have God in your heart and life can you have this kind of love. This is God's nature and we were born in the image of God. We were born to serve Him. We are the salt of the earth and we need to let our light shine for Jesus. James 1:27, Pure religion and undefiled before God is this, to visit the fatherless and widows in afflictions and to keep ourselves unspotted from the world. It is our Christian duties to take care of the widows and children who have no parents to take care of them. What are you doing to help? You can see that just believing in Jesus is not enough. If you are one of His then you will be obedient to Him and do what He has told you to do. I myself feel I have done very little for the cause of Christ. There's so much work to be done and He's looking for His children to get it done. We need to get out of our comfort zone and get busy doing His work of taking care of these people. II Pet.3:14, Be diligent that you may be found of Him peace without spot and blameless. Blessed are the pure in heart for they shall see God. Do you have peace with God? He said we can have peace for He gives the peace that passes all understanding. Tim.1:5, The end of the commandments is love out of a pure heart, good conscience and of faith unfeigned, natural love. This kind of love is not a put on one, but it's real because it comes from deep within your heart and soul. It's God's love living inside of you for God is love. Ps.24:3-4, Only the pure and spotless will enter into the Kingdom of Heaven. Who shall assend unto the hills of the Lord or who shall stand in His presence? They that has clean hands and a pure heart and has not lifted up their soul into vanity or sworn deceitfully. All is vanity except what you do for the Lord. Don't waste your life on things that won't last or is of no value. You can have joy, peace and a good life here in happiness living for the Lord and then others will want this kind of life that you are living. Paul said that he was to be a good example for others to follow. He said if we follow Jesus Christ then we want others to follow in the same foorsteps also. We are to be an example to the believers in word, conversation, charity, spirit, faith and in purity. Be careful of your conversations with others, make sure they are clean and pure. Do not be a part of bad jokes and foolishness, vulgar or foul talk and jesting. Put your faith in action in all thing show yourselves a pattern of good works in doctrines showing uncorruption, gravity or grounded which is sincerity. Be grounded in the Lord always. Live godly, honest and true in all things at all times. Don't waver or wishy washy so to speak. Let your nays be nay and your yayes be ayes. Be able to be trusted in everything by everyone. James 5:10, Be an example in sufferings and afflictions with patience. How do you act when you are going through problems, sickness and afflictions? Do you grumble and complain or do you praise the Lord and show joy? You don't praise the Lord for your problems but you praise Him because you know He's going to bring you through them. Blessings come out of the praises to the Lord. It's easy to praise and show joy when everything is going good but we have to do the same when things are not going so well and trials are coming our way. Many times others are watching our actions on how we handle our troubles and problems. Do we act like the world or do we act as Jesus would act? He has been the pattern for His children to follow. He went through temptations and troubles, suffering like no other has ever done and ever will be but He never failed or complained. Even at the cross He prayed to the Father that if it was His will to let that cup pass from Him but He didn't complain. You may be saying, yes but He was God. He was God but He was man also and He felt the pain as you and I do today for He was as human as we are. He walked as man upon this earth but He was still God. He died and rose again and was ascended into Heaven where He is sitting on the right hand of the Father interceding for you and me waiting for the Father to say to Him, go get My children. He's coming back for His bride, the true church. If you are one of His and you are following Him then you are among His bride. Are you one of His? If not then you should accept Him today and make the decision to follow Him. Don't wait until it's too late for today is the day of salvation. He's waiting for you so come to Jesus Christ so you can be ready.

What matters most in your life?

Acts 20:24-27, But none of these move me, neither count my life dear unto myself so that I may finish my course with joy and the ministry which I have received of the Lord Jesus to testify the gospel of the grace of God. Paul was saying, my life is worth nothing unless I am doing the work of the Lord that was assigned to me by Jesus Christ and the work of telling the good news about God's wonderful kindness and love. He said, I am pure from the blood of all people, record this day that I am pure from the blood of all men. He was saying, no one can damn me or place the blame on me if they reject the message of Jesus Christ. I didn't shrink or stray away from all God wanted me to do. I have told you all about what God wanted me to tell you and how to live a holy life. For whosoever loses their life shall find it and whosoever will save their life shall lose it. If you give your life to Jesus and die daily to self then you will be saved in the end. But if you live the way that you want to and not follow Him then you will lose your life in the end is what he is saying. This life is just a short one but the next life is eternal. This life is full of troubles and trials but the next life will be all happiness and full of joy forever. Rom.6; 13, Don't yield yourselves to instruments of unrighteousness unto sin, but yeild yourselves unto God as those that are alive from the dead, and your members and your members as instruments if righteousness unto God. Those who follow Christ are alive because they have died to self and to sin. James 4:7, Submit yourselves therefore to God, resist the devil and he will have to flee. We live in this world but we are not of the world for we are different and we are separated from the world. The things of God mean much more to me than anything else in this world. There is pleasure in sin for a season but it's not fulfilling. The only thing that is fulfilling is what we do for the cause of Christ and what He does for us. Phil.3:7, Paul said, what things were gain to me those I count loss for Christ. Yes, I count all things but loss for the Excellency of the knowledge of Christ Jesus my Lord for whom I have suffered the loss of all things and I count them as dung that I may win Christ. He is saying, none of the things that I thought I enjoyed are any joy or good to me now. I traded them all for the sake of Jesus Christ. We are to be like Paul, for he didn't want anything that the world had to offer him for he had made up his mind to serve Jesus and Him only. The things of God were the only things that brought him joy and fulfillment. Gal.2:29, I am crucified with Christ, never the less I live, yet not I but Christ lives in me and the life I now live in the flesh, I live by faith of the Son of God who loved me and gave Himself for me. We live by faith in Jesus Christ and not by our own desires or the way someone else wants us to live. This is what should matter the most in all Christians lives for it's only what we do for Christ that will last and count. I Thessalonians 5:23, And the very God of peace sanctify you wholly and I pray your whole spirit, soul and body for to be preserved blameless unto the coming of our Lord Jesus Christ. He will sanctify you in the Holy Ghost and keep you. If you will give your all to Him then He will take care of you. Prov.23:26, My children, give Me your heart and let your eyes see My ways. His ways are higher than our ways and His thoughts are deeper than our thoughts, so we are to keep our eyes on Him and let Him lead us all the way. If your heart is right with Him then the rest of your body will be right also. If we be dead with Him then we will reign with Him. They that are Christ's have crucified their flesh with the affections of lust. Gal.5:25, If you are living now by the Holy Spirit then follow His leading in every part of your life. Don't let your flesh get in your way for the flesh wars against the Spirit. Acts 23:1, Paul said to the counsel, men and brethren, I have lived in all good conscience before the Lord until this day. He had no regrets for he knew he had lived a good life in Christ and done everything he could to please God. We are to strive to live the same way for Paul was a good example to us. We are to set a good example for others, our family and especially our children. Whatever God has called you to do, do it with all of your might.

What satisfies your hunger and thirst?

Ps.26:8, David said, Lord I love the inhabition of Your house and the place where Your glory dwells. He was saying, I love the things in your house, the people and especially You God. God's people are in His house, prayer, singing, praising and worshipping of God is there. Do you love it there? Ps.42:1, As the deer pants and longs for the water brooks so I long for You Lord. On a hot day when you are thirsty and dry, just knowing where the water is won't quench yout thirst. You have to look for it and find it and then drink it before it helps you. It's the same way about knowing about the Lord Jesus Christ, for you have to know Him to reap the benefits that He has promised His children. There are many that say, I wanted to go tp the house of the Lord, BUT, they find so many excuses not to go. They are not thirsty and hungry enough to make their move as the deer is to find water. We are to desire to go to the house of the Lord as the deer pants for water. What are you hungry and thirsty for? Many watch TV, watch movies, play games, listen to music, have social gatherings or go on vacations. Some go on a buying spree, they buy cars, houses, clothes, shoes, furniture and do other things to try to satisfy themselves and to make them happy and content. Some even strive for success and recongnition at work or even in church to be content. Some even try new relationships. These are not all bad things but they are not fulfilling and what you really need to satisfy your soul. Jesus is the only one that can satisfy your soul and life completely. Things will satisfy you for a short while but they will not satisfy the empty places in your heart and life. We were designed by God to be filled with only Him and by Him. The great hunger and thirst in our heart and soul can only be filled with the presence of God. When the music is turned off, the party is ended for most people. The movie ends and the TV gets boring, the clothes wear out, or you get tired of wearing them. The vacation time is up, the desire of success fades away and you're right back where you started. None of these things would fill the hunger and thirst in you life like you thought they would for they all were for a season. There's nothing left but hunger and thirst and that empty feeling again. Eventually, everything's coming down to just you alone. There's nothing that you can hold on to except the presence of Lord Jesus Christ. The truth is, God is Immanuel, God with us. Draw near to Him and He will draw near to you. God wants you to know who He is and not just to know about Him. He wants you to long for Him. He wants you to seek Him so He can satisfy your desires, your hunger and thirst. Ps.63:1-5, David said, God, you are my God and earnestly I will seek You. My inner self thirsts for You, my flesh longs and faints for You in a dry and thirsty land where no water is. I looked for You in the sanctuary to see Your power and Your glory. Your loving kindness is better than life. I will bless You where I live, and I will lift up my hands to You in Your name. My whole being shall be satisfied as with marrow and fatness amd my mouth shall praise You with joyful lips. You will see that Psalms is full of praises of David to God. He said his whole being followed hard after God and he was clinging close to Him. That's what God wants of all of His children and when we know Him as David did He will fill all of our needs according to His riches in glory. David found God because he searched for Him. You too can find Him if you seek for Him. You can't have Him if you're still holding on to the things of the world. If you've got one hand on Him and the other one holding on to the things of the world then you will miss out on the things that God has for you. You have to be on one side or the other. We live in this world but we are not of the world. John 7:37-38, If anyone is thirsty let them come unto Me and drink. You can come just as you are. They who believe in Me shall flow out of their hearts rivers of water and will never thirst again. God will go with you and give you rest, meet all of your needs and fill you to the fullest. He will put into the right relationship, the right job and cause you to be content wherever you are. He will satisfy your soul so let Him be your guide and be your life. Ex.33:15, Moses didn't want to go anyplace without God's presence going before and with him. He also hungered for God, not just for what he could get from God but because he loved Him and hungered and thirsted for Him. The more you desire Him the more His presence will be with you. The more you worship and praise Him the closer you will be to Him and the closer He will be with you. In the world the more you will achieve the more you want because you are never satisfied. That's why the Bible says that, hardly will a rich person enter the kingdom of Heaven for they are greedy and greed takes over the most of them. With greed a person is never satisfied for they long for more and will get it anyway they can even is it's dishonest. I'm not saying everyone that is rich got it dishonest but many do. It's not money that is evil, but the love of money that is the root of all evil. That's not my words but it's the Word of God. Many worship their money and what it can buy. Ps. 33:20, Our souls wait for the Lord, our deepest desires can only be satisfied by Jesus Christ alone. He's our creator, our Father and the love of our life. This should be our earnest desire to seek Him always, seek always for the Lord and wait upon Him for He loves you. We are to be like David in Ps.38:9, Lord all my desires are before you. This means everything in his life was dependant upon the Lord and that's what he yearned for.

The power of praise and worship to the Lord

The more you praise God for His goodness the more you will see Him manifested in your life. That's the hidden power of praise. Praise Him even when things are not going good for you. Never doubt that God is good no matter what is going on in your life and around you. In bad times we have to keep reminding ourselves that God is good and He cares for us and He's working out all things for our good. God is good all of the time for He's God on the mountain and He's God in the valley. He is the God of mercy, love, grace and in all things. Ps.100:4-5, His mercy is everlasting and His truth endures to all generations. How great His goodness is to all who trust Him and fear Him. His goodness shall follow us all the days of our lives and we shall dwell in the house of the Lord forever. There is no where else in the world and there's no one else in the world that you can find such love, mercy and grace but of the Lord. God wants us to praise and worship with our whole heart, mind, soul and strength. He's not asking anything hard for you and me to do. This comes naturally when you have Him in your heart and life. Ps.1:1-3, Blessed, happy are the ones who walk and live not in the counsel of the ungodly and walk after them and do the same things that they do and tell them to do. For they delight in the desires of the Lord to do the things that He wants them to do. Their desires are on the laws and preceipts of God. God promises prosperity to those who are in Him and meditate on Him always. When you give God first place in your heart and life you can expect to prosper in all of your ways. It is God's will that you prosper and be in good health just as your soul prospers. God will fill your hunger and thirst when you hunger and thirst after righteousness. Ps.16:8, David said, I have set the Lord continually before me, He is at my right hand and I shall not be moved. This is the life style we should have just as David did. David had his eyes and heart fixed on the Lord and what He wanted him to do. This is what I desire of the Lord. I want to be as close as I can to Him and do the things He wants me to do. Forgetting the pass and reaching for the higher goal and victory in Jesus Christ. We can make it through Him but we have to stay in Him and keep our eyes and hearts on Him always.

Isa.40:29-31, Those who wait upon the Lord shall renew their strength for they shall run and not be weary. The way that we should wait upon the Lord is to spend time with Him in praise and worship. To receive the power of God we have to praise and worship Him. This requires obedience to Him, prayer, reading and studing His Word and keeping a good relationship with Him. Keep the lines open all of the time so His power can flow through you. You can't live the life after the flesh and live the way you want without Him and expect for Him to release His power in you. You have to surrender all to Him. Worship is surrendering your whole life totally to Him so that He can be powerful in you and demonstrate His power through you. Our faith and actions have to rest in Him and His power. Power of praise and worship lead us to holiness and without holiness we won't see God. We have to live holy for God is holy. Col.1:22, Help me to be holy for You are holy. Establish my heart, holy and blameless before You. Give me clean hands and a pure heart. O God help us for we need You so. We should always pray, Lord don't let us lift up our souls into vanity or be deceitful. Let me always be honest, truthful, loving, kind, gentle, patient, merciful and longsuffering as You are. God will feed us the Spiritual food if we ask for it and seek for it. Seek the Kingdom of God and His righteousness first and then all of these other things will be added unto you. God wants His children to have the very best. The truth is that you have to have your heart and soul right with Him first of all and then you walk with Him doing His will and not yours to have all of the things that He promised His children. All of the promises in the Word of God are for His children. He will fulfill His promises but we have to be obedient to Him to be able to obtain them. This is His Word, let Him fill you right now.

You are what you eat

John 6:53-54, Jesus said unto them, verily,verily I say unto you, except you eat of the flesh of the Son of man and drink of His blood you have no life in you. Whosoever eats of My flesh and drinks My blood has eternal life and I will raise them up at the last day. Jesus is talking about eating and digesting His Word. He's not talking about actual drinking His blood but accepting the Son of God and believing that He died and rose again for you. It's His blood that washed away all of your sins and cleanses you from all unrighteousness to be able to serve Him and enter into the Kingdom of Heaven. I Pet.2:2-3, Just like new born babies desire milk to grow then we should desire the milk of the Word of God for food for the spirit, body and soul. You cannot live by bread alone but by every Word that proceeds out of the mouth of God. David said, how sweet are the Words of the Lord to my taste, yes they are sweeter than the honeycomb in my mouth. Jer.15:16, Thy Words were found and I did eat them and Thy Word was unto me joy and rejoicing to my heart for I am called by Your name O Lord God of hosts. His Words are spiritual foods to us, His children. Isa.52:2, Hearken unto Me and eat what is good and let your soul delight itself in fatness. John 6:51, I am the living bread which came down from Heaven. If anyone eats this bread they shall live forever and the bread that I will give is My flesh which I will give for the life of the world. The Word of God is food for our souls. We need to seek the Spiritual food as well as the natural foods. We can survive with natural foods but you can never survive without Spiritual food from God. Natural foods don't feed our souls. And we have to have Spiritual food to be saved and live forever in the Kingdom of God. Luke 6:21, Blessed are they that are hunger for thay shall be filled. If you are hungry for the Spiritual food then God will feed to over flowing. He will give you all you want and desire, for the Spiritual food never runs out, for God has an abundant supply, you will be filled and satisfied with the fatness of your house. The Lord satisfies the mouth with good things. It satisfies the longing of your soul and fills the hungry soul with goodness. The Lord gives food to all flesh and His mercy endures forever. The Lord will satisfy your soul in drought and make fat your bones. Heb.5:13-14, Everyone who is on milk is unskillful in the Word of righteousness for they are babies. Strong meat belongs to them that are of full age in the Lord for they can discern both good and bad. We are to grow in the Lord to get to the meat of the Word. We need to stay full of the Word of God. If you eat Spiritual food then you will be Spiritual and you will grow stronger and stronger in the Lord. You can tell who are on the Spiritual food by the way they carry themselves and how they believe and act. So you see, you are what you eat Spiritual.

Our bodies are what we eat natural as well

We know that certain foods go against out health. Some foods cause a lot of different health problems. Over weight is a big problem and a killer to many all because of over eating or eating the wrong foods. In the health news we have seen many times of how different foods or drinks cause lots of problems even death to some, things such as caffeine, red meats, alcohol, some seafoods, sugar, sodium, too many starches and organ meats. They are saying and have proven that different foods causes high blood pressure, strokes, hign blood sugar, high cholesterol and diabetes. Over eating causes obesity and this in itself causes lots of health problems. Certain foods can change your brain chemistry. Certain foods can disrupt your sleep cycle. It can also cause behavior changes. So you can see that we are what we eat whether Spiritual or natural eating. God tells us to be wise in all things so we need to think and be healthy Spiritual and natural. Our bodies are the temple of the Lord so we should always take care of them. We all can eat healthy if we desire. When we put God first and let Him lead you then you can do all things through Jesus Christ who gives you strength. Nothing is impossible with Him. No where does it say that it was going to be easy but it is possible with Christ. Eat the Spiritual food first and then God will help you with the natural food.

Whose economy are you depending on?

Matt.6:33, Seek ye first the Kingdom of God and His righteousness and all of the other things will be added unto you. When you put God first in your heart and life then you have the right to expect Him to give you all you need, fill your desires and to do the work in your life that He called you to do. But understand this, you have to put Him first place over everyone and everything. He will do what He said He would do but you have something to do also. You have to be obedient and faithful to Him and follow where He leads you. Lots of people are worried about the economy, even Christians, about what's going to happen. We as Christians have to live and look to God's economy. He's the one who will take care of you and me. He said that He would take care of His children and He will. You have to trust His Word and look to Him in these hard times that we're facing. David said, I have never seen the righteous forsaken or His seed begging for bread. Phil.4:19, My God shall supply all your needs according to His riches in glory by Jesus Christ. He didn't say that He was going to give us everything that we wanted but He said He would take care of our needs. So why do you weary and fret? Don't look at the world's economy but look to God and accept what He has told you in His Word. He will do what He says. III John 2, Beloved, I wish above all things that you be in good health and prosper just as your soul prospers. He wants us to prosper spiritually, physically and financially. The whole gospel is for the whole person. From the beginning of the first Word in Genesis 1:22 all the way to the ending of the Bible in Revelation it is clear that the Lord of glory desires to bless and prosper His children. He wants us to be happy, contented and free to serve Him. Jesus Christ is the source of all blessings when a person gets saved then they get into God's economy system. Don't forget this, you have to seek Him first and all His righteousness and the rest of your body can prosper just as your soul prospers. How is your soul? Are you growing in the Lord? Are you closer to Him now than you were in the beginning when you got saved? If you're not prospering then you need to check youself to see why. It's surely not God's fault. He has laid the plans and the ground work and all we have to do is follow in Jesus Christ footsteps. Jer.29:11, For I know the plans I have for you says the Lord, plans to prosper not to harm you, plans to give you hope and a future. Prosper means to grow and have a good life even though the road may get a little rough at times, we can still prosper in the Lord. We don't have to waste our life because of trials that we have to go through. Our Christian life is a journey of faith and the end will be prosperous is we endure to the end with Him. The Word tells us that we will go through testing times, trials and troubles here if we follow Christ. But this way can and will be prosperous for we will have the blessings of God. The Holy Spirit will lead and guide us all of the way. I do believe that God want the very best for His children for He said so, for He never says anything that He doesn't mean and stick by it. Stand on His Word and claim your prosperity today, whatever the need He will fulfill it if you're one of His children. Don't let the devil steal from you what God has for you.

Health prospering

I Pet.2:24, Jesus bore our sins in His body on the tree that we being dead to sin should live unto righteousness by whose stripes we were healed. Jesus is our healer and He wants us to live a healthy life. We bring a lot of sickness on ourselves by the way we live, eat, work, worry and many other things. Sin brings sickness in our bodies. Sin was brought on by Adam and Eve in the beginning and it's been handed down since then. We were healed by the stripes of Jesus for we know that one day all will be healed completely and there will be no more sickness or sin. But until then we will suffer in our bodies the sin of the world. Paul said that if we follow Christ we would have trials and tribulations all the days of our life here on this earth. Yes, Jesus died for our sins but there are still sins in the world and there are sicknesses also. We are not exempted from troubles, trials or even sicknesses. But if we do get sick we can call on Jesus and He will heal according to His will. James 5:14-15, If anyone is sick among you let them call upon the elders of the church, let them pray the prayer of faith, anoint them with oil and the prayer of faith shall save the sick. God made a way through His Son Jesus Christ in case we were to get sick then He could heal you. By faith we can be healed in Jesus name. Sickness is cause by the fall of Adam and Eve. Jesus never turned anyone away that needed healing in His ministry on this earth. There are times that some are not healed on earth for whatever reason but if they are Christians then they are healed if they should die because there will be no sickness in the Kingdom of God. While we are praying for some people to be healed they are praying that God would take them. So you have to believe that there are some who want to go home to be with Jesus. I believe that Jesus in all of His mercy hears and gives them their desire. Whatever the case we still know that God does heal. I remember my sister telling me after she had fought the fight with cancer for over six years, don't pray for me to live anymore for I am tired and I want to go home. She asked me to pray that God would take her home and I had to honor that prayer for her. She knew that she was ready to go. We believed together for all of those years that God was going to heal her and God did have it put into remission for a long time of terminal cancer and she was grateful. We don't know how many others desire the same thing and are praying that same way. We need to let God be God and just follow His leading for He knows best for His children. Sometimes God heals immediately, sometimes He waits awhile and sometimes it is through death that He heals. We don't understand when someone has such faith to be healed and even claims their healing and then healing never comes until death. God has a plan for all of His children and we need to let Him have His way and trust Him, for as I have said many times before, God knows best and He never makes a mistake.

Soul propering

Phil.3:12-14, Paul talks about his never ending desire for getting closer to God. He wanted to know Him more. He wanted to be confounded in the image of Jesus Christ. No matter how much we have grown in the Lord there's still room for more growth. I press toward the high calling of God in Jesus Christ. I want to know Him and the power of His resurrection. For your soul to prosper is the most important, for your body and your whole being depends on it. This is your foundation for all other prosperity. We must grow spiritually to be able to overcome all of the things we have to go through in this life. God is our strength, He's our fortress, our keeper, our salvation, our healer and our comforter. We have to live above all sin and lust of this world. We can live free from sin in Jesus Christ. He is the One who sees us through this life and takes us to the Kingdom of God eternally. We need to press on to the high calling of God just as Paul did. We need to know Him and His resurrection not just to know about Him. Many know about Him but they don't really know Him for they have no relationship with Him. We should have that never ending desire to love Him and live close to Him always doing the things that pleases Him. Some Christians get discouraged and give up or take a step in the backward direction when they have troubles or sicknesses. They know they need to get closer to Him but don't seem to really know how. Some feel thay have plenty of time to get where they need to be with Him. Then they wonder why they don't get the victories over their problems or get their desires met. To get the victory we have to stay in Jesus and stay true to God even when we don't understand God's timing or His ways. His ways are higher than our ways. Don't ever doubt or stop believing what you have asked for. Sometimes He says yes, sometimes no and sometimes He says wait awhile. Don't let anyone or anything hinder your faith in Him. Sometimes He may even want you to wait to learn patience. Put it all in His hands and leave it there. Stay in God's Word, pray and seek His will for your life and you will draw closer to Him. The more you yield to Him the closer you will be drawn to Him. Stand in His strength and His righteousness. Many times it takes fasting with praying to get to another level with God and to get some prayers answered. Many things come out only by fasting and praying. The closer one gets to Him the more knowledge He will give them. Make sure that you are on the meat of the Word and not just milk. When you fast you are denying yourself of all natural foods in exchange for the Spiritual food of God. It's the Spiritual food that gets you closer to God. Jer.32:8, There is a spirit in man and the inspiration of the Almighty gives them understanding. Prov.20:27, The spirit of man is the candle of the Lord searching all the inwards parts of the belly. Rom.8:8-16, We cannot please God in the flesh, for as many that are led by the Spirit of God are the children of God. You have to be led by His Spirit and not by your spirit. His Spirit bears witness with our spirit that we are the children of God. Let the Spirit of God lead you for He will not lead you where He will not keep you. He will make a way where there seem to be no way. Just trust and lean on Him for He will see you through whatever problem you're going through. Prosper in all of His ways for this is His will for you.

Stay away from the lusts of the world

I John 2:15-17, Do not love or cherish the world or the things of the world. If anyone loves the world the love of the Father is not in them. For all that is in the world, the lusts of the flesh and the lusts of the eyes, these do not come from the Father but they are from the world. The world passes away but they that do the will of the Father shall live forever. You can conquer these lusts with the Word of God. We are in the world but we are not of the world. The world and the things of the world are of the devil. He is the ruler of the world as we know it today. The world's system is based on selfishness, greed, dishonesty, immoral sexual acts, hatred, murder, stealing and lies. The world's system stands against God's system that's written in the Word of God, the Bible. Everything seems to be based on fear and hate. Our natural birth was borned in the world's system but not our second birth for it was born of God. When we accepted Jesus Christ in our heart and life as our Savior and Lord we were changed into God's system. Praise the name of Jesus. You can see the world's system coming through the soap operas, talk shows and even the news. Of course, I never see the world's system coming through the soaps because I never watch them. Years ago I did and didn't want to miss a one but God changed all of that. There was nothing but a world of sin. When God convicted me of them and let me know they were not for me to look at I stopped. I praise Him for convicting of my wrongs and there have been more, for I am not the same persom I once was thanks to Him.

David says in Psalm to be careful of what you allow your eyes to look upon, your ears to hear and where your feet take you. The things of the world are the lust of the flesh, ears, eyes and mouth. We can either operate our finances and lives by the world's system or God's system it is your choice. In the end there is no profit in the world's system for all is vanity. Only what is done for God and His Kingdom will last and stand. You are going to be with God or with out Him for there is no in between. All lust will pass away along with all other sin. Lusts come from your intent appitite to have something or to do something that flesh wants. It lures you out of God's will. Gal.5:16-17, Walk and live in the Holy Spirit then you won't fulfill the lusts of the flesh. For the desire of the flesh opposes to the Holy Spirit and the Holy Spirit opposes to the things of the flesh. They war against each other so that you cannot be free. So how can you get the world's system out and the lusts of the flesh out and God's system in? You have to walk in the Spirit of God. It's not what you don't do, but what you do to get away from the lustful things of the world. Jesus said that if you were of the world then you were not one of His. He said that you would either hate the world or love Him. You can't have both for you will love one or the other. Draw near to God and He will draw near to you. Once you start serving God with all of your heart it won't be hard to drop the things of the world for you will find that you're enjoying God and His love so much that you don't need or want anything else. You will find yourself lusting after the things of God. You will have such a desire to follow Him that you will do whatever it takes to please Him and to do His will. Die to self daily and follow Him all of the way. David said, my heart is fixed, I will serve the Lord. Is your heart fixed on Him and your desires on the things of the Lord? He said He would feed you, clothe you and meet all of your needs, what more can you ask? He carries you through every load and problem and gives you the strength to do what you have to do. He gives you wisdom, knowledge, understanding and the peace that passes all other understanding. The world doesn't offer you that now or never will. The world will take away what God gives you if you let it. You cannot live in the flesh and live spirituall at the same time. The only way you can please God is to live by faith in Him. The just shall live by faith. If you try to please man then you do not please God. You have to choose today whom you will serve. We have taken our stand in our household for we have chosen with Joshua, for me and my house we will serve the Lord. We have found that the world has nothing to offer us but God has it all. His way is everlasting and life here is fulfilling with Him. In serving the Lord you have prosperity here and then life everlasting to come. If you follow the world now all you have to look forward to is eternal hell in the end. The sorrows that you have now will never end for they will only be worse in hell. Why won't you change the system that you're serving and living under now? There's nothing stopping you but you yourself. In the world's system you have worries about the economy and what's going to happen to you. In God's system it's all in God's hands for He said that He would take care of His children. Be an overcomer of this world and accept God's way. He is waiting for you to say yes. He will never leave or forsake you for He said that He would go with you all of the way. Free yourself of the burdens that you carry for He said to bring your burdens and heavy lading and give then to Him and He would carry your load. Don't wait any longer, come now just as you are. Do away with all of the lusts of the flesh and of this world and live for Him.

Are you satisfied with the fruit of your mouth?

Prov.12:14, From the fruit of you mouth you are filled with good things as surely as the works of your hands reward you. You will see from these scriptures that what you say is what you get. If you speak negatively you will reap negative things. If you speak positive you will reap positive things. Don't go around confessing you're sick all of the time and those things will never get any better. Speak good things and look for the best. You hold the keys of life and death in your mouth. When one speaks without thinking it can bring much trouble and harm. Those who guard their tongue and their mouth keep themselves from calamity. Prov.21:23, From the fruit of your lips a person enjoy good things but the unfaithful have a craving for violence. Those who guards their mouth guards their life but those who speak rashly will come to ruin. The tongue is a small part of the body. James 3:1-12, tells us about taming the tongue. It is like a great forest fire set aflame with just a small spark. The tongue is a fire and it corrups the whole body, the whole person. All animals, birds and creatures can be tamed by humans but no one can tame the tongue. The tongue is reckless, evil and full of deadly poison. With the tongue people praise the Lord and Father and with the same tongue they curse human beings who have been made in God's own image. Some even curse God. Out of the same mouth come blessings and cursing. This should never be so. Can fresh water and salt water come from the same cistern? Can a fir tree bear olives, grapes or bear figs? God says, neither can salt water bring forth fresh water. What's inside of a person will come out as I have said before. If we will just listen to ourselves we will find out just what's on our inside of us. We need to try to tame our tongues. God has said that no one can tame them but we can surely do better. The key to controlling the tongue is to oversee the source from which our words flow. Think about what you're going to say before you speak.

Matt.15:18-19, The things that come out of the mouth comes from the heart and these makes a person unclean. For out of the heart come evil thoughts, murder, adultery, sexual immorility, theft, false testimonies and slander. The mind thinks it, the mouth speak it and then it's committed. Sin starts in the mind and the mind speaks to the heart and then you allow flesh to actual fall into temptation. Temptation is not sin but to yield to temptation is then sin. There are a lot of people that miss out on blessings because of what they speak. Many pray to God and ask for something and they don't receive it because they have spoken negative or they have spoken words of doubt. They don't get what they ask for they asked amiss or they didn't believe what they prayed for. Always speak positive words even though you don't see what you have prayed for yet. Be careful of what comes out of your mouth. Prov.24:9, The thoughts of foolishness is sin and the schemes is an abomination unto the Lord. Don't answer a foolish person according to their folly for they will despise the wisdom of your words. Don't slander a servant to their master. Don't let the words come out of your mouth to condemn anyone. Don't cut people down but lift them up. If anyone talks negative to you about someone else you need to say something that will lift them up instead of agreeing with them about whatever they have been speaking. Ecc.10:12, Words from a wise person's mouth are gracious but the lips of a fool will swallow up himself. Don't ever betray another person's confidence by the words that you speak. Don't let bad words come out of your mouth for it becomes a habit. You are going to answer for all of the idle words that you speak says the Word of God. Prov.16:24, Pleasant words are like a honeycomb, sweet to the soul and health to the bones. Prov.25:11, A word spoken is like apples of gold in pictures of silver. 17:27, They that have knowledge spare their mouth. Matt.5:37, Let your communications be yes and no. We have enough scriptures to show us that our tongues are like a fire and we need to try with everything that's within us to do the best we can to tame them. We have the mind of Christ so we need to think like Him. We are to be quick to listen and slow to speak. Many times if we would just think first before we speak it would be the right thing to speak. Never form your opinion and speak it when you don't know all of the circumstances. Many do this and pass it on to others and it hurts others and God as well.

Power of Christian witnessing

Ps.30:1, David said, I will watch my ways and keep my tongue from sin. I will muzzle my mouth as long as the wicked are in my presence. He was saying, I will be careful in what I say and what I do so I won't mislead anyone or be a bad influence to the lost. He was afraid of what he would say or do when the believer was near to him or in his presence and then he would dishonor God so he kept silent. I can remember my dad saying, if you can't say anything good then don't say anything at all. We need always be careful what we say, what we do and where we go. People are watching you especially to those who call and confess themselves to be a Christian. We have to be different from the world and sinners. Matt.5:14-16, You are the light of the world a city built that is set on a hill that cannot be hid. Neither do men light a candle and put it under a bushel but on a candle stick so it will give out light unto all who are in the house. Let your light so shine before others so they can see your good works and glorify your Father which is in Heaven. Unbelievers will recognize God in you and give Him praise. This is the power of Christians witnessing.

Wherever we go everyone should be able to see Jesus in us. That's why we have to make a difference in our lives. When you are living a Christian life you don't even have to tell others because they will see it in you.

This is the power of witnessing of the tongue

Prov.12:18, Reckless words pierce like a sword. Solomon warns how crucial it is that we guard our tongues when we're in the company of those who don't know God. We should guard our tongues wherever we are. They that keep their tongue keep their life. Our tongue is a powerful organ. It can hurt or it can help. It can bless or it can curse. It can lift up or it can tear down. Nothing should ever come out of our mouth except what will bless the Lord. Isa.50:4, The Lord has given me the tongue of the learned that I should know how to speak a word in season to them that are weary. God gave us a tongue to speak good things that would help others. Speak with wisdom, truth and grace. Job 6:24, Job said, teach me and I will hold my tongue. Verse 25 says this, how forcible or potent, powerful, mighty and strong are right words. Keeping the tongue is most important. Ps.15:3, David asked the Lord, who can enter the Kingdom of Heaven and this is what He told him, they that back bites not with their tongue and among other things as well. He was saying not to speak evil of anyone in secret. Do not gossip about anyone or say something that would hurt or cause someone to fall. Don't be busy bodies. Ps.119:172, My tongue shall speak of Thy Word for all Thy commandments are righteousness and testimonies. Ps.145:11, Christians should speak of the glory of Your Kingdom and talk about Your power, God's power. Prov.18:21, Death and life are in the power of the tongue and they that love it shall eat of the fruit thereof. This is where we get the phrase, what you say is what you get. If you speak negative things then you will eat of the negative things and if you speak of the positive things then you will eat of the positives things.

Every tongue has to confess that Jesus Christ is Lord to be saved

Isa.45:23, Every knee shall bow and every tongue shall confess that Jesus Christ is Lord. Rom.14:11, For it is written, as surely as I live says the Lord, every knee shall bow and every tongue shall confess to God. Phil.2:11, And every tongue shall confess that Jesus Christ is Lord to the glory of God the Father. When you receive Christ into your heart and life then you are a witness for Him. God has a work for you and all of His children to do. Be a witness everywhere you go and in everything you say. He will help your weakness to be able to be strong and faithful to Him. Be a living sacrifice for Jesus Christ. Let the world see Jesus in you. Kind words can lead a sinner to Jesus Christ but condemning words can run them away. If you condemn others then you are condemning yourself as well. Don't forget, you will answer for every idle word spoken at the judgment seat of Christ.

CHAPTER EIGHT

No Change No Gift

CHAPTER 8

No Change, No Gift

Rom.6:23, For the wages of sin is death but the gift of God is eternal life. The gift is ours to accept. You can accept it or reject it for it's your choice. If you accept it you have to make a change in your life. If you reject it then there is no gift within you. The gift of salvation is free to all who will accept it. For God so loved the world that He gave His only begotten that whosoever believes in Him shall be saved. Thanks to God for His unspeakable gift. Epe.2:8, For by grace are you saved through faith and not of yourself it is the gift of God. When you accept this gift you have to make a complete change in your heart, mind, soul and life for you are a new person now in the Lord Jesus Christ. You have to keep your temple, which is your body clean for He won't live in a dirty mess up temple with sin in it. You are to keep your temple holy for He is holy. Rom.8:1, Therefore there is no condemnation to them that are in Christ Jesus who walk not after the flesh but after the Spirit. You don't do what your flesh wants to do anymore for you follow Jesus now. Your sins are all washed away by the blood of Jesus and you are not condemned for your past sins and wrong doings. They are covered by the blood never to be remembered anymore by God. He said that when He forgives He cast your sins as far as the east is from the west in the deepest sea never to remember them anymore. Now, you don't go and pick those sins back up and live in them anymore, for if you do then you are backslidden and you can lose your salvation. Never sin willfully for to know to do good and doeth it not it is sin. If and when you make a mistake you have an Advocate, Jesus Christ, who you can go to and ask forgiven and God will forgive. But if you continue in sin and do them over and over again knowing you are wrong then you are no longer walking in the Lord. John 5:24, Verily, verily I say unto you that whosoever hears My Words and believes on Him that sent Me has everlasting life and shall not come into condemnation but is passed from death unto life. You have to believe in the Lord Jesus Christ to be saved for there's no other way but through Him. Isa.55:7, Let the wicked forsake their ways and the unrighteous their thoughts and let them return unto the Lord and He will have mercy on them and our God will abundantly pardon them. This tells us that if you do sin then you can come to the Father and ask forgiveness and He will forgive. I John 1:9, If we confess our sins then He is faithful and just to forgive us and cleanse us from all unrighteousness. Not only will He forgive but He will baptise you with the gift of the Holy Ghost. No one is perfect for we are still in this flesh after we have been born again but we are to be lead by the Holy Spirit and not lead by the flesh. The flesh will lead you to sin but the Holy Spirit will lead and guide you into all truth.

Acts 2:38, Repent and be baptized every one of you in the name of Jesus Christ for the remission of sins and you shall receive the gift of the Holy Spirit. You have to sanctify yourself with the washing of His Word. You have to get clean and stay clean. You are sanctified by the washing of the blood of Jesus. There is no other way to get clean and stay clean but in Him. Keep a good relationship with Him, communicate with Him always for He desires your fellowship and love to Him. You are now justified by faith so live the life that He has called you into. We have access to grace through faith in Him. All who believe in Jesus Christ are saved and justified in Him when you live your life for Him and follw Him all the way. No, you won't be perfect for there is no one perfect but Jesus but you are to strive to be perfect just as He is perfect. The Bible says that all have sinned and come short of the glory of God. But praise the Lord, there is forgiveness for everyone that asks in Jesus name and continues in Him. I Cor.6:11, We were all sinners but now we are washed and justified in the wonderful name of Jesus and by the Spirit of God. To be justified means, it's like you have never sinned because when you come to Jesus, accept Him in our heart and life then repent of our sins, He forgives and forgets our past. He never brings them up to us again for He says He forgets them. People won't because they will continue to remind you but we are to forgive and forget as well. Your past is past so leave it there and press on with Jesus in your new life with Him. The Bible tells us that whosoever looks back at the plow is not worthy of the Kingdom of God. You can't change one thing in your past and it can only bring hurt and pain. Many times it has brought oppression in lives but God doesn't want this to happen that's why you should never look back. Yes, it is good to know where God has brought us from so we can be thankful to Him for giving us another chance for keeping us and forgiving us. Oh what a Savior we have and what love, mercy and grace He shows to His children. Gal.3:24, The law, the Ten Commandments were given to us for a school master to teach us right from wrong and to bring us to the Lord. The law won't save anyone but we are to keep the commandments of God. It is only through faith in Jesus Christ that anyone can be saved. It is the gift of God by grace through faith. You can't buy it or work for it for it is a gift of God. After you receive the gift then you are to live by God's Word to keep this gift for it is possible to lose your salvation if you follow any other way but God's way. You must endure to the end to be saved. The Bible teaches this, they that endure to the end the same shall be saved. Don't let anyone deceive you to make you think you can live any old way and still be saved just because you once accepted Jesus as your Savior. Jesus said that He would blot your name out of the Lamb's book of life if you didn't stay true in Him to the end. You can find that in Revelation and other books of the Bible too.

Spiritual loss, loss of you soul

Mark 6:36, For what does it profit you if you gain the whole world and lose your soul? Luke 6:49, Whosoever hears the Word and does not obey is like one without a foundation that builds a house upon the earth or on the sands and when it rained it beat against it, which the stream did beat vehemently and immediately the house fell and the ruins of the house was great. Nothing will stand on this earth unless it's built upon Jesus Christ. Only if you build a house upon Him will it stand. It's only what we do for Him that will last and stand. Build upon the rock and that rock is Jesus. If you build on anything else it will soon fall and fail you. We're talking about our temple now which is our spiritual house. We will have troubles and trials to come upon us and they will cause us to fall like the waves, winds and the rains did upon the house on the sands if you let them. But if you have built your spiritual house upon Jesus then He will help you stand for He said that He would carry our burdens and lighten our loads and you can rest upon His Words for He will always do what He says. He said to lean on Me and trust in me for I will carry you through. I Cor.3:15, If anyone's work shall be burned they shall suffer loss but they themselves shall be saved. Even if you should lose everything like Job did you will be saved. Don't keep your eyes on the things of this world but take care of your soul. If you should gain the whole world and lose your own soul what will it profit? It's your soul that's most important and will live forever. It will either live in Heaven or hell for your soul will never die. So think about it and make sure that your soul is made right with God before you leave this world for after death there is no other chance to make it right with God. Your preparation for eternity is right now. Rom.6:23, For the wages of sin is death. There is a price to be paid for sin. Sin will never profit anyone for ever, it may profit you for a season but then it's all over. Jesus died on the cross for all, He paid the great price with His blood for you and me once and for all but you have to accept Him and His forgiveness and then follow Him all of the way. You don't want to just profit for a season do you? Sin brings eternal death to all who continues to commit sin and denies Jesus Christ. Heb.11:25, For there's a pleasure in sin for a season. For what does a person profit if they gain the whole world and lose their own soul. Treasures of wickedness profit nothing and there is no reward for the evil person. The candle of the wicked shall be cut off. The light of the world is Jesus Christ but if you're not living for Him then you do not have this light and you live in darkness and that's why your candle has gone out. The darkness is of the wicked and that's of the devil. Your hateful ways shall not prosper. II Pet.2:13, You shall reap the reward of the unrighteousness which is death and hell. Hateful ways does not come from the Lord for He is love, peace, joy, happiness and life. Heb.2:3, How shall we escape if we neglect so great salvation which began at the first to be spoken by them that heard the Lord and was confirmed unto us by them that heard Him. The only way to profit is to be saved and live godly and righteous in Jesus Christ in this world that we now live. Keep His commandments and laws which He has commanded you. Isa.55:2, Eat what is good and let your soul delight itself in fatness. Care for your soul for that is the only part that will live through out eternity. Eat the Word of God and delight yourself in it is what Isaiah is saying to us. We can have the joy and peace of this life if we delight ourselves in the Lord. David tells us in Psalm that if we delight ourselves in the Lord He will give us the desires of our hearts. What better can we do but delight and enjoy the Lord all the days of our life and receive the blessings that He has for us? If you go any other path and follow the ways of the world you will have this to look for. Rom.3:16, Destruction and misery are in the ways of the wicked. Jer.5:25, Your sins will withhold good things from you. God doesn't even hear sinners unless they are calling on Him to repent and to be saved. Don't let sin short change you. Sin destroys all good things and will keep you from going to Heaven. Sin leads to death and destruction, death and hell.

Prov.13:15, The way of the transgressor is hard. If you follow the devil you will always br getting into trouble for he will lead you to destruction and hell. It may seem good for a while but you will always have to reap what you sow whether good or bad. Of course, it is good to reap good seeds and a harvest but not the bad because that's when it becomes hard. Epe.5:11, Have no fellowship with the unfruitful works of darkness but rather reprove them. Change the works of darkness to the works of light and of fruitfulness. When you are in the Lord Jesus Christ you have to do the works of Him for you have the gift of salvation now and you are a changed person in Him. Be faithful in Him in all things, endure to the end and you shall be eternally saved. Lean on God and trust Him in all things, be obedient and submissive to Him at all times. He will lead and guide you into all truth and He will be your strength. Prov.3:5-7, Trust in the Lord with all your heart and lean not upon your own understanding. In all your ways acknowledge Him and He will direst your paths. Don't be wise in your own eyes but fear the Lord and depart from evil. Verse 9, Honor the Lord with your first fruit and all of your increase. Be sure to give your tenth of what you earn to the Lord for it belongs to Him. If you don't give the tenth to Him then you are robbing God. You can find this in the book of MalachI. Prov.4:20,23 and 27, Attend to My Words and incline your ear unto My sayings. Keep your heart with all diligence for out of it are the ssues of life. Remove your foot from evil. God tells us how to use the parts of our body, our ears, feet, wisdom, heart, eyes, mind and our actions. Our giving is part of our action. God didn't leave any instructions out so there is no excuse for not following Him. Prov.7:2-3, Keep My commandments and live, keep My laws as the apple of your eye. Bind them around your fingers and upon the tables of your heart. He is saying, write them and obey them in everything you do and everywhere you go. If you have made a change in your heart and life then you have the gift of life in you through Jesus Christ. You must always walk in the newness of the Spirit of God. Separate yourself from the world and the lust of the flesh. Stay away from the evil ones. The Bible teaches us to stay away from them and have no fellowship with the sinners. We are to love them but not their sins and don't engage in the things with them. Stay in the Word of God and pray always. He will carry you through and be with you always through everything you have to go through in this life, as I have said many times before. Whatever you do, don't turn back to sin and don't lose your salvation which is the gift of God. Show the world who you stand for and win all you can for Jesus Christ.

Cleave unto the Lord

Acts 11:23-24, When he came (Barnabas) and had seen the grace of God he was glad and exhorted them all that with purpose of heart they would cleave unto the Lord, for he was a good man full of the Holy Spirit and of faith. And many people were added unto the Lord. Many were saved because of his faith and stedfastness to cleave unto the Lord. God's Spirit drew the people to Him. He used Barnabas to tell them there at the revival at Antioch in Syria. We have to also purpose in our hearts to cleave unto the Lord, to love and serve Him. Ps.108:1, David said, my heart is fixed for he had made up his mind to cleave unto the Lord no matter what went on and what happened. Ps.45;17, He said, I will make Your name to be remembered an all generations. To survive this life we have to cleave unto the Lord always. We have to keep out heart, soul, mind, eyes, ears, hands, feet and our whole being on Him. Just to start this walk with Jesus and then stop is to no avail. For the ending is better than the beginning. We have to endure to the end to be saved. A sheep has to be close to the shepherd to be safe and we are the sheep and Jesus is the Shepherd. To survive Spiritually we must cleave unto the Lord Jesus Christ. Job said, though he slay me I will trust God. We will have troubles and trials in this life but we are overcomers in the Lord. Just because we are children of the Lord doesn't exempt us from troubles in this life. Acts 14:22, Tribulations will follow you even when you serve the Lord for it is a part of your earthly walk here. Job 5; 7, A man is born unto troubles. Job 14:1, Man is born of a woman is of a few days and full of troubles. Verse 22, His flesh upon him is full of pain and his soul within him shall mourn. Ps.116:3, David said, the sorrows of death compassed me and the pains of hell got hold of me and I found troubles and sorrow. Even though we may go through many trials we know this, God gives to us what is good in His sight, wisdom, knowledge and joy. The joy of the Lord is our strength. I Pet.4:12-13, Beloved, think it not strange concerning the fiery trials which is to try you as though some strange thing is happening to you. But rejoice inasmuch as you are partakers of Christ's sufferings that when His glory shall be revealed you may be glad also with exceeding joy. Rom.5:2-6, We rejoice in hope knowing that tribulation works patience, patience works experience, experience works hope and hope makes not ashamed because the love of God is shed abroad in our hearts by the Holy Ghost which is given us. For yet while we were sinners and without strength in due time Christ died for the ungodly. God now gives us grace and mercy to go through all we have encountered here while on this earth as long as we cleave unto Him. Ps.108;12, God gives us help from troubles. Verse 13, God shall tread down our enemies. James 5:11, Behold we count them happy which endure. You have heard the patience of Job and have seen the end of the Lord that the Lord is pitiful, full of compassion and of tender mercy. To grow Spiritually we must cling to the Lord as I have already said but it's worth repeating. We have to fast, pray, read and study God's Word faithfully. Draw near to God and He will draw near to you. We need to praise and worship Him more. He wants to have an intimate relationship with His children. He gives us agape love and He wants us to love Him back. When you love someone you have a relationship with them. He wants you to talk to Him regularly and not just once in a while when you need something from Him. So many times when a Christian goes through problems they turn away from God. Some even blame God for their misfortunes instead of growing stronger they fall away. There are blessings in trials and testing. We are to learn from our troubles and grow stronger in faith. Sometimes God sends trials to us to make us grow closer to Him and to grow spiritually. II Cor.4:17, For our light afflictions which is but a moment works for us a far more exceeding and eternal weight of glory.

Job 23:10, Job said, God knows the way that I take when He has tried me I shall come forth as gold. He knew he could count on God no matter what he had to go through. Job was a righteous man and he followed God. His problems didn't come on him because he was a sinner. God allowed the devil to tempt him because he knew Job would stand strong in Him. God knows your heart also. When God allows things to come your way be as Job was. Stand strong knowing that God will make a way for you and you will be stronger in the Lord than before. In the end Job had more than he ever had before because of the blessings of the Lord. I Pet.1:7, The trial of your faith being much more precious than gold that perishes though it be tried with fire might be found unto praise, honor and glory at the appearing of the Lord Jesus Christ. When we cleave unto the Lord and endure to the end it will be worth all of the problems, sufferings and afflictions. The end will be so much better than the beginning like Job's was and even better than His for it will be eternal. Let's be like David, lets make His name be remembered to all generations through this life we live. Let people see and hear your testimonies of what God has done and still doing for you. Your family and others are watching you so be careful to follow the Lord and cleave to Him no matter what else goes on around you and what happens to you. Ministry flows out of cleaving unto the Lord. God can't use you if you're not cleaving unto Him. What is it that you feel God is calling you to do? Do it with all your might. Acts 11:24, Barnabas was a good man and full of the Holy Ghost and faith. Many people were saved and added to the church because of His ministry and personal work and cleaving unto the Lord. He didn't save them but he led them to God and He saved them. When we cleave unto the Lord we will stay full of the Holy Spirit and faith. We will work in the Spirit and we will live in the Spirit. God can use us then just as He used Barnabas and many others to bring the lost to Him. God will give us the mercy and grace to do the work. Job 23; 10, But He knows the way that I take and when He has tried me I shall come forth as gold. Let God have His way with you and He will use you for His Kingdom. I Pet.1:7, The trial of you faith is much more precious than gold. Gold perishes but our faith will not. Faith will bring us praise, honor and glory at the appearing of our Lord Jesus Christ. Our life will be tested and tried, spiritually and physically as well, but have faith in God and Jesus Christ will keep us if we cleave unto the Lord and endure to the end. Rev.21; 4, All sorrow will be banished away when we get to Heaven with Jesus. All tears will be wiped away from our eyes and we'll never cry anymore. There will be no more pain, sorrows, hurts, troubles,death and no more sin for all old things will be passed away and behold all things will become new. These promises are for all Christians who cleave unto the Lord and endure to the end of this life. It will surely be worth it all. Whatever we may have to go through doesn't compare with the greatness of Heaven. Praise the Lord. Ps.46:1, God is our refuge and strength and a very present help in time of troubles. He is always with you and me, all of His children. He will carry you through. When troubles start He is right there with you for He is always present. You can count on Him. Be a cleaver unto the Lord and help others to follow the same path.

You can't love God and not love your brother

I John 4:7-18, Beloved let us love one another for love is of God and everyone that love is born of God. He that doesn't love does not know God for God is love. We must have brotherly love toward one another because God first loved us and sent His Son to save us. That is real genuine love, agape love that manifested God's love toward us that we might live through Him. We love because He first loved us. He sent His Son Jesus Christ to be the propitiation, a sacrifice for our sins. Since God loved the world then we are to love one another. No one has ever seen God at anytime but if we love one another God lives in us and His love is perfected in us. We are complete in Him. We know how much God loves us and we have to put all of our love and trust in Him. We believe in Him because He is love and they that dwell in love dwells in God and God in them. As we live in God our love grows more perfect in Him. We will not have to be afraid of the judgment day but we can face Him with confidence because we are like Christ here in this world. There is no fear in love because love cast out all fear. They that fear are not made perfect in Him. These verses need no explaining for they are clear and understanding, that we must love one another if we are of God and He in us. Love is commanded of God and there's life and power in the Word. Mark 12:30-31, Thou shall love the Lord thy God with all your heart, with all your soul, with all your mind and with all your strength, this is the first commandment and the second is like it namely this, you shall love your neighbor as yourself. There is none other commandment greater than these. If you love God then you must surely love others who are made in His image. We should pattern our love for others after Christ Jesus. When you love God as He has said you should, then you will meet the demands of His laws and His other commandments for all the other commandments hang on these two commandments of love. You cannot pick who you will love for this is sin unto God. James 2: 8-9, If you fulfill the royal law according to the Bible, you shall love your neighbor as yourself, then you do well. But if you have respect of persons then you commit sin and are convinced of the law as transgressors. Love does good to others and not evil, love fulfills the law of God. God is love but it is also tough and demanding of us, for love is the greatest gift. We know that a gift such as this is worth fighting for, whatever it takes and whatever the cost we have to love. It's a compassionate commitment to do whatever is necessary to conform others and to bring them into the knowledge of Jesus Christ. Remember this, love will motivate you. We were made in His image and we have to act upon that at all times. You can never hide or run away from the love that God has for you. His love and mercy endures forever. Let it be known that your love for Him and others will last forever as well. Real and sincere love never dies but grows deeper and deeper.

The danger of hate and not loving your brother

Verses 20-21, If a person say, I love God and hate their brother they are a liar, for they that doesn't love their brother whom they have seen how can they love God in whom they have never seen? This is the commandment of God to love one another, our brothers and sisters in the Lord and even our enemies. I John 3:14-15, We know we have passed from death to life because we love the brethren. He that does not love their brothers and sisters abide in death. Whosoever hates their brothers and sisters is as a murderer and you know no murderers will have eternal life abiding in them. This is strong teaching and it came from the Lord Himself. Verses 17-19, What we do when we have love. Whosoever has this world's goods and sees their brothers and sisters in need and they shut up their bowels of compassion to them, how does the love of God abide in them? In other words, if you have enough money and goods to live well yourself and you see someone in need and you refuse to help them how can God's love abide in you? We are our brothers and sisters keeper the Bible teaches us. This is a command of God. We need to stop just saying we love each other and really show it by our actions. It is by our actions that we show the truth we're living in. We are to live in deeds, in truth and not just by words. The real test is how we live and not what we say. And hereby we know that we are of the truth and shall assure our hearts before Him. Meaning, When we do these things we show the world and everyone and most of all God, that we abide in Him and He in us. We can be assured of this. Prov.25:21, If your enemy is hungry give them bread to eat and if they are thirsty give them water to drink. We will be held accountable if we let them go hungry and thirsty. Matt.5:42, Give them that ask of you and don't refuse them that ask to borrow from you. Oh my, how many times have I failed to do this? It doesn't say who they are or what they have done but it plainly says to help them. This brings to mind all of those we see standing on the streets with a sign in their hands saying, help me. I believe God expects us to be wise about what we give and how much. There are alcoholics and drug addicts that you cannot give money to because they will only go buy more. But the Word of God says not to let them go hungry and thirsty. Acts 20:35, Paul said, we are to support the weak and to remember what the Lord says, it is more blessed to give than to receive. Whatever we render out will be measured back to us. If you give sparingly then you will reap sparingly. Give and you shall receive… You can never out give God. He said to give and it shall be given back to you. So love, love, love,

We are to go beyond our duty

Matt.25:43, This scripture tells us of our duties beyond our calling. I was a stranger and you didn't take me in, I was naked and you didn't clothe me. I was sick and in prison and you didn't visit me. Jesus said that when you do these things then you do them unto Me. When you don't do these things then you go against Christ and His Word. James 1:27, Pure Christianity and undefiled before God and the Father is this, to visit the fatherless and widows in their afflictions and to keep yourselves unspotted from the world. The Bible calls it true religion but I like to think of it as Christianity because it sounds more like Christ. Of course, the Bible is never wrong for it is all truth. When I think of religion I think about what we do all of the time, on a regular basic like going to work, eating, going to school and all of the things we do religiously. We are to praise and worship God the same way, religiously. Rom.15:1-2, We are to be burden bearers and not to please ourselves. We who are strong ought to bear the infirmities of the weak and not to please ourselves. We are to deny self to help others. This will help their faith to grow in Christ Jesus. Jesus helps all and we are to follow Him. We need to let our light shine for Him in the dark places for others. Phil.2:4 Do not be interested in just your own life but be interested in the lives of others. We are to care for others especially for the household of faith. Acts 20:35, Paul said, I show you in all things how you should work as I did and help the weak. I taught you the Words of Jesus, it is more blessed to give than to receive. Ezek.18:7, Feed the hungry and clothe the naked. God has told us from the very beginning what we should do as Christians if we are to follow Jesus. There is much more to being a Christian than just going to the house of God and confessing that you are a Christian. You must be a doer of the Word and not just a hearer only. You must go beyond the duty of your calling. I look at so many churches today that have plenty but are not taking care of the needy as God has told them. They have big building, good heat, water, bathrooms and all of the good comfort of a home but never use it for a shelter for the homeless. They only use the building several times a week for services or for whatever they desire. I just can't believe that God is pleased with this for He has told us what to do and how to do it. Some have nice big homes but never take anyone in to shelter them from the cold or heat and to feed them. I know we have to be careful and wise on who we take into our homes but God has told us to make sure the hungry are fed and the naked are clothed, the sick and those who are in prison are visited. Pray and seek God and He will lead you in the right direction for He said that He would take care of His children. We have to do it God's way and not ours. God blesses and honors our motives. We have to start doing something for the needy. Heb.13:1-3, Keep on loving one another as brothers and sisters. Remember to welcome strangers in your homes because some have welcomed and entertained angels unawares. Visit those in prison as though you were there in prison with them. Remember those who are suffering as if you were suffering with them. We are to feel and care for the unfortunate ones. Many are stressed out and hurting because of finances. Many have lost their jobs and are even losing their homes because they have no way of paying for them. There are many that have no food or the medicines that they need. God is going to hold His children accountable if we don't help. You can go to church every time the doors are open and confess that you are a Christian but if we don't do it God's way then you're going to miss out. There should never be any of God's children doing without. The first Christians sold everything that they had and carried the money to the temple so there would be enough in God's house to take care of everyone. Christians are still giving much today to the churches but many are only building bigger buildings or doing things to fulfill their wants and desires. Many don't even fill the buildings that they have with people. I believe that if they would share with the poor as they should then God would fill their churches and then they would have to build bigger buildings. You know who are going to answer for not giving in this case? The shepherd who is the pastor and the leaders of the churches will be held accountable. This is happening everywhere for you can see it all of the time. Now, there are many churches that do have a great program of giving for they feed, clothe and shelter the homeless and you can see their growth in attendance and growth Spiritual as well.

Helping the weak and needy

Ps.41:1-3, Blessed are they that have regard for the weak for the Lord will deliver them in time of trouble. The Lord will protect and preserves their lives. He will bless them in the land and not surrender them to the desire of their enemies or foes. The Lord will sustain them from their sick bed and restore them from their bed of illness. What a blessing God has promised us just for helping the weak and needy. If every Christians would abide by God's Word and do what He says there would be less sickness in this world today I believe, for God never lies and He always does what He says He will do, for He keeps all of His promises. Ps.82:3-5, We are to defend the poor and the fatherless, do justice to the afflicted and needy. Deliver the poor and needy, rid them out of the hand of the wicked. We are to rescue them. They know not, neither will they understand for they walk in darkness all of the foundation of the earth is out of course. Some of these poor and needy have no understanding of the Word of God or how to prosper in life. They have never been taught or led in the right way. Many are wasteful and have no knowledge of living according to their level or standards. They are walking in darkness and need to be taught as well as helped in their weak and needy situation. Prov.14:21, Blessed are they that are kind to the needy. Prov.18:17, Those who are kind and give to the poor lends to the Lord and He will reward them for what they have done. We get our rewards from God, Himself. Money can never buy the kind of blessings that God gives. But doing good deeds and being obedient to Him brings these kinds of blessings that cannot be bought. You can never out give God. Matt.10:42, If anyone gives a cup of water to one of these little ones because they are My disciples, I tell you the truth, they shall never lose their reward. We are to be especially good to our brothers and sisters in the Lord. You are His dsiciple if you follow Him. II Cor.9:6-9, Whosoever sows sparingly will also reap sparingly but whosoever sows bountifully shall reap bountifully, or generously. Each should give what they have decided in their heart and what you are able to give not under pressure, compulsion or grudgingly, for God loves a cheerful giver. God is able to make all grace abound to you so that you in all things at all times having all that you need, you will abound in every good work. It is written, He has scattered abroad His gifts to the poor for His righteousness abides forever. The joy of giving is an expression of thankgiving to God who has given us Christ. This is why we should always give without regret or dread. God gave His very best when He gave His Son, Jesus Christ. Are you doing and giving your best? Prov.29:7, The righteous consider the cause of the poor and has mercy to help them.

I John 3:17-18, They that has this world's goods and sees their brothers and sisters have needs and they shut up their bowels of compassions from them, how does the love of God dwell in them? My little children let us not love in word neither in tongue but in deeds and in truth. Christ told His disciples when He sent them out, freely give and you will feely receive. Like I said before, we are His disciples and He is saying the same to us today. Don't just say that you're going to do something but make sure that you do it for Jesus said, don't just think it or say it but you are to do it. Some people make pledges and never fulfill them and this is wrong for it is a lie and no liars will enter into the Kingdom of Heaven. Make sure that you always keep your word especially your vows. Matt.19:21-24, Jesus told the rich man to sell all he had and give to the poor if he wanted to be perfect. The rich man told Jesus that he had kept all of the commandments and done all of the things that he was supposed to do from his youth. Jesus asked him to sell what he had and give it to the poor. He was a rich man and he couldn't do this that Jesus had asked of him, so he went away sorrowful for he had great possessions. That's the way of a lot of rich people today, they want to hold on to all they have and don't want to share with others who are in need. Jesus said, verily, verily I say unto you, that a rich man shall hardly enter into the Kingdom of Heaven. And again, I say unto you, it is easier for a camel to go through the eye of a needle than for a rich man to enter into the Kingdom of God. Money is not the root of all evil but the love of money is. Luke 6:38, Give and it shall be given unto you, good measure pressed down and running over shall men give unto you. For what measure you measure out it will be measured back to you. Prov.22:9, A generous person will be blessed for they shall share their food with the poor.

Prov.28:27, They that give to the poor will lack nothing. If you are struggling then ask yourself this question.Why? Why are things like this in my life? Check yourself, are you giving to the poor and needy as you see a need? Are you giving to God His tenth that He requires? He said that He would meet all of your needs and He will even do more. If you will be obedient to Him then He will meet all of your needs according to His riches in glory. Rom.14:1, Accept those whose faith is weak without passing judgment on disputable matters. We need to see that they see the truth of God's Word. We were once weak in our faith too and God sent someone to help us. We learn by reading and hearing the Word of God. Gal.6:2, Carry each other's burden and in this way you will fulfill the law of Christ. We are to encourage the timid, help the weak and be patient with everyone. Good will come to those who are generous. You can count and rely on this, God has promised good things to those who help others. He talks much about giving and helping where there's a need. I Tim.6:18, Command them to do good and be willing to share, to be rich in deeds and to be generous. In doing this you will lay up treasures in Heaven, Remember that whatsoever you do unto others you do it to God. If you even give a cup of water in Jesus name you will be blessed. God never ask anything of us that's beyond our abilities but we must go beyond our duties. All else outside of what you do for Christ is vanity. This life is but a short time but the life after this will last forever. If you want to get into the Kingdom of Heaven then you will have to do it God's way and follow Jesus Christ for He has made the way for us.

We need to be good examples

I John 13:15, Jesus said, I have given you the example to follow. Do as I have done. Your attitude should be the same as Jesus was and still is. We are to be like Him for we have the mind of Christ. Col.3:12-17, God chose us to be a holy people, tender hearted, merciful, full of kindness, humble, gentle and patience. Forgiving others for Jesus forgave us. Love because it binds us together in perfect harmony and love is the greatest gift. Let the peace of God rule in your hearts. Always be thankful. Let the Words of God rule in your hearts to make you wise and to use His Words to teach others and counsel them. Whatever you say or do let it be representative of the Lord Jesus Christ all the while giving thanks through Him to God the Father. Read and study God's Word so you can know and tell the truth to others in order to help them. II Tim.2:15, Paul said, study to show yourselves approved unto God a workman that needs not to be ashamed, rightly dividing the Word of truth. We were called because Jesus suffered for you and me leaving an example that we should follow His steps. We are to be examples to all believers and unbelievers as well, in what we teach, in the way we live, what we say and where we go. Let your life, love, faith, purity be like Jesus. We must be good examples by doing good deeds. Let everything you do reflect the honesty and seriousness of your teaching and living. John 5:10-11, Look at the examples of patience of the people who spoke in the name of the Lord. Job is a great example who endured patience. Jesus is our prime example amd most important example for He was completely perfect and did no sin. Paul exhorts us to be good examples in working. II Thessalonians 3:6-13, Stay away from Christians who walk dishorderly, in idleness and doesn't follow the tradition or examples which they received of us. Paul said, we were never lazy or even accepted food from anyone for we worked for what we needed and we paid for it. We worked hard day and night so we wouldn't be a burden on anyone. He said, it wasn't that we couldn't ask you but we wanted to be examples for you to follow. If anyone will not work then they should not eat. He said, we hear of some of you are idle and refusing to work and wasting time meddling into other people's business. Idleness is the devil's workshop. He said, we command you to settle down ands get to work, earn you own living. To the rest of you brothers and sisters, never get tired of doing good. Be an example in everything you do. People are watching you and actions speak louder than words so let your life show it everywhere you go and everything you do and say. Paul has spoken plain and open so that all can understand what he is saying.

They that look back is not worthy of the Kingdom of God

Luke 9:62, Jesus said, no one having put their hand to the plow and looks back is fit for the Kingdom of God. Gal.1:6, I marvel that you are so soon moved back from Him that called you into the grace of Christ unto another gospel. Whatever you do don't fall for every wind of false doctrines. Looking back can be a bad thing but it can also be a good thing if you look back positive. Most people that look back are only hurt and they get upset with themselves and others. Some even fall completely away from serving God and feel, what's the use for I have completely failed. There are some who never find themselves back to God. The devil makes them believe that they have gone too far and is of no good. Don't ever believe that lie of the devil for Jesus is always waiting for you to come back to Him. He's a forgiving and loving Lord and Savior. You cannot change a thing in your past so you have to press forward reaching for the higher goal in Jesus Christ. When I think of the past I thank God for where He brought me from and all of the patience, longsufferings, mercy, love and grace that He has shown me. He gave me another chance to get my life right with Him. It makes me appreciate and love Him more to know that He didn't leave me back there when I was not serving Him. Heb.10:38, Now the just shall live by faith but if anyone draw back my soul shall have no pleasure in them, this is what Paul was saying. You can't have pleasure with one that is not serving the Lord Jesus Christ for you have nothing in common with them. If you fall back then you won't have fulfilled pleasures within yourself either. I know that I didn't, for my wrong was always before me for I knew what was right and what was wrong. I am so happy that God was always tugging at my heart to do what was right and to come back in full fellowship with Him. You cannot have true, genuine happiness outside of Jesus Christ for I know for I have been there. There is nothing like the peace and joy that He gives. You may not always be happy in everything that you have to go through but you can still have the joy and peace of the Lord. II Pet.2:20, Once you come to the Lord and are cleaned up by the blood of Jesus Christ and then you fall back into the world of sin and you stop serving Him the latter end is worse then the beginning. Don't let the devil put a guilt trip on you and make you feel you're not fit because of what you've done in your past. Come back to God and change your way of living and God will take you back, forgive you and give you another chance for He loves you. When He forgives He forgets and doesn't bring your past back up to you again, you shouldn't either. Thinking of your past can hinder your spiritual growth in the Lord and affect your spiritual living, so be careful and let it all go. Don't let it have you in bondage for when Jesus forgave you then you were set free.

Acts 7:36, God brought them out after He had shown them signs and wonders in the land of Egypt and in the Red Sea and in the wilderness for forty years. Verse 39-43, They began to look backwards, they turned back to Egypt and entangled themselves back to making and serving others idols. They were following the man and not because they loved God or wanted to serve Him but for their own self gain. Moses led them all the way with God leading and making a way for them and giving them everything they needed. God let them do what they wanted to do for He makes no one serve Him. God gave them up to worship their own idols and do what they wanted to do. They couldn't wait on the Lord so they did it their way. They had no patience to wait for Moses while he was on the mountain talking with God. That is where God gave Moses the Ten Commandments and because he stayed longer than what they though he should they said, we will make our own god and worship it. Because they made other gods and worshipped them God told them, I will send you into captivity far away into Babylon. They had to live in their own consequences because they brough it on themselves. So many today are bringing calamities in and on their life because they choose their own way instead of God's way. If you are pretending to follow God and it's not coming from your heart then it won't work for God said that you have to love Him with all your heart, soul, mind and all of your strength, and He won't accept anything less. You don't serve Him because someone else does but because you want to. They had seen the miracles of God and they knew who He was but they wanted to do their own thing their own way, God knew they were not serving Him from their hearts and because they loved Him. He knows your heart and your motives. Many pretend to follow God for what they can get from Him for self gain. Some because their family does and they think they are following them, some for rituals or by habit or traditions and some for other selfish reasons. Some accept Jesus in their hearts at an early age but they drift away. Some go through the rituals because someone else does or to please someone to get them off their backs. These kinds of people have no roots and they are tempted and just fall back completely away. That's why many fall back into the world of sin because they were never really planted on the Rock which is Jesus Christ. They never sought Him with their whole heart. God will let you do what ever you want to do for He will never make you serve Him. But remember this, you will have to suffer the consequences for your sin of rejection. My husband has a great testimony of how someone in the church just kept on talking to him about the Lord and about coming to church. He said to get that person off his back he finally gave in to go to church. It wasn't long after that before God got a firm hold on Him and he accepted Jesus in his heart and life and was born again and he's been walking with God every since. Praise God this person that was witnessing to him was persistant and wouldn't give up on him. That's the way we should be, but make sure you do it in pure love. There are times when you can run people away but God says to use wisdom. Ask God for wisdom and He will give you the right words to say and the right time to say them.

Prov.14:14, The backslider in heart shall be filled with their own ways and a good person shall be satisfied from himself. Matt.24:12, Because sin shall abound the love of many shall wax cold. Acts 28:27, For the heart of His people has grown gross or vulgar, and their ears are dull of hearing and their eys have they closed. II Tim.3:7, They are ever learning and never able to come to the knowledge of the truth. A backslider is one who at one time served God but has left Him to serve the devil. You may be thinking or saying, I don't serve the devil just because I walked away from God. If you're not serving God the Father then you are serving the devil for there is no in between, you cannot serve them both. Rom.1:18, For the wrath of God is revealed from Heaven against all ungodliness and unrighteousness of men who hold the truth in righteousness. They know the truth but don't walk in it or obey it. God doesn't want you to worship the things that He made but He wants you to worship Him, the God and Creator of all things. Rom.1:20, There's no reason or excuse for not knowing God for you can see Him in all creation, that only He could have made. He is the Almighty God and Father of the universe and all of Heaven. You can see from these scriptures that if you walk away from God and aren't obedient and following Him then you are a backslider and a backslider will not enter into the Kingdom of Heaven. It's each and everyone's own choice to serve God or not. Pretending to serve Him is not good enough for God knows your heart.To deny the Lord Jesus Christ is blaspheming and that is the sin unto death because you cannot be forgiven for that. This is the unpardonable sin the only sin that cannot be forgiven for. To say there is no God and to reject Jesus Christ and say He is not the Christ and Savior of the world is blaspheming against the Holy Ghost. Matt.12:31-32, Wherefore I say unto you, all manner of sin and blasphemy shall be forgiven unto men but the blasphemy against the Holy Ghost shall not be forgiven unto men. Whosoever speaks a word against the Son of man it shall be forgiven him but whosoever speaks against the Holy Ghost it shall not be forgiven him neither in this world or the world to come. Many people before they were born again and accepted Jesus in their lives said all kind of evil against Him, they even called His name in vain, some even cursed Him. But when they came to Him and asked forgiveness He forgave them. If they would have continued to be in the sinful state and denied Him to the end then they would have blasphemed against the Holy Ghost and would have been forever lost. Please don't wait until it's too late to come to Christ and give your heart and life to Him. Ask Him to forgive you of all of your sins and then follow Him and be obedient to him. He will forgive you and will go with you until the end here and then you will have eternal with Him and all of the saints of God.

Just look what the Jews went through because they rebelled and wouldn't serve God, they turned away from Him and served idols and other gods. Many of them are going to have to go through the seven years of tribulation because of their rebellion and rejection to God. You will too if you reject Him and be disobedient to Him as they did. What a terrible time that's going to be here on this earth after all of the saved has been raptured and taken to Heaven. The saved will be taken in the rapture, caught up to be with Jesus when He comes in the clouds of glory. The tribulation period will be a time like never before and will never be again. You think times are bad now, it is nothing that's compared with the great tribulation. You don't want to be here for that, so get prepared to go with Jesus in the rapture or through death, should that come first. After death you will not have another chance to prepare for today is the day of salvation. The Bible tells us about all of this in Daniel, Zechariah, Revalation and some of the other books as well. God is real, I know because I feel Him in my heart, soul and spirit. You can't buy or work for this flight of salvation for you have to come by faith in Jesus Christ and accept Him as your Lord and Savior. It has to be real for you can't just pretend, for God knows your heart and everything about you. He knows your thought even before you speak, He knows your motives and He even knew you while you were still in your mother's womb. You were the child that He made and you were made in His own image. That in itself should draw you to Him and cause you to want to serve Him. Don't ever think that you are a nobody, because God made you and He loves you. God never made junk. Are you saved, are you sure? Are you ready should He call you through death or comes in the rapture to get His church? Jesus is coming soon so be ready, waiting and watching for Him. He said that He was coming for those who are waiting and watching for Him.

If there's something that's in your past that the devil keeps bringing up to you just come against him in the name of Jesus and tell the devil he's a liar and the father of them. Tell him that Jesus has reinstated you're your past and everything has been made new in you. No matter what you have done in the past it cannot keep you from Jesus once you have come to Him and have been forgiven and covered by the blood of Jesus. Only Jesus can reinstate our past and give us a new start in life. Don't look back but look forward and press on the mark of the high calling of God. He has a work for you to do and your past cannot disqualify you from whatever God has for you to do. Your strength is in Him so stay in His Word and pray always and He will lead and guide you in everything. Keep a good relationship with Him, fellowship with Him on a regular basic. Stay in tune with Him and He will carry you through to the end. Whatever you do don't look back for you can't change a thing in the past. The Bible says, when I was a child I spoke like a child but when I became a man, or grown, I put away childless things. So now you have grown up and you're a child of God and you have grown in Him. Keep on maturing in Him, think like Him, act like Him, walk like Him and talk like Him always and everywhere you go in everything you do. Give Him the praise and the glory for everything in Jesus name. To Him be the glory and honor forever. There is life in God's Word, Amen

Reflections and radiant lives

Prov.27:19, As water reflects a face so a man's heart reflects the man. When you look into clear water you will see your face. In the same way when someone looks at us they should see our heart. David said, I will praise Him who is health of my countenance and my God. He is saying, God is the health of my face, it was because David had God in his life and it was showing on his face. God's people should be the happiest people in the world and it should always show on our faces. We have no reason to walk around with long, gloomy and sad faces, for the joy of the Lord is our strength and that joy should always show in our faces. There are some Christians who you hardly ever see them smile or seem to be happy. You can be happy in the Lord no matter what's going on in your life and around you. Christians should live radiant lives and it has to show for you can't hide happiness and joy. Matt.5:14, You are the light of the world, a city that is set on a hill cannot be hid. What kind of light are you putting out? Is it a very dim one or a blinking light? We are to let out light so shine that others can see and be saved. No one when they have lit a candle puts it under a bushel but on a candle stick that all can see. Our light should be a good influence to others. Without Jesus in your heart and life you don't have this kind of light. Flesh is weak and full of worries, doubts and all kinds of things that cause you to be looking sad and unhappy. You are bound up with all of the cares of the world without Jesus Christ in you. II Cor.3:18, But we with all open faces reflect the Lord's glory and we are changed into the same likeness which comes from theLord who is the Spirit of the Lord. When you have Jesus living in you it changes your reflections. Even in troubles and trials we can let our light shine to this lost and dying world. Steven did in Acts 6:15, When he was cast into prison for preaching the gospel, all who sat in court looked at him seriously. They saw his face as if it had been the face of an angel. Steven had seen the Lord and the joy of his soul shone on his face. God said to let our light shine out in darkness. This was a dark moment for Steven but his light was still shining. God made the light to shine in our hearts so we are to let it shine out to others. We should especially let it shine when we are going through problems to let the world know that we have Jesus living in us and we are different from the world. John the Baptist was a burning shining light. What kind of reflection and light are you?

Radiant faces

Ps.34:5, Those that look upon Him are radiant, their faces are never covered with shame. Their brightness shines even though the hard and difficult times. For with you is the fountain of life, which is God. In you there is light, Jesus Christ. No one whose hope is in the Lord will ever be put to shame. We will not be disgraced or feel guilty about the light we are shining. Let others see the God in you that makes you happy and have a radiant face. Isa.49:3, God said to Israel, you are my servants in whom I will display My splendor, My shining face and My great talent. Even though He was talking about His chosen people Israel, it still goes for His children today for the Gentiles were grafted in. He doesn't want His children to walk around with sad faces. He wants to shine through us. Ps.34:1-3, David said, I will extol, lift You up, exalt, manify and glorify you at all times. His praise shall always be on my lips. My soul will boast, brag and magnify in the Lord. Let the afflicted, distressed, grievous and the harassed hear and rejoice. Glorify the Lord with me, let us exalt His name together. Do this always in all things no matter what the situation you're in or what's going on around you. Verse 10, A righteous person may have many troubles but the Lord delivers him or her out of all of them. This is why we can be happy when we are going through problems, because the Lord has told us that He will help us and deliver us out of all the problems. The righteous are, upright, devout, godly, holy, earnest, straight and true Christians. That doesn't mean they are perfect but they are striving to be perfect to be like Jesus. Matt.13:43, The righteous will shine like the sun in the Kingdom of their Father, those who have ears let them hear. We can taste of the Kingdom here during the times of Spiritual communion with Jesus and the Holy Spirit through prayer, reading God's Word, fellowshipping with Him and among other Christians. To live a kingdom life you have to leave self interests behind and walk into the life through Jesus Christ. What are your chief hindrances not to follow God's Word?

Standing in the gap

We are to stand in the gap for our weaker brothers and sisters who are of a little faith and are going through troubles and trials. Those who are hurting we need to lift them up to God and stand in for them in prayer. Many times one will have such a load that it seems that they just can't reach God so we need to be there for them. I know I have been in this situation. It's easy to just see the problems and not see the problem solver which is God. It's not that God wasn't there but sometimes we let flesh get in the way and it causes us more problems. I thank God for my spiritual family as well as my own blood family.

I thank God that when I was down and in need He sent someone to lift me up to Him. You have to remember we are still living in the flesh and the flesh is weak and we allow it to over ride the spirit at times. Doesn't mean that you have fallen away from God but it just shows we are human. We won't be spiritual until we are changed from this mortal to immortal body to be like Christ. I have never heard of anyone that has never felt like this at some point in their life. Even to Paul, the great man of God that he was, had problems and this is what he said. II Cor.4:8-9, We are troubled on every side yet not distressed, we are perplexed but not in dispair, persecuted but not forsaken, cast down but not destroyed Verse 10 tells us the most important issue we need to always keep. We are to always show forth in our bodies the dying of the Lord Jesus that the life of Him might be made manifest in our own body. We are to be Christlike no matter what goes on with us as Christians. We have to die to self daily to be like Him. Ps.106:23, He would have destroyed them, the Israelites His chosen people had it not been for Moses who stood in the gap or had been a breach before Him to keep His wrath from destroying them. The Israelites had forgotten God and all that He had done. They murmured and complained and were disobedient to the Lord their God. But because one man stood in the gap and asked the Lord not to destroy them God hearkened to his cry. Verse 30, Another time God hearkened to another cry for help for the people was when the people were worshipping baal so God sent a plague upon them and Phinehas stood up and intervened for them and God stopped the plague. A righteous person is a believer, a mediator, someone standing for others, even if they are not righteous people. It's like a familiar image in the Old Testament and a powerful shadow of the Supreme mediator Jesus Christ. They were looking for Jesus to come for He had not yet come. We are to help our Christian families as well as others too. Sometimes Christians do get weak under such a heavy load and we need to fast and pray, lift them up to the Lord and stand in the gap for them. We are to always stand in the gap for the lost and show them the way to Jesus Christ.

I Cor.12:28-31, And in the church God has appointed first of all, apostles, prophets, teachers, workers of miracles, those having the gift of healing, those who are able to help others, those with the gift of administration and those who speak in other tongue. He said to earnestly desire the greatest gift, which is love. God gave these gifts because He knew there were people that needed Spiritual help to endure this life. We are to reflect Christ to a broken world. We are to encourage, lift up and edify believers through humility and unselfishness. We are not to think of ourselves but to think upon others with humility and care. We need to stand in the gap for our country, church, community, our family and all of the lost everywhere. God is still looking for faithful Christians to stand in the gap and intercede for others before Him. We as Christians need to show others the faithful way of life through following our faithful God and Savior Jesus Christ. Where are your feet standing? David said, my feet ate standing on level ground in the great assembly and I will praise the Lord. He prayed to God to teach him His way and lead him in the straight path. He said that God made his hind feet like the feet of the deer. He enabled him to stand on the heights for he stood high. He said that God lifted him out of the slimy pit, out of the mud and mire and set his feet on the rock and gave him a firm place to stand. God delivered him from death and his feet from stumbling so that he could walk before God in the light of life. Ps.66:9, He has preserves our lives and kept our feet from slipping. How is this? Because His Word is a lamp unto out feet and a light unto our path. Paul said in Rom.10:15, How beautiful are the feet of those who bring good news. We are to shod our feet with the preparation of the gospel of peace. Our feet are very important parts of our body as you can see. Watch and be careful where they take you. Stand firm, stand sure, stand always in the will of the Father, and stand in faith believing all that the Father has promised to His children He will do. Epe.6; 13, When you have done all you can to stand, stand. Don't ever give up on God and give in to the devil. You are a winner in the Lord and you do have the victory through Jesus Christ. Always remember, there's life in the Word. God's Word makes life work bountifully, beautiful, worth living and then eternal life after this life is over. If you want to live many good days you have to follow God's commands for there is truly life in the Word. You can choose life or death and I pray you will choose life through Jesus Christ.

CHAPTER NINE

Seven Precious Things Peter Taught

CHAPTER 9

Seven precious things Peter taught

The living stone, Jesus Christ

I Pet.2:6, Wherefore I lay in Zion a chief cornerstone, elect precious and all that believe on Him shall not be ashamed. First we look at the cornerstone. A cornerstone is an immaterial thing upon which something else rests. A cornerstone is a firm foundation, a bed rest and keystone, something that you can rest on and you will not fall. This cornerstone is Spiritual not made with hands or with material. Jesus Christ is this cornerstone that Peter is talking about. He is the firm foundation, He's our bed rest for we can rest in Him, and He is the keystone, the main stone. He is the solid rock and He is the only way. Jesus was chosen by God the Father to be the one and the only Son of God to be the cornerstone, the Savior of the world. He is elite and the chosen one. God search through Heaven and couldn't find one that was pure enough to be the Savior and Lord of His people. Jesus was chosen and precious is He. Something precious is costly and lovable. It cost Jesus His life to be the cornerstone and there is no greater love than this. They didn't kill Him for He laid down His life for you and me. He could have called ten thousand angels to loose Him but He died because He loved us. Isa. 28:16, Therefore said the Lord God, Behold I lay for a cornerstone, a stone, a tried stone, a precious stone and a sure foundation. He that believes shall not make haste. They will not be dismayed, discouraged or disappointed. A person will never regret believing in the Lord and they won't be disappointed that they are serving Him. A true Christian will be content in Jesus Christ. In the world there are diisappointment and discouragements but in Him there is fulfillment and peace for He is the place of rest and a firm foundation to lean on. Matt.7:24, Whosoever hears these Words of Mine and does them, I will liken unto them wise ones who built their house upon a rock. I Cor.3:11, None other than a person can lay that is laid, which is Jesus Christ.He is the only sure foundation, the only foundation that is rewarding and will give you eternal life in the Kingdom of Heaven. II Tim.2:9, The foundation of God stands sure, having this seal. The Lord knows them that are His. Everyone that names the name of Christ shall depart from iniquity, which is sin. You can be sure of this foundation because there is hope and there is life. You can take your rest in safety if your heart is fixed on this sure foundation, Jesus Christ. You don't have to be afraid of the evil one, the devil, because you are trusting in the Lord. You don't have to be afraid of the terror by night or by the arrows by day for God is with you all of the way, He will never leave of forsake you.

The precious blood of Christ

I Pet.1:19, But with the precious blood of Jesus as of a lamb without blemish and without spot. We were not bought with material things that are corruptible but with the blood of Jesus Christ. You cannot do your own thing anymore because you were bought with a price and you are not your own anymore for you belong to Him. He is your life now. Matt.26:28, For this is My blood of the New Testament which is shed for all for the remission of sins. Being justified by the blood we shall be saved from wrath to come. We are saved by grace through faith in Jesus Christ, it is a gift of God and not of works lest any should boast. You can't work for it or buy this gift. I John 1:7, If we walk in the light as He is in the light we have fellowship one with another and the blood of Jesus, God's own Son cleanses us from all sin. Jesus loved us and washed us from sin in His own blood. He is our atonement and salvation for there is no other way to be free from sin. You can be free from sin but you are not free to sin. But if you do sin or make a mistake He is there to forgive you if you ask Him. Praise God for Jesus and what He did for us. When you really see Him on the cross of Calvary as He hung there nailed by His hands and His feet as He suffered and died with His blood dripping down in all of the dreadful and agony pain, it will make you to love him more and want to serve and follow Him for what He did. Because of His love for you and me He did this. It was all because of love of human beings. The first Adam sinned but the second Adam which is Jesus Christ never sinned or knew no sin for He was pure and spotless. Without faith in Him and washed in His blood can anyone be born again and saved.

The believer's faith

II Pet.1:1, To those through the righteousness of our God and Savior Jesus Christ have received a faith as precious as ours. Faith comes by hearing and hearing by the Word of God. Faith is the substance of things hoped for and the evidence of things not seen. Heb.11:1, For whoever is born of God overcomes the world and this is the victory that overcomes the world, even our faith. Believe in the Lord your God so you can be established. Faith in Christ secures our salvation if we continue in Him. Whosoever believes in Him should not perish but have everlasting life. Whosoever has faith in Him and confesses with their mouth and believes in their heart that God raised Jesus from the dead shall be saved. Just confessing with the mouth that you believe is not enough to have salvation, for it must come from the heart. Then you must be obedient and faithful to Him and follow Him all of the way. They that endure to the end the same shall be saved. The just shall walk and live by faith, for without faith you cannot please God. We have no righteousness of our own for our righteousness is as filthy rags so we walk in God's righteousness. When you walk in faith you have the peace of God in your life. When you come to Jesus and accept Him as your Savior and Lord of your life, you can't live anyway your flesh wants you to. You have to die to self daily and live to please God. Seek His will for your life and live according to His will and not yours. No where in the Word of God does it say that it will be easy, but it's rewarding here in this life and then life eternal with Him. It's a good life serving Him even through the problems here in this life you can have peace and joy in the Lord for He is our strength and joy.

The fiery trials

I Pet.1:7-9, That the trial of your faith being much more precious than of gold that perishes though it be tried with fire might be found unto praise, honor and glory at the appearing of Jesus Christ. Receiving the end of your faith, even the salvation of your soul, our faith will be tested and tried if we will stand for God. We will have problems in this life but problems help us to grow in the Lord. The Word of God tells us that we will have trials and tribulations all the days of our life if we follow Jesus. The good thing is, He will be there with you all the way, through every trial you may have and He said that He would make a way for you through the problems. He never said that He would take away all of your problems but He would make the load and way easier so that you may be able to go through them. He said He would make a way where there seem to be no way. You can depend on Him always for He will do what He said He would do. People and even Christians will fail you but He will never fail you or leave you as long as you are following Him. That's a promise from God. James 1:2-3, Count it all joy when you fall into diver temptations, knowing that the trying of your faith works patience. Verse 12, Blessed are the ones that endure temptation for when they are tried they shall receive the crown of life which the Lord has promised to them that love Him. II Pet.2:9, The Lord knows how to deliver the godly out of temptation. You can't deliver yourself but He can for He is your strength and protector. II Tim.2:12, If we suffer with Him we shall reign with Him also. In this life we will face a lot of hardship, hurts, trials, sufferings and sorrows but don't lose your faith and hope for you are overcomers in the Lord Jesus Christ. You have the victory in the end if you will endure in Him. There is coming a day when there will be no more of the bad things but all will be good, but until then we have to continue to endure whatever comes our way. There are some teaching that if you are a child of God you don't have to go through any of these bad things, for all you have to do is name it and claim it. That simple is not true. Jesus said that we would go through these things here on this earth but not to fret or give up or give in to them for He would make a way of escape. If Jesus said it you can depend on it for it's truth. We live in a world of sin and hurts because of the sin of Adam and Eve but God has made a better way through Jesus Christ for those who will believe, accept and follow Him.

The meek and quiet spirit

I Pet.3:4, Let it be the hidden man of the heart in which is not corruptible, even the ornament of a meek and quiet spirit, which is in the sight of God of great price. A meek and quiet spirit is highly honored in God's eyes. To be meek we have to be humble, showing no signs of pride. Many times it's better to listen than to speak. We need to have a quiet spirit and not to be boisterous when we talk. These two important qualities go hand in hand for they go together. You need to put on the robe of righteousness, that's God's righteousnes for our righteousness is dirty and unfit. The only thing good in us is Him. You have to be clothed in the garment of salvation. You have to put on the garment of praise also. Let the beauty of Jesus be seen in you. There has to be a right Spirit in us and that's the Spirit of Jesus Christ our Lord and Savior. Job 29:14, I put on righteousness and it clothed me, my judgment was as a robe and a diadem, a crown. Don't lift yourself up but live holy and righteous in the Lord. To do this we have to be meek and have a quiet spirit in us. This is the seventh precious thing that Peter taught us. To be meek we have to be humble, long suffering, patient, merciful, kind hearted and most of all loving. These are the precious things needed to make it into the Kingdom of Heaven. Gal.5:22-23, The fruit of the Spirit is listed here and all God's children have to have them. The fruit of the Spirit is made up of all these things. These are a must in a Christian's life. They are all Christ like and Christians are Christ like. Matt.5:5, Blessed are the meek for they shall inherit the earth. Isa.61:10, I will greatly rejoice in the Lord, my soul shall be joyful in my God for He has clothed me with the garment of salvation. He has coved me with the robe of righteousness as a bride adorns herself with jewels. You have to be saved first of all to have these qualities of Jesus. Rev.21:3, One day we will have a Spiritual adorning body for we are Christ's bride. The Christians, the church is the bride of Jesus Christ. He is your Spiritual husband and one day He is coming back for you and me. Just as you have to be faithful and true to your earthly husband here you are to be faithful and true to Him. Many commit spiritual adultery because they aren't faithful to His Word. He is a jealous God and He wants nothing or anyone to come before Him. Rev.22:14, Blessed are they that do and keep His commandments that they may have the right to tree of life and may enter through the gates to that city, New Jerusalem. We will live forever in happiness, good health, pain free, sinless and praising God forever. Rev.3:5, They that overcome shall be clothed in white raiment and I will confess their names before My Father and before His angels. They that overcome shall inherit all things and I will be their God and they shall be Mine. You have to stay clean and pure to enter into the Kingdom of God. God said, be ye holy for I am holy.

Ps.22:26, The meek shall eat and be satisfied, they shall praise the Lord and shall live forever.
Ps.37:4, The meek shall inherit the earth and shall delight in the abundance of peace.
Ps.147:6, The Lord shall lift up the meek.
Ps.149:4, The Lord shall beautify the meek with salvation.
I Thessalonians 4:11, Study to be quiet and to do your own business and work with your hands as we have commanded you.

More promises God has given His children

Knowledge

II Pet.1:1-11, Peter a servant of Jesus Christ has given ua a call to godliness and tells Christians of the gifts and promises of the gospel of Jesus Christ. God will bless His children with special favors and wonderful peace as we come to know Jesus our God and Lord better and better. God, Jesus Christ and the Holy Spirit are all ONE. They are three manifestation of ONE God… God the Father, Jesus Christ the Son and the Holy Spirit are ONE. John 1:1-4, In the beginning was the Word and the Word was with God and the Word was God. The same was in the beginning with God. All things were made by

Him and without Him there was nothing made without Him. And in Him was life and the life was the light of men. John 1:14, And the Word became flesh and walked among us and we beheld His glory, the glory as of the only begotten of the Father, full of grace and truth. Verse 18, No one has seen God at anytime, the only begotten Son, which is in the bosom of the Father, He has declared Him. John 10:30, Jesus said, I and My Father are ONE. Verse 38, The Father is in Me and I in the Father. John 14:9-10, He that has seen Me has seen the Father. I am in the Father and He is in Me, the Father that's in Me does the work. Verse 26, But the Comforter which is the Holy Spirit whom the Father will send in My name will teach you in all things. John 15:26, When the Comforter is come, I will send unto you from the Father, even the Spirit of truth which preceeded from the Father, for He shall testify of Me. II Cor.13:14, The grace of the Lord Jesus Christ and the love of God and the communion of the Holy Ghost be with you all, Amen. I Pet 1:2, Elect according to the foreknowledge of God the Father through sanctification of the Spirit, unto obedience and the sprinkling of blood of Jesus Christ, grace unto you and peace be multiplied. In Genesis 1:1 We see that God said He created the heavens and the earth. In Heb.11; 3, We see that by faith we understand that the worlds, more than one, were framed by the Word of God. Now go back to John 1:1, Who is the Word? In the beginning was the Word, and the Word was with God and the Word was God. The same was with God in the beginning. Here you can see two in ONE. Now in John 1:3, All things were made by Him, Jesus, and without Him was not anything made that was made. Epe.3:9, God created all things by Jesus Christ. Col.1:15-16, Jesus who is the image of the invisible God and the first born of all creatures. For by Him were all things created that are in Heaven and in earth, visible and invisible for all things were created by Him and for Him. In Gen.1:2, The Spirit of God moved upon the face of the waters. Job 26:13, by His Spirit He has garnished the heavens. Ps.104:30 Thou sent forth Thy Spirit, they are created and Thou renewed the face of the earth. Now, this is telling us that the Holy Spirit is the creator. God, Jesus and the Holy Spirit were all One, the creator. I don't believe you can separate one from the other for they are all ONE. Isa.45:5-7, I am the Lord and there is none else, there is no God before Me. There is none beside Me for I am the Lord and there is none else. I formed the light and created darkness, I make peace and create evil, and I the Lord do all these things. Deut.6:4, Hear O Israel, the Lord our God is ONE Lord. I Tim.3:16, And without controversy, great is the mystery of godliness, God was manifest in the flesh, justified in the Spirit, seen of angels, preached unto the Gentiles, believed on in the world and received up in glory. How else can you explain this? The Word of God tells us that this is the mystery of Jesus Christ. Col.2:2, Let your hearts be comforted and knited together in love and unto all of the riches of the full assurance of understanding to the acknowledgement of the mystery of God and of the Father and of Christ. I Cor.2:7, But we speak the wisdom of God in a mystery, ever the hidden wisdom which God ordained before the world, unto our glory. I Cor.2:9, God reveals His secrets and mysteries to His servants and prophets by His Spirit, for the Spirit searches all things, yes the deeper things of God. This is why every Christian should not only read but study the Word of God. He will show you great things. No one will ever know all, for the secrets belong to God. These scriptures that I have given you I plea with your to study them. II Tim.2:15,You should never take the work of anyone but study to show yourself approved unto God a workman that needs not to be ashamed, rightly dividing the Word of truth. It doesn't say read but to study. God will reveal many deep things to you. Not all see the same things but He will give you peace of mind in what you believe. I know this has been deep for it is deep for me as well. When I think of how big and great God is, and how He came from Heaven to come to earth and walk here as man then died for me it just overflows me of how He could love me that much. It's hard to comprehend the love of God the Father, His Son Jesus Christ and the Holy Spirit.

It didn't stop there, for He has taken care of me all through these years and is coming back to take me with Him to live forever. Even if I go by the grave I will be with Him forever. I only regret that I have not been as faithful to Him as I should have been through the years of my life. I have always loved to study His Word and have done so most of my life. I have a sister that told me when I was just a little girl about 11 years old, and I quote, all you do is read the Bible. She wasn't being ugly but it has stuck with me all of my life. I only wished

I would have listened to God and to His calling on my life then. I have always been one to write down what I studied and have kept most of the studies in the last 30 odd years. Little did I know that God was going to call me to write Christian books. He has written through me about 50 songs since 1969 that only my family and I have sung. I never dreamed I would be writing books. He did lay a Scripture upon my spirit and heart many years ago, Ps.145:1, My tongue is the pen of a ready writer. Now we know that was talking about speaking prophecy but He would never let me go of this. It just kept coming to me and one day I felt the call and desire to write. I had said to my husband a number of times that I didn't believe that God just gave me all of these studies just to let them lay in a file drawer. Little did I know that He was preparing me to write Christian books over all these years. I do not take any credit or glory for any of this for I give Him all of the glory, honor and praise. I could never do this on my own but it's through His knowledge and wisdom that I can do this. I am still learning so much more about His Word, about Him and I still want to learn more for there's so much more to learn. We can never know it all but I praise Him for all He's taught me and I want to share it with others. I want to see people saved, helped, healed and on their way to Heaven. I pray that the books I write will help do all of this. If you have not read my first book, "There's No Room for Doubt", I urge you to get it and read it. Praise the Lord forever.

Abundance is promised

Ps.36:8, He gives us joy.They shall be abundantly satisfied with the fatness of Thy house and shall make them drink of the rivers of Your pleasure. This is saying, you will be completely satisfied with the goodness and pleasures that the Lord has and He has it all. Happiness is of the Lord's house, happiness comes from Him for He is the fulness of your joy. He said He would fill you with everything you need and He gives us more than what we need as well. The joy of the Lord is your strength. He is joy unspeakable and full of glory. You can have joy of the Lord even through sorrow and troubles. You may not show happiness in times of sorrow but you can still have the joy on the inside because you have the Lord. That joy will carry you through because in that joy you can have peace. There's no joy like the joy of the Lord in your soul and spirit.

John 10:10, He gives us life. I am come that they may have life and have it more abundantly. There is no other good and fulfilling life outside of Jesus Christ. Life is good living when you have Him in your heart and you are serving Him. He wants us to enjoy life here to the fullest for He wants His children to have the best. He has everything we need and He will give it to all who will follow Him and be faithful to Him. He said to ask and you will receive. We will have trials and tribulations in this life but He will be right there with you to make a way for you. We grow through our hard times and we learn to trust Him more. If we never had a problem then we wouldn't know that He could solve them. He loves to work when our backs are against the wall and we don't know what to do or where to turn. Just turn to Him and you can have joy knowing that He will carry you through. He doesn't want us to go around mourning and complaining all of the time, just praise Him for He works through the praises of His people. The more you praise Him the closer you will get to Him and you will be abundantly filled with His presence. You can have a good life here and then life eternal with Jesus and all of the saints when this life is over. Praise the Lord.

II Cor.9:8, He gives us grace. And God is able to make all grace abound toward you, always having all sufficiency in all things, made abound to every good work. Grace will always abound in your good works. God will not lead you where He won't keep you. When God calls and gives you a work to do He will be right there with you to help you and show you how He wants you to get the job done. He will bless your every efford for His grace is sufficient as He told Paul when he was going through a time of testing in his life. God may not always give you what you think you want for it may not be the right thing for you at the time but He said He would fill your every need. You can always depend on His grace for it is just as sufficient today as it has always been. His grace never changes as His love never changes for you and me. He never changes for He's the same today as He was yesterday, He will be the same tomorrow as He is today. Thank God for His mercy, love and grace toward us.

Epe.3; 20, He gives us power. Now unto Him that is able to do exceedingly, abundantly above all that we ask or think according to the power that works in us. It's God's power that works in us for He is our power and strength. When we are weak then He is strong. He has given us power to walk on serpents, (snakes) and they will not hurt us. He has the power to build up and the power to tear down. There's no power such as His. His power works through Christians to lay hands on the sick and they shall recover. He gives us power to cast out demons and drives away evil in Jesus name. God has promised us in Mark 16:17-18 that all believers are given the power to perform miracles, drive out demons in My name and speak in other tongue. This is the power of God and not of man. Are you using what God has given or entrusted you with?

Phil.4:19, God gives us supplies. But my God will supply all of your needs according to His riches in glory by Jesus Christ. He didn't say that He was going to give you everything you wanted but He would supply your needs. What are you in need of? Ask yourself what your problem is if your needs are not being met and fulfilled by Him. Matt.5; 6, Blessed are they that hunger and thirst after righteousness for they shall be filled. Are you hungry and thirsty after the things of the Lord? There are Spiritual needs and there are physical needs. First, above all else we are to meet the needs of our Spirit and soul. Jesus said, seek ye first the kingdom of God and then all of these other things will be added unto you. Mal.3;10, He said to bring all of your tithes and offerings into the storehouse of the Lord and He would open up the windows of Heaven and pour out you a blessing that you wouldn't have room to receive. So if you're not getting your needs met it's not God's fault, you best check yourself out to see where and why, you are missing out. You can rest assure it's not God's fault for He will do what He says. He never said that you can have everything that you wanted but that He would meet your every need and give you the desires of your heart if you would be obedient and faithful to Him. What more could a person want?

II Pet.1:11, He will give you entrance. For so an entrance shall be ministered unto you abundantly into the everlasting Kingdom of our Lord and Savior Jesus Christ. What more could we ask for, that what He has promised to all who will receive Him in their hearts and lives here on this earth and then eternal life with Him in His Kingdom forever. Jesus will be standing at the gate to welcome all of His children who have endured to the end to enter in. What a time, what a time. What a day that will be, Heaven will surely be worth all of the things that we have to endure here on this earth in which we live now. Are you making your plans to go to Heaven? You have to make your preparation here now to be able to enter in. Remember, it's only what you do for Christ that will last for all else is vanity and will be done away with in the end.

God has promised so much for His children here and now and then eternal life but you have to faithful and obedient to Him and do His will. Lev.26:5, The Israelites were God's chosen people but all of the promises then are still for God's children today. You shall eat of your bread to the fullest and dwell in your land safely. You will not grow hungry or thirsty. Deut.30:9, The Lord your God will make you plenteous in every good works of your hand, in the fruit of your body, in the fruit of your cattle and in the fruit of your land for good. The Lord delights in your prosperity for He said that it was His will that you be in good health and prosper just as your soul prospers. If you're not prospering it may be that your soul isn't prospering in the Lord. That has to be the first prosperity and then all of the other things will be added unto you, says the Lord. Jesus Christ who laid the foundation so all we have to do is follow Him if you want to prosper in everything. Mal.3:16-17, God has promised that all who follow Him will be saved in the end. Those who fear the Lord will follow Him and be saved. God keeps a rememberance book, a record for all who love and are obedient to Him. He has a Lamb's book of life and if your name is written down in that book and you continue to follow Him in faithfulliness and obedience to Him you are one of His children and He is your God. You will be among His people when He makes up His treasured possessions. He said I will spare you as a father spares his son. Those who fear My name, the Son of righteousness will rise with healing in His wings. Keep My commandments and laws and the greatest of all is LOVE. Love the Lord with all your heart, mind, soul and strength and your neighbor as yourself. All of the other commandments hang on these two commandments. You can never be saved without the love of God in your life.

We shall prosper according to our obedience to God

Isa.1:9, If you are willing and obedient you shall eat of the good of the land. You will see that to inherit the good things of the Lord there are requirements. Here you have to be willing and obedient. Ps.132:15, I will abundantly bless your provision, I will satisfy the poor with bread. Prov.3:10, Your barns shall be filled with plenty and your presses shall burst out with new wine. Ps.67:6, The earth shall yield her increasee and God our own God shall bless us. You shall reap crops from your work tilling the land that you sow. You will reap the seeds that you sow. Luke 11:28, Even more blessed are we that hear the Word of God and put it into practice. Obeying God's Word makes you prosper and be blessed. John14:23, All those who love Me will do what I say, My Father will love them and We will come to them and live with them. This is too marvelous to even comprehend, the Father and Son Jesus Christ will abide in us and with us. Prov.11:25, The liberal soul will be made fat, meaning to have much. 22:9 says this, Blessed are those that are generous. Luke 6:38, Give and it shall be given you, good measure, pressed down, shaken down and running over, for what you measure out it will be measured back to you. Jesus said, Ask and it shall be given unto you, seek and you shall find, knock and it shall be opened unto you. A lot of times we don't have because we don't ask, seek and knock. You have to make your requests made known to others and to God. Deut.29:9, Keep the Words of the covenant and do them that you may prosper in all you do. I Chr.22:13, You shall prosper if you keep the commandments and fulfill all of the laws and statues that the Lord has given you by Moses. Be strong and be of good courage, don't be dismayed or dreadful. Stop worring about everything, trust and lean on God for He will do what He said and you have to do your part as well. Ps.1:3, You shall be like a tree planted by the rivers of water that brings forth fruit in its season, where their leaf will never wither and whatsoever they do shall prosper. When you stay in the Spirit of the Lord you will stay filled with His goodness, mercy and grace. The water David was talking about here is the Holy Spirit for He is the living water. You cannot survive without the Spirit of God living in you. Your soul and spirit will always prosper in Him. The Bible says to seek first the Kingdom of God and His righteousness and all of these other things wll be added unto you. So you can see here that you must be obedient to God to prosper and have the things that He wants to give you.

What does the Lord require of you? He will always do His part but there's a part that you must do also. Deut.10:12, God requires of you to fear the Lord your God, walk in His ways and to love Him. Serve Him with all your heart and with all your soul. Joshua 24:14, Honor the Lord and serve Him whole heartily, serve Him and Him alone. We are to serve Him with a willing mind and a deep desire to serve Him because you love Him. You don't serve the Lord because you have to but because you want to. If you know the story of Joseph you can see that God bless him in all that he did. He did not have an easy life for his life was filled with hate from his earthly brothers, but he was a God fearing person and God rewarded him for that. Nothing else really matters outside of serving the Lord and being obedient to Him. For if you do these things then God will bless the rest of you life for He said He would. Why don't you trust Him? The Bible teaches, trust, try and prove the Lord and see if He won't perform the things that He said He would. He will never fail you. There's another command from God that we need to keep. Ps.122:6, All who love the city of Jerusalem will prosper. If you love Jerusalem then you will pray for her. The Lord has told us to pray for the peace of Jerusalem, this is a the command of the Lord God.

I Tim.4:8, Godliness is profitable unto all things having promise of the life that now is and that which is to come. When you live godly we have all of the promises that God has promised and then life eternal for the life to come. I Tim.6:6, Godliness with contentment is great gain. There is a true and faithful saying, that they which have belived in God might be careful to maintain good works. These things are good and profitable unto all. He's saying here, it is profitable to all of My children, those who are faithful and obedient to Him. God said, be ye holy for I am holy, for without holiness you will not see God. You are to cleanse yourself of all filthiness and lusts of the flesh and to live holy and righteous all the days of your life. You are to fear the Lord, which is love. We are to follow peace with all people with holiness. Be holy in all conversations, live sober, righteous and godly in this present world. Ps.92:12, The righteous shall flourish like the palm tree, they shall grow like cedar trees in Lebanon, and they shall be strong and tall. There are great rewards for being obedient to God and keeping His commandments and there will be rewards in the next life. You can never lose by serving God and living for Him. There are trials that we all face but we don't have to face them alone for He is with us all the way. Jesus Christ is the only way to Heaven and the only way to prosper here in the Spirit. If you will study the Scriptures I believe that you will be a changed person. The Bible was writen to show everyone the way to live but if you don't read and study it you will fail. God will give you the knowledge and understanding of His Word as you study. If you want to prosper then you will have to do it God's way.

Things that are made known to us

Seven great certainties that can be known of the believers. Job 19:25-27, For I know that my Redeemer lives and He shall stand at the latter day upon the earth. I myself will see Him with my own eyes. How my heart yearns within me. We can know that our Redeemer lives because He lives within our hearts. We will see Him one day, oh what a day that will be. I believe that is going to happen soon, and I get excited and yearn to look upon His face and to sit down and talk with Him and Him with me. Many have believed because of His Word for all have not seen Him. John 20:29, Jesus said to Thomas, because you have seen Me you have believed but blessed are they that have not seen Me and yet have believed. Believe on the Lord Jesus Christ and you shall be saved. There are many Scriptures that tell us this. There are many more to be saved yet so we have to continue to pray and believe for our children, grand-children and great-grandchildren.

Never give up on anyone but keep striving in the Lord to see them saved and come into the fold. If you believe in your heart that Jesus Christ was born, lived, died and rose from the grave on the third day ascended up to Heaven and then and is coming again, you are saved. Now you have to serve Him, live for Him, be obedient and faithful to Him all the days of your life. You are His child and He is you Father and God. Nothing and no one can ever take that away from you. Only you can walk away from Him for He will not leave you but you can leave Him. I pray you will never forsake Him and go back to your old life in the world.

Rom.8:28, For we know all things work together for good to them that love the Lord and are called according to His purpose. Why do we worry or fret when things don't go the way we think they should or we want them? God is still in control of our lives if you are His child. He knows what He's doing for He never makes a mistake.Now if you walk ouside of His will, His protection or His covering and brings things on yourself then you have a problem. You will surely reap what you sow whether good or bad seeds. This doesn't mean that God won't help you. There are penalties for doing wrong. If you are in His will and things go wrong then He said He would work all things out for your good. That's a promise and knowledge that He has given all of us who are serving Him and loving Him. One thing is for sure, if you love Him then you will serve Him and be obedient and faithful to Him. I love this scripture, II Cor.5:1, For we know that if this earthly house of this tabernacle was dissolved we have a building of God, a house not made by hands but eternal in Heaven. We know when these bodies are gone and decayed we have the Spirit of God living in us and at the resurrection we will be given a new body that will never have to die again. Remember, our body is the temple of God. We know we are to keep them clean, pure and holy and acceptable unto Him. You are not to defile your body in any way for the Spirit of God lives in you and He will not live in a temple messed up and dirty with sin. You can know how to live for it's all in the Word of God. There are many things that we can know from the Holy Words of God. We know that we have to love Him with all of our heart, mind, soul and strength. We know we have to love our neighbor as ourself. We know we have to live holy and righteous in Him. We know we have to please Him and not ourself. We know that when we come to Him He will not turn us away. We know that when we come to Him and ask forgiveness that He forgives all of our sins never to remember them anymore. We know we are to keep all of His commandments and statues.

II Tim.1:12, We know in who we have believed and are persuaded that He is able to keep that which we have committed unto Him against that day. We can know that we are saved and that Jesus Christ is able to keep us from the terrible days that He has told us about, the seven years of the great tribulation that is coming upon this earth after the church, the believers has been caught up with Jesus Christ in the rapture in the clouds to be with Him forever. When He tells us that He is going to keep us then we can count and believe that. He is our salvation and our keeper. I John 3:2, We know we are the children of God and when He shall appear we shall see Him as He is. Verse 14, We know we will pass from death to life if we love the brethren for love is the greatest gift. We may not like a person but we are commanded to love them. We also know we need to seek understanding, knowledge and wisdom from God. Prov.3:13, Happy are they that seek wisdom for they will get understanding and knowledge. All can receive if they only ask. God's wisdom, understanding and knowledge leads to eternal life. John 17:3, This is eternal life that they might know the only true God and Jesus Christ.

We know God's children are married to Jesus Christ

Have you been saved? Have you accepted Jesus Christ as your Lord and Savior? Then you are married to Him. You are the bride of Christ and I believe He's coming soon for His bride. The question is, are you ready, waiting and watching? Isa.62:5, For as a young man marries a virgin, and rejoices over the bride so shall thy God rejoice over you. When you accept Jesus Christ as your Savior then you become married to Him and He rejoices over you for He loves you. Just as we are faithful to our spouses we are to be faithful to God all the days of our lives. II Cor.11:2, God said, I am a jealous God over you with godly jealousy for I have married you to one husband that I may present you as a pure virgin to Christ. You are not to put anyone or anything else before Him. You are to stay true to Him always. It thrills me that He would choose me to be His bride. I feel so unworthy to have such an honor to belong to Him. Rev.19:7, Let us be glad, rejoice and give honor to Him, for the marriage of the Lamb is come and His wife has made herself ready. The wife is the church, the bride of Jesus Christ. Are you among the bride of Christ? I never want a divorce from Him for I intend to serve Him all the days of my life. He's been so good to me all of my life. We are one in Him, He in us and we in Him. I Cor.6:15, Know ye not that your bodies are the members of Christ. Epe.5:30, For we are members of His body, flesh and bones. When you become saved you become one of His and Jesus lives in you. God's Spirit comes into you and lives within your heart and life. He will never leave you but you can stray from Him if you have sin in your life. Rom.7:4, Wherefore My brethren you are become dead to the law by the body of Christ that you should be married to another. Paul is saying, be faithful to the one that was raised from the dead in three days. We are to bring forth fruit unto Him, fruit of the Spirit. We are to do good unto Him, be obedient to His will. We are to have joy, peace, longsuffering, patience, kindness and always be honest. Epe.5;23, Just as the husband is the head of the wife even so Christ is the head of the husband and the church and He's the Savior of the body and soul. So then, Christ is the head of our bodies if we belong to Him. Deut.14:2, For you are a holy people unto the Lord and I have chosen you to be a perculiar people unto Himself. He was talking about Israel here but it's meant for all of the church.

Don't be like the foolish virgins in Matt.25:1-13, Ten were invited to a wedding celebration. They took lamps to meet the bridegroom. Five of them were wise and took oil in their lamps and five of them were foolish and took no oil.While the bridegroom tarried they all slept. At midnight there was a cry made, the bridegroom comes, go out to meet him. All ten virgins rose up and trimmed their lamps. The five foolish ones ask the five wise ones to give them some oil for their lamps for they had none and their lamps went out. But they said no, because we may run out ourselves. Go out and buy some oil for yourselves. While they went out the bridegroom came and those that were ready went in to the marriage celebration and the door was shut. The foolish virgins came back and cried out, Lord, Lord, open the door to us but He answered to them and said, I don't know who you are. Watch therefore for you know not the day or the hour when the Son of man comes. You have to be ready at all times because when Jesus comes back in the rapture for the church, His bride if you're not ready you won't have time to get ready for it will be too late. He said He was coming for those who are ready, waiting and watching for Him. You may even go before the rapture through death but you have to be ready for after death there is no other chance for you to prepare. Many think they have plenty of time but no one knows when Jesus is coming or when death will strike. You don't want to miss Heaven, for nothing here is more important than going to Heaven for eternity with Jesus Christ. Are you ready? If not, today is the day of salvation for you may not have another day so accept Him as your Lord and Savior and serve Him with all your heart, mind, soul and strength. You can do this right where you are right now, just call out to Him.

God's people

We have learned that God's people are peculiar people. We have learned that we are chosen by God and His people are exalted above all nations. We are guided like a flock and we are prepared for service. God's laws are written upon the hearts of His children. Pet.2:9, You are a chosen generation, a royal priesthood, a holy nation, a peculiar people and you shall show forth the praises of Him who has called you out of darkness into His marvelous light. Praise God that He has chosen you. We have so much to praise Him for. James 2:5, God has chosen the poor of this world, rich in faith and heirs to the Kingdom. He chose us before the foundation of the world that we should be holy and without blame before Him in love. He has set aside or apart those who are godly for Himself. The Lord will hear when you call upon Him and He will answer. I Pet. 2:10, The Gentiles were adopted or grafted in to be God's people. They shall be fellow heirs of the same body and partakers of His promises in Christ by the gospel. It was prophesied by Isaiah that the Gentiles shall come to Thy light.

All who love the Lord and serve Him are His children and heirs to His Kingdom. All who call upon the Lord shall be saved. Confess with your mouth, believe in your heart, believe that God raised Jesus Christ from the dead and you shall be saved. God has redeemed His people for He has saved them from their sins by the washing of the blood of Jesus. You are to live in holiness and His righteousness all the days of your life. Jesus Christ is our Redeemer because of the mercies of God the Father. It's a new beginning when you come to Christ and become one of God's children. Jesus is our light and He guides our feet into the path of peace, joy, happiness and then in the end eternal life. I thank God for His salvation, love, mercy and grace. Rev.22:14, Blessed are those that wash their robes that they may have the right to come to the tree of life and enter into the gates of the city.I'm so glad that I'm a part of the family of God. I've been washed in the fountain cleansed by His blood, joined heirs with Jesus as I travel this road. I'm so glad I can sing this song and mean it from the heart. Can you? Listen to His call and heed to it for He loves you.

Master key to Heaven

Keys are instruments that open doors, locks, gates and vehicles and so on. They are symbolic of power, authority and control. There are many keys to blessings and rewards in a Christian's life but only one key to Heaven. Prayer is the key to Heaven but faith unlocks the door. Jesus Christ is the master key to Heaven and the only key by the way that you have to go. There is no other way to enter into the Kingdom of God and Heaven outside of Jesus Christ for He's the only way. Isa. 22;12, The key to the house of David I will lay on his shoulder so He will open the doors that no one shall shut and He shall shut and no one can open for His children. Rev.3:7, These things say that are holy, true and that has the key of David. Jesus opens and no one closes and He shuts and no one opens. He has the power to do all things. Matt.16:19, Jesus Christ will give to His children the keys for He is the master key to Heaven. Without Him in your heart and life you have no key. He is the way, the truth and the life and no one comes to the Father but by Him. You may have some of the other keys that we'll be talking about but without Him you won't make Heaven your new home forever. You can have the key to blessings here on this earth and still miss Heaven. You may be saying or thinking, how can this be? We will see as we study further. Matt.28:18, All authority has been given Jesus in Heaven and on earth. He is the key to salvation and to Heaven. You have to be born again first of all and then give yourself totally to Jesus and follow Him. Rev.22:13, Jesus said, I am Alpha and Omega, the beginning and the end, the first and the last. There are conditions to enter in. You have to be washed in the blood of the Lamb, which is Jesus. When you accept Him as your Lord and Savior and you ask Him to forgive you then you are washed and He cleans you up but you have to stay clean. You are to live holy, obedient to Him, be faithful to Him and be doers of the Word and not just hearers only. You must endure to the end to be saved. Once you come to Christ you have to live for Him for you can't live any way the flesh wants you to live for you belong to Him now. When you accept Him in your heart and life you become a new person for the old person is done away with in Christ Jesus. Rev.1:18, Jesus holds the key to death and hell for He holds the key to all things.

Qualities to keeps us on the way to Heaven

Prayer is the greatest force and the greatest weapon to keep us in line with the Word of God. The prayers of the saints are precious. You have to have faith to believe what you pray for. You have to work but works without faith is dead. You have to continue to seek God. I Chr.16:11, Seek the Lord and His strength, seek His face continually, and pray always. We are to pray always with all prayer and supplication for all the saints. The Bible says to pray without ceasing, stay in a prayerful spirit. Watch and pray so that you won't fall into temptations. Our flesh gets weak but God is our strength so we need to always call on Him and ask for His strength. He said to call upon Him and He will answer. He said that He would go with you through your trouble for He is a very present help in time of troubles. Seek Him in everything you do. So many fall into temptations because they don't seek the Lord first. Financial problems come from not seeking God many times. Then when these problems come upon you it can and will affect your marriage, your family, and your walk with the Lord. We need to make sure that nothing hinders our walk and relationship with the Lord. You can't make it through this life without talking to the Lord. He wants to have a close relationship with His children. The more you talk to Him the closer you will get. II Chr.7:14, If My people who are called by My name will humble themselves and pray, seek My face and turn from their wicked ways then I will hear from Heaven, forgive their sins and heal their land. Always seek God and pray, turn from all sin and grow spiritually in Him. We are to fast and pray for there are things that don't happen without fasting and praying. Matt.17:21, Howbeit this kind does not go out but by prayer and fasting. When you deny yourself food and other things that you enjoy doing for the sake of others or some need that you have, God will bless and honor you. If you have never fasted you have no idea how it feels to be in the presence of the Lord when you deny yourself for spiritual things of the Lord. You grow stronger in Him, your physical body feels good for when you do without foods it cleanses your body. It's really a detoxation to your body. In a fast He will show you things that you don't normally see and know. Fasting prepares you for a deeper relation with Him and more powerful ministry. We will look at a few fastings in the Bible and see how God moved and used them. Do you want God to move in your life into deeper things?

Ex. 34:28, Before Moses wrote the Ten Commandments he fasted forty days and nights. He didn't eat bread or drink water. Now, before you try something like this you make sure it's the will of God, for you can live without food for a while but not without water. If God leads you to do it then He will keep you for it will be for a real dire need or reason. Moses was lead of God and He kept him. Daniel 10:3, Daniel fasted for three weeks on vegetables before God gave him the vision of what was coming in the last days. You can find these visions in chapters 10 through 12. He had to prepare himself for these visions of God. Luke 4:1, Jesus fasted forty days and nights, He ate or drank nothing while in the wilderness, this was preparing Him for the temptations of the devil for forty days and nights in the wilderness. The devil knew that He was probably hungry and He would give in but Jesus never gave in to him. Jesus told him, you can't live on bread alone but by every Word of God. Jesus always had the right Words for the devil and the devil had to flee. I encourage you to read this scripture and get the full account of Jesus being tempted and how He resisted all of the temptations of the devil. Jesus said, draw near to God and He will draw near to you, resist temptation and the devil, and he will flee from you. Jesus never told us to do anything that He hadn't done before Himself. He is our leader and out guide, our model to follow.

There a key of power and Jesus holds that key. There's power in the name of Jesus and His blood. All power and authority is given to Him in Heaven and on earth. He gives us power and strength. Luke 10;19, Behold, I give unto you the power to walk on scorpions and serpents and over all the power of the enemy and nothing shall by any means harm you. WOW what power! Isa.40:31, They that wait upon the Lord shall renew their strength. Acts 1:8, You shall receive power after the Holy Spirit shall come upon you. Acrs 4; 33, Great power was given the apostles and they were witnesses of the Lord's resurrection and great grace was upon them all. Dan.11:32, The people that know their God shall be strong and exploit, take action. When you know God personally you will pray and fast and have power in the Holy Ghost. The more you fast and pray the closer to the Lord you will get and He will give you the power to do great things and the things that He wants you to do. We can do all things through Christ Jesus.

There are keys to giving. God has asked for only ten percent of our first fruits. But He has told us in many scriptures to give and it shall be given unto you and it is more blessed to give than to receive. Prov.11:25, The liberal soul shall be made fat and they that water shall be watered unto them. If you give freely to others then it will come back to you. To give liberally means not to give grudgingly or complain about what you give but to give it out of your heart and because you want to give. If you complain then you will lose your blessing of giving. Prov.22:9, They that have a bountiful eye shall be blessed. Mal.3:10, Bring all of your tithes into the storehouse and I will open up the windows of Heaven and pour you out a blessing that you won't have room to receive. How many Christians do you know that have been blessed so much that they don't have room to receive it? We need to check ourselves to see what's wrong with us. What more can we do, where are we failing? Blessings don't have to be money only. So you get discouraged think about all of the blessings and things that the Lord has rained down upon you. All good things come from the Lord. Luke 6:38, Give and it shall be given to you, pressed down, shaken together and running over shall men give to your bosom. God uses people to bring blessings to us many times. Whatever good happens to you, always give God the glory and thanks for them.

I Cor.9:6, They that sows bountifully shall also reap bountifully. If you want to receive then you have to give. Some say, I don't have enough to give. The Bible says to give out of your needs and you will be blessed. As far as tithing, you can't afford not to give for it is a command of thr Lord to give the tenth of what you earn or get. You owe that to Him, and if you don't give it to Him then you are robbing God and no thieves will enter into the Kingdom of Heaven. You can read all of this in the book of MalachI, the last book in the Old Testament. Prov.26:27, Whosoever gives to the poor there shall be no lack. What God is saying here is, He will meet all of your needs when you take care of the poor and needy. The doors of Heaven will be opened unto you and He will pour you out blessings and fill your every need. You have to have this key of giving in order to be blessed to the maximum by God. God will bless all of those who are His followers and who are His children but in order for Him to pour you out a blessing that you don't have room to receive you have to give as He has said.

There is a key of caring and intercession we must have also. We are to care for others and stand in prayer for them. We are our brothers and sisters keeper and we are to stand in the gap for them when they are going through troubles and sorrows. John 17:9, Jesus prayed for the church, He said, I pray for them not for the world but for them which You, God, has given Me for they are Your's. He was talking about His children and you are His child if you have been born again and are washed in His blood and following Him. Moses prayed for

Israel. Hezekiah prayed for the people. Jesus prayed for Simon Peter that his faith would stand strong and fail not. Luke 22; 32, Jesus told him that satan desired to have him and sift him as wheat. That's what the devil would like to do to us, all of the believers of Jesus Christ. That's why we always need to pray, fast and interceed for each other. Pray for others needs as well as yours. James 5; 16, The effectual fervent prayer of the righteous avails much. God hears our prayers and He will answer. It may not be in our timing when we want things but He is never too late for He is always on time and He never makes a mistake. God has given us these keys so we can use them and whatever you do don't lose them. You can lose the key to salvation and with it all of the other keys. Stay in the Lord Jesus Christ and He will keep you for He's the keeper of our salvation.

Revelation chapters 2 and 3 Jesus warns us seven times about overcoming and enduring to the end. You can't just start with the Lord and walk with Him for a while and then quit but you have to endure to the very end in Him. The end is what? You have to continue in Him until He comes after us in the rapture or you go by the grave through death, which ever comes first. Jesus said these Words, They that overcome I will not blot their names out of the Lamb's book of life. This tells us that if we don't follow Him to the end then He will take our names out of the book of life. If your name isn't in that book then you won't make Heaven and hell will be your final home. If this happens then you will lose your key to Heaven and eternal life. Jesus said, to them that overcome I will grant them to sit with Me on the throne with My Father. This surely does away with the teaching once saved always saved, doesn't it? If you couldn't lose your salvation then He would have never said that your name could be blotted out of the book. It had to be written in the book at one time to be blotted out. Does this mean that we never make a mistake? Of course not, for we are not perfect but we are striving to be perfect as He is perfect. This doesn't mean that we have to be afraid of losing our salvation every time we make a mistake. But if you continue to sin willfully after you have accepted Christ as your Savior then you can lose it. When God reveals to us that we're doing wrong then we need to ask forgiveness and don't repeat that same wrong again and He will forgive. They that know to do good and doeth it not to them it is sin. If you have to wonder or guess whether a thing is wrong then the best thing for you to do is not do it. Pray about it first and if you feel in your spirit that it's not right then leave it undone. God will lead and show you what is right and what's wrong. Rev.3; 19, Jesus said, As many as I love I rebuke and chasten so be zealous and repent. Verse 16, He said, because you are either cold or hot and you are lukewarm I will spew you out of My mouth. In other words, you make Me sick, for you are trying to live two lives and you can't do that. You are either for Me or against Me. You are on one side or the other. There are only two sides, Me or the devil. Either I'm your Father or the devil is your father. There's no in between, no such thing as straddling the fence. Verse 22, Listen to Me and do what I say for I will never leave or forsake you as long as you abide in Me.

Rev.3:11, Behold I come quickly, hold fast to what you have so that no one can steal your crown. If it were not possible to lose your crown or keys to eternal life Jesus would have not told us this. We are heirs to the Kingdom of God so let's not lose our crown, rewards and keys to Heaven. Jesus is coming back for His children and I believe soon. All who endure to the end will be saved. Be faithful to Him and to your brothers and sisters in the Lord. Be ready for you won't have time to get ready when He comes in the rapture for His church. He's coming in a twinkling of an eye and we'll be gone from this earth to meet Him in the clouds of glory. Hold on to your keys and endure to the end. God bless you and keep you in His care always. Amen

CHAPTER TEN

God's Grace Is Sufficient

CHAPTER 10

God's Grace is Sufficient

Epe.4:7, But every one of us is given according to the measure of the gift of Christ... Whatever the gift, that amount of grace is given us. Verse 11, These are Spiritual gifts from God. And He gave some apostles, some prophets, some evangelists, some pastors and some teachers. Why were these gifts given? They were given for the perfectiong of the saints, for the work of the ministry and for the edifying of the body of Christ. How long were these gifts for? Verse 13, Til we all come in the unity of faith and of the knowledge of of the Son of God unto a perfect man unto the measure of the statue of the fullness of Christ. Meaning, until we all grow up to be a mature Christian and be in unity with Jesus Christ and have Spiritual knowledge of Him and perfect ourselves to His likeness and to become in the fullness of Him. So this means that it will last forever until we come into the Kingdom of Heaven for we will not be in perfection until we are changed from this mortal body to a mortality one. So we need to continue to grow in Christ Jesus until He comes and then we will be like Him forever. We won't need to have faith anymore for we will be there with Him forever. What then is spiritual growth? Verses 14-15, Henceforth we be no more children tossed to and fro and carried away with every wind of doctrine by the words of men and women and cunning craftiness whereby they lie in wait to deceive, but speaking the truth in love may grow up into Him in all things which is the head even Christ. From whom the whole body fitly joins together and compacted by, that every joint supplies according to the effectual working in the measure of every part maketh increase of the body unto the edifying of itself in love. The gift of faith will have to work as long as we are in this body and in this world. We have to live by faith for without faith we cannot please God. As long as we live we are to continue to grow in Christ to be like Him. It doesn't stop with just an individual body but it has to reach the whole church body. We are to help others grow in the body of Christ as well as ourselves. We are are called to do a work in the body of the church and all are fitly joined together. Not everyone is a hand or a foot but they have to work together to make up a whole part.

Epe.4; 6, I beceech you brethren that you walk worthy of the vocation in which you are called. Be humble and gentle, be patience with each other making allowances for each others faults because of your love. Always keep yourselves united in the Holy Spirit and bind yourselves together with peace. We all all one body and we have the same Spirit and have been called to the same glorious future. One Lord, one faith and one baptism. One God and Father who is over all and in all living through all. Paul was begging us to walk the walk that God has called us and to be sure we are worthy of the work that God has called us to do. Live a life that is worthy, always follow the direction of our Lord and Savior Jesus Christ. Don't be critical or judge others but be understanding when others make mistakes because none of us are perfect but we have to strive to be perfect. We are to be patience and humble with each other. If we want to win others we have to work together in unity and peace. Our work ie never finished here until Jesus comes. So don't give up or grow weary for we will reap if we faint not. God's grace is divine and sufficient and is freely given to all who will accept it. He will not lead you where He won't keep you. I Cor.15:10, God's grace impowers us for service. By the grace of God I am what I am and His grace which was bestowed upon me was not in vain but I labored more abundantly than they all, yet not I but the grace of God which was with me. God gets all the glory for whatever we do for Him. II Tim.2:1, Be strong in the grace of Jesus Christ. Grace enables us to lead a simple life but a good one.

II Cor.1:12, For our rejoicing is this, the testimony of our conscience, that in simplicity and godly sincerity not with fleshly wisdom but by the grace of God, we have had our conversation in the world but more abundantly to you. God didn't call us to live high and mighty as some of the world do, but He simplied things for us to live godly, be sincere, keep a good conscience and have godly wisdom which all comes by the grace of God. Much grace is given to the humble and meek. James 4:6, He gives more grace wherefore He said, God resists the proud but gives grace to the humble. The Bible says that a proud look comes before a fall. There is never a thing we should be proud about because whatever good we do all the glory goes to the Father. Ps.138:6, Though the Lord is high He looks down on the lowly and the humble, but the proud doesn't come from the Lord for that's one of the devil's traits. If you want more grace of the Lord Jesus then you have be more humble. Grace will see you through and will keep you through for it is sufficient for all your needs. II Cor.12:9, When Paul was going through much with the thorn in his flesh and had prayed three times the Lord said, My grace is sufficient for you for My strength is made perfect in your weakness. When we are weak and feel we can't go on then His strength in us is strong. He said to lean upon Him and trust Him in all things for He will carry us through and make a way that seems to be no way. He has done this for me so many times. There are times when everything looks so bleak and nothing is going right for us, but hold on for help is coming. Just remember what He said, My grace is sufficient for you. He knows what you're going through and what you need and He will be right on time for you because He is never too late. It may seem to be too late for you but He knows what's best for you and when to give it to you. Just wait upon the Lord and trust Him an all things.

Grace is a mark of faithful servants and ministers. II Cor.6:1, We beseech you not to accept the grace of God in vain. You must believe what you are teaching and preaching and work diligently with the Lord. It is the minsters duty to exhort and persuade their hearers to accept the grace that is offered to them. Work for God and His glory and for lost souls and for their good. They should be faithful to God and their labor will be effectual. Never be conceited or think more highly of yourselves but work and give all the glory to God the Father who has called you into His ministry. Do not be argue mental, but be understanding and long suffering like Jesus was. Do what you do in love and above all be truthful to the Word of God. Always be sincere with the Word of God and don't compromise but have the knowledge and wisdom from God to be able to reach everyone. Stay on guard and test the spirits to make sure you are receiving the right Spirit, which is of God. Today is the day of salvation so do whatever it takes to win souls. Don't give any offense as to hinder a soul from getting saved. Endeavor in all things to approve yourselves faithful to the ministry and to God. Thank God for His mercy, grace and love and for trusting you in His ministry and for calling you to do a work. Do it with all of your might, give it all you've got and remember, Jesus Christ is your example. Let the Holy Ghost lead and guide you all the way. Don't lean on your own understanding but trust God in all things. He will not lead you where He won't keep you for His grace is sufficient. Ps.103:8-12, The Lord is compassionate and gracious, slow to anger and always abounding in love. He never changes for He's the same today as yesterday and He will be the same tomorrow. He will not always accuse nor will He harbor His anger forever. He does not treat us as our sins deserve or repay us according to our iniquities. For if He did none of us would make it into the kingdom of Heaven for we have all sinned and fallen short of the glory of God. Thank God for His love, mercy, grace, patience and long sufferings for all of us. For as high as the heavens are above the earth so is His love for those who fear Him. As far as the east is from the west, so far He has removed our transgressions from us. Rom.8:1, There is therefore now no condemnation to them that are in Christ Jesus who walk not after the flesh but after the Holy Spirit. Our sins are gone through the blood and name of Jesus Christ.

Ezra 9; 13, What happened to us as a result of our evil deeds and great guilt and yet our God has punished us less than we deserved and have given us a remnant like this. The grace of God could never be more beautifully described. As sinners we have caused Him pain yet He responds to us differently than we do to others who hurt us. When someone does us wrong and hurts us we feel we need to repay back the same way but not Jesus for He's so loving and has forgiveness to us for everything if we would just ask Him. We need to do unto others as we would love for them to do unto us.We deserve God's wrath and punishment but He gives us compassion, love, mercy, grace and forgiveness instead. He treats us the very opposite way than what we deserve. I praise Him that He has not given me what I really deserve for all the wrong I have done in this life. He forgives and forgets and continues to love, for His love endures forever.

Rom.12:9-21, Paul tells us how Christians should live. Love must be sincere, hate what is evil, cling to what is good. Be devoted to one another in brotherly love, honor each other above yourselves. Never be lacking in zeal but keep your spiritual favor serving the Lord. Be joyful in hope, patient in afflictions and faithful in prayer. Share with God's people who are in need. Practice hospitality, bless those who persecute you and and curse not. Rejoice with them that rejoice and mourn with them that mourn. Live in harmony with each other. We have been taught how to live according to the Word of God so lets do it with all our might, with God's help. Let us be eager to do good and let us keep our feeling of doing good. Be of the same mind one with another. Do not be proud but be willing to associate with people of low positions. Do not be conceited or feel better than thou. Never repay anyone back with evil for the evil they have done to you but pay back with good to them. Do not revenge yourselves but rather give place unto wrath, for it is written, vengeance is Mine says the Lord for I will repay. If your enemy is hungry feed him and if he is thirsty give them to drink for in doing this you heap coals of fire on his head. Do not be overcome with evil but overcome evil with good. When you do good to those who do you wrong it will make them think and feel bad about what they have done to you. They will see that you are different and this could cause a change in them.

Matt.5:7,11-12, Blessed are the merciful for they shall obtain mercy. Blessed are you when people insult you, persecute you and falsely accuse you and say all manner of evil against you for My name sake. Rejoice and be exceedingly glad because great is your reward in Heaven. For in the same way they persecuted the prophets before you.

Jesus called us to a higher standard of life and righteousness that can only come from walking close to Him. We should always do what is pleasing to Him and not ourselves.

20 ways we can aim and love each other the way God loves us. God has given us grace, love and mercy so that we can show the same to one another.
1 - Love must be sincere
2 - Hate what is evil
3 - Cling to what is good
4 - Be devoted to one another
5 - Honor one another
6 - Have compassion one with another
7 - Keep your spiritual zeal or feeling
8 - Be joyful in hope
9 - Be patient in afflictions
10 - Be faithful in prayer
11 - Share with people who are in need
12 - Bless others that persecute you
13 - Do not curse those who do you evil or wrong
14 - Rejoice with them that rejoice
15 - Cry and mourn with those who cry and mourn
16 - Live in peace with everyone if at all possible
17 - Be not conceited or proud
18 - Do not repay evil for evil
19 - Do what's right in the eyes of the Lord and everyone.
20 - Grow in love for God and others everyday and thank God for His grace, love and mercy.

God never stops loving us

Ps.30:5, For His anger lasts only for a moment but His favor for a lifetime, weeping may last for the night but joy comes in the morning. His love last forever here and in Heaven. He never stops loving us. He loves us so much that He gave His only begotten Son to die for us so that we can live eternal and have a good and abundant life here on this earth as well. God is love and it's pure without spot and never ending. Not many of us in this fallen world will experience a human relationship that remains steadfast and loving from the time we were born to the moment we die. Friends come and they go. Not all parents love unconditionally. Children break our hearts, even many spouses don't stick around for better or worse. We seem to love conditionally but God's love is unconditional. He loves us when we aren't even lovable.What a profound comfort it is to know our Creator, the lover of our souls will never stop loving us. God will be angry when we sin and He will discipline us because He loves us and wants us to do what is right. He never hold a grudge for His nature is gracious not wrathful. We can rejoice for we are utterly secure in God's everlasting and unfailing love as long as we are in Him. His love will never be separated from us but we can separate our love from Him if we fall away and stop serving Him. Ps.36:7-10, David said, how priceless is Your unfailing love. Both high and low among men we find refuge in the shadow of Your wings. We feast on the abundance of your house and it gives us to drink from Your River of delights. For with and in You is the fountain of life, in Your light we see the light, for You are the light and the life. We can depend on Your continued love to those who know You and Your righteousness to the upright in heart. Your love O God reaches to the Heavens and Your faithfulness to the skies. God not only loves us but He is faithful also.We can always find refuge in Him for He never leave or forsakes His children. As I have said before, His love, mercy and grace endures forever.

God's orders for Christians

Ps.37:8, Refrain from anger and turn from wrath, do not fret for it leads only to evil. You don't get anger and wrath from God it's from the devil himself for he is evil. No evil ever comes from the Lord. There are times when we get upset with others and we can be angry but sin not. Never let anger turn to hate or to wrath for then it is sin. Verses 30-31, The mouth of the righteous utters wisdom and their tongue speaks what is right and just for the law of God is in their heart. The Lord loves the just and faithful ones and will not forsake them and He will always forgive and protect them for ever. David said not to let the sun go down on your anger. Make sure you make things right with another before you go to sleep at night. Ps.33:18, Our hope is in His unfailing love. The Lord is good and His love endures forever. His love is so great that He keeps us. We could never keep ourselves in this flesh we live in. God has angels assigned to each one of His children to protest us wherever we go whatever we do as long as we stay in Him and do His will and commands. God has given His children and followers commands to follow and we are to be faithful and obedient to Him. He has never given us anything hard to do. If you will love Him and put Him first place in your heart and life then your life here will be a happy and prosperous one and you will want to follow His commands. It hurts Him when His children aren't faithful to Him just like we that are parents are hurt when our children are rebellious towards us and refuse to be obedient.

Wisdom is Supreme

What is wisdom? The Webster's dictionary says, sound judgment, discernment, careful, dispensing justice, insight, understanding, brilliance, sense, the ability to understand inner qualities or relationships. I Cor.3:19-20, For the wisdom of this world is foolishness with God for it is written, He takes the wise in their own craftiness. And again, the Lord knows the thoughts of the wise that they are vain. This wisdom descended not from above but is earthly, sensual and devilish. True wisdom comes from God above. James 3:17, The wisdom from above is first pure then peaceable, gentle and easy to be entreated and full of mercy and good fruits without partiality and without hypocrisy. This is the wisdom we are looking for and we have to have, not man's wisdom for that is of the world. Luke 21:15, If any of you lack wisdom ask of God. He said He would give you a mouth of wisdom which all of your adversaries shall not be able to resist. This is one way we can learn to control our tongues is from the wisdom of God. God's wisdom cannot be valued with gold, onyx or the sapphire. Wisdom is better than rubies. Happy are they that find wisdom and who get understanding. If you are wise you will search for the wisdom of God and you will be strengthened. God gives to the good and just persons in His sight, wisdom, knowledge and joy. Ecc.2:26, But to the sinners He gives travail to gather and heap up so that He can give it to the good and righteous ones. God will take from the evil to give to His children is what the preacher is saying here. It's only what you do for Christ that will last; for everything else is in vain and sooner or later you will lose it. Dan.3:21, He gives wisdom to the wise and knowledge to them that know understanding.The fear of the Lord is the beginning of wisdom and to depart from evil is understanding. Wisdom is knowing that the ways of the Lord are right and that the just shall walk in them. To be just we have to walk with God for He lives in us and us in Him. Only God is just and righteous but we have to walk in His righteousness for our righteousness is as filthy rags. The only good thing in us is Jesus Christ.What ranks in God's economy is not a sharp mind but a discerning heart and spirit. The only thing that Solomon asked God for was wisdom, when he became king, God blessed him tremendously for choosing such a spiritual and meaningful gift. I Kings 3;5-14, Solomon assures his listeners that they too will receive honor, grace and joy if they would diligently pursue wisdom, no matter what the cost. It does cost you something to follow Christ. It cost you yourself, for you have to die daily to self to follow Him. You can't live to please yourself for you were bought with a great price, the blood of Jesus Christ. You are not your own anymore for you belong to Him if you have accepted Him in your heart and life. This is why we need the wisdom of God and His understanding. Prov.8:35-36, For whosoever finds Me finds life and receives favor from the Lord but whosoever fails to find Me harms themselves, all who hate me, (wisdom) love death. Those who lack good judgment and fail to pursue wisdom, folly will follow them. God is saying, this is foolishness and lack of good sense. If you don't follow God then you will follow the devil. There is a quote that was written by Reinhold Niebuhr in 1926 which says, God grant me the serenity to accept the things that I can't change, courage to change the things that I can and the wisdom to know the difference. Wisdom enables us to know the difference between what gives life and what leads to death. Blessed are the ones who find wisdom. Wisdom is found on the lips of the discerning ones, the wise ones. James 1:5-6, If anyone lacks wisdom let them ask of God who gives generously freely to all without finding fault. Ask and it shall be given you. Wisdom is supreme so get it for it is from God. Wisdom will save you from the ways of the wicked and evil one. Reads Proverbs Chapter 1 about the wisdom of God. Whosoever will listen to the Words of God will live in safety and be at ease without fear of harm. Those with wisdom store up knowledge and a person of understanding has wisdom. The mouth of the righteous brings forth wisdom with humility for all good things come from God. The teaching of the wise is a fountain of life. The wisdom of the prudent, careful or discreet is to give thought to their ways. The wise will think about what they are doing, what they say and where they go. Wisdom rest in the heart of the discerning Christian. Discernment is a gift of God.A person of wisdom guides their mouth and is careful what they speak. The fear of the Lord teaches wisdom for when you fear the Lord you will walk close to Him, for to fear Him is to love Him. A person who has wisdom discerns from these two things that the Lord hates. Prov.17:15 and verse 24, He that justifies the wicked and he that condemns the just, they are both abominations unto the Lord. A discerning person keeps wisdom in view. They know the difference in the guilty and the just and know how to handle them. The fountain of wisdom is a bubbling brook. Col.4:5, Walk in wisdom to those who are on the outside, for we who are the family of God should always show the lost the way to Jesus Christ and to life. We are to make the best of every opportunity we have to seek and get the lost saved. We can't save them but we can show them the way.

There are sixty do nots in Proverbs .1:8-31, Do not forsake your mother's teaching, do not go along with sinners, and do not set foot on their paths. Do not forsake My teaching, do not lean on your own understanding, do not be wise in your own eyes and do not despise the Lord's discipline. Do not resent His rebukes, do not let sound judgment and discernment out of your sight. Do not fear sudden disaster or ruin that overtakes the wicked, do not withhold good from those who deserve it, do not put off until tomorrow what you can do today and do not plot against your neighbor. Do not accuse a person for no reason and do not envy a violent person or choose any of their ways. More do nots in chapter 4:4-25, Do not forget My Words or swerve from them, do nor forsake wisdom, do not set foot on the path of the wicked or walk in the ways of the evil ones, do not travel on the way of the evil and do not let My Words out of your sight. Chapter 5:7,8 and 25, Do not turn away from what I say, do not go near the door of an adulterous and do not lust after them. Chaper 8:33, Do not ignore My instructions and wisdom. 9:8, Do not rebuke a mocker for he will hate you. 20:13 and 22, Do not love sleep or you will grow poor and do not say, I'll pay you back for the wrong, for God says revenge is Mine I will repay. Chapter 22:22-28, Do not exploit or use, the poor because thay are poor, do not crush the needy in court, do not make friends with a hot tempered person, do not associate with one easily angered and do not shake hands in a pledge or put up security for debts and do not move a boundary stone or line set up by your fore fathers. 23:3:31, Do not crave a ruler's delicacies for it is deception, do not wear yourself out to be rich, do not eat the food of a stingy person, do not crave their food, do not speak to a fool for he will scorn you and make fun of your words, do not withhold discipline from your child and do not let your heart envy sinners. Do not join those who drink too much wine or gorge themselves on meat, which are glottens and drunkards, do not despise your mother when she is old and do not gaze at wine when it is red, when it sparkles in a cup when it goes down smoothly. In chapter 24 you will finds these do nots. Do not envy wicked ones, do not desire their company, do not lie in wait like an outlaw against a righteous person's house, do not raid their dwelling place, do not gloat when your enemy falls, do not let your heart rejoice, do not fret over evil ones or be envious of them and do not join with the rebellious. Do not testify against your neighbor without a cause or use your lips to deceive and do not say, I'll do to them what they did to me. 25:6-9, Do not exalt yourself in the king's presence, do not claim a place among great men, do not bring hastily to court and do not betray another person's confidence. Chapter 26 and 27, Do not answer a fool according to their folly, do not boast about tomorrow for you don't know what a day may bring, do not forsake your friend and the friend of you father and do not go to your brother's house when disaster strikes. Chapters 30 and 31, Do not slander a servant to his master and do not spend your strength on women. There are some of these do nots mentioned more than once. Listen to these proverbs and you who are wise and will shine like the brightness of the heavens. Dan.12:3, Get wisdom and live.

The wise will follow Christ

Prov.1:5, A wise person wil hear and increase learning and a person of understanding shall attain unto wise counsel. They will listen and heed to wise instructions. The fear of the Lord is the beginning of wisdom and understanding. Fools despise wisdom and instructions. A fool is a person who lacks good sense or judgment. They are a dummy, a dodo, a dope, an adoit, moron, loser, lunatic and even a hard head. If sinners try to entice you to follow them, never concent to them or follow them. Resist temptations, resist the devil and draw near to God and the devil will have to leave. Being tempted is not sin for it's when you yield to temptation that it becomes sin. Be careful not to follow the wrong people but follow Christ. Rom.6:13, Don't yield your members as instruments of unrighteousness unto sin but yield yourselves wholly to God and your members as instruments of righteousness unto God. Don't use your hands, feet, mouth, eyes, ears or any part of your body to the things of this world of sin. Be careful what you let your eyes see on TV, books, movies or upon any lusts of the flesh. Don't listen to dirty jokes or engage in any bad conversations. Keep your whole being upon the things of God, have a righteous and holy living. Follow Christ and you will be wise and live eternally with Him and all of the saints of God. Epe.6; 13, Put on the whole armor of God so you can be able to stand in the evil day and having done all to stand, stand. Be careful lest you be led away with the errors and mistakes of the wicked and fall away from your steadfastness with God. Beware of the devil's cunning ways for you can fall from grace if you turn from serving God and following Him. Don't walk in the way of sinners, stay away from their path for they run to evil and the ways of the devil. The Bible tells us to be a separate people to keep ourselves unspotted from the world. If you are among the wrong people you can be tempted to join their evil ways and fall back into sin again. II Pet.3:31, You shall eat of the fruit of your own way and be filled with your own devices. If you sow good seeds then you will reap a good harvest of good things in life but if you sow bad seeds then you will reap a bad harvest. You will reap what you sow whether good or bad. God has warned us to listen and heed to His

Words, be obedient and faithful to Him and we can live a quiet and peaceful life. It doesn't mean that we will never have a problem or have any troubles in this life but that He will be with us through it all and give you peace in the midst of the storm. Prov.11:19, Just as righteousness tends to life so to those that pursue evil to their own death. You have a choice. You will hear some say, I don't believe that a loving God would send someone to hell. He doesn't for you send your own self because everyone has a choice to serve God and have eternal life or serve the devil and end up in eternal damnation in hell. In God's Word He has told us how to get to both places. The Bible is the road map to Heaven. Jesus Christ is the only wy to Heaven for there is no other way, He is the truth, the way and the life and no one can come to the Father but by Him. There are only two places to choose, Heaven or hell. Which road and way will you take? The preparation time is now while you are still living for after death it will all be over for you will go to one or the other places. Why not make your plans to go to Heaven. Epe.18:4, The soul that sinneth shall surely die. For the wages of sin is death but the gift of God is eternal life through Jesus Christ our Lord and Savior. Isa.59:2, Sin will separate you from God. Your sin will hide God's face from you so that He will not hear you. Heb.2:3, How shall we escape if we neglect so great salvation of the Lord Jesus Christ? I Pet. 4:18, If the righteous scarcely be saved where shall the ungodly and sinners appear? This is a very serious question of Peter. You need to follow Him always, all the way. If you are wise you will follow Him. Only Jesus can give you the peace that passes all other understanding when you are going through the trials and troubles in this life. He said to trust, try and prove Him to see if He wouldn't do what He said He would do.

Jesus Christ is indispensable. He will never be done away with for He has always been and He will always be. Gal.1:4, He gave Himself for our sins that He might deliver us from this present world to the will of God and our Father. He gave Himself for that He might redeem us from all iniquity and putify unto us Himself a peculiar people zealous of good works. He is the good shepherd and He gave His life for the sheep. He died for all and it's up to each individual to accept Him and follow Him or deny Him. He is our only interceeder to God the Father for He is ever interceding for His children, the church. Luke 22:32, Jesus prayed for the weak for He said, I have prayed for you that your faith fail not and when you are converted, strengthen your brethren. He prayed for the weak believers and we are to do the same to help them. Just as He stands in the gap for us we are to do the same for all in need, especially the weak in faith. Luke 23:34, Jesus prayed for His enemies and said, Father forgive them for they know not what they do and we are to pray for our enemies and all who come against us. He has shown us how to pray and who to pray for. John 14:16, He prayed for a comforter for He said, I will pray to the Father that He will send a comforter to abide with you forever. Thank God for the Holy Spirit that is the Comforter to lead and guide us as well as protect us from the evil of this world. If you are His child then He lives within you and keeps you always. Jesus knew He was going away to Heaven to be with His Father and He knew that we couldn't make it on our own so He prayed to God the Father to send the comforter, the Holy Spirit to help us. We can't see Him but we know He's with us because we can feel Him. Praise God. John 17 is the love chapter of Jesus praying for His children because of the love He has for us. He prayed a special prayer for the church. He prayed to God and said, I pray not for the world but for all of the believers and followers that God has given Me for they belong to God. He didn't leave us comfortless, praise His holy name. He will save all who call upon His name and come to Him for it is His will that none perish but all have eternal life. Jesus loves to make intercession for His children for He cares for you and He wants the very best for you. He cares for our safety and well being.

Jesus is the only remedy and way to be saved. John 3;16, For God so loved the world that He gave His only begotten Son that whosoever believes in Him should not perish but have everlasting life. They that hear My Words and believes on Him that sent Me has everlasting life, Jesus said in John 5:24. He said, I am the resurrection and the life and they that believe on Me and He that sent me shall live. Jesus said, I am the bread of life, come to Him and you will never be hungry and you will never thirst again for He will give you that living water. He is the light of the world and He is all you need. He is our spiritual nourishment, the food that gives us strength for He is the bread of life and the one who can quench your thirst forever. Ps.13:5, He prepares a table before us in the presence of our enemies and anoints our head with oil, our cup runs over. Jesus anoints us Himself. When you come to Him your joy will be filled because He is joy and it remains in you. You can be filled with the fulfillment of the Lord and His love. He loves you with an everlasting love.

Jesus is the only source of truth, John 6; 68, Jesus has these Words of eternal life. His Word is all truth. There is no salvation in any other name for there is no other name under Heaven that anyone can be saved. All hope of eternal life is built on Him and in Him. No other foundation can anyone lay that has been laid but on Jesus Christ. He's the only way, the only salvation and the only hope and source. Phil.2:9-11, God highly exalted Him and has given Him a name above all names, that at the name of Jesus every knee shall bow of things in Heaven and in earth and under the earth. Every tongue shall confess that Jesus Christ is Lord to the glory of the Father. Rev.19:16, He has written on His thigh and His vesture, King of kings and Lord of lords. Jesus is the only foundation, He is our Rock and Fortress, He is the light of our salvation and the strength of your life and mine. He is a very present help in time of trouble for He's always there with us. Isa.12:2, For the Lord Jehovah is my strength, salvation and song. He's the one who we can always lean on for He never fails and He is never indispensable.

Jesus is the only door for He said, I am the door and by Me if anyone shall enter in they shall be saved and go in and find pasture. You will be satisfied for you shall find food and drink that will always sustain you. He said that He will keep us safe from that evil day to come. The day He's talking about is the great tribulation when the anti-christ shall reign after Jesus has taken His church out by the rapture of the church. If you follow Jesus He said that He would give you life and life more abundantly. Rev.3:8, Jesus said, I have set before you an open door which no man can close. Jesus is that opened door and no one but you can close it. Jesus aid, I am the door of the sheep, the way, the truth and the light and no one can come to the Father but by Me. Matt.7:13-14, Enter in at the straight gate, because straight is the gate and narrow is the way which leads to life and a few therein find it. Wide is the gate that leads to hell and destruction and many will find it and go there. You do not want to go on this road and be lost forever. Stay on the straight and narrow road that leads to Heaven and eternal life.

Jesus is our keeper. We can't keep ourselves without Him. Gen.28; 15, I am with you and I will keep you in all places wherever you go. I do not slumber or sleep. He sees everything and knows everything for He's everywhere at the same time. You can never hide from God. II Tim.1:12, Paul said, I know Him and am persuaded that He is able to keep me. Jesus said, fear not for I am with you, I am your God and I will strengthen you and will help you. I will hold you with My right hand of My righteousness. Right hand means power. He said I will carry you for I have made you and I will deliver you. He will keep you in perfet peace whose mind is stayed on the Lord because you trust in Him. If you want God to keep you then you have to trust Him, follow His Words and do His will. The peace of God which passes all other understanding shall keep your hearts and minds through Jesus Christ. He will never make anyone follow Him for it's your own free will, you have to choose to follow Him. This world is too big and full of troubles to handle it on your own. You need Jesus to lead and keep you. You will still have some problems because the Word tells us that if we follow Him we will have troubles all the days of our life but, Jesus said that He will make a way for you that will help you go through whatever it is that you have to go through. I can't imagine being alone with no help in some of the troubles I have had to go through. Jude 24:25, Now unto Him that is able to keep you from falling and present you faultless before the presence of His glory with exceeding joy, to the only wise God our Savior, be glory, majesty, dominion and power both now and forever. Amen and amen. He is the only One who can keep our salvation and bring us faultless before God the Father. He is our divine keeper forever. When you walk with Him you will never have to walk alone for He will carry you all the way.

Jesus is the Prince of life

John 1:4, In Him was the light and the light was the light of men. 5:16, For as the Father has life in Himself so has He given to the Son to have life in Himself. I have come that you may have life and have it more abundantly. I am the good Shepherd and the good shepherd gives His life for the sheep. 11:25, Jesus said, I am the resurrection and the life, they that believes on Me though they be dead yet shall they live. 14:6, I am the way the truth and the life and no one comes to the Father except through Me and by Me. I John 5:12, Jesus is the only source of life and they that has the Son has life.

Jesus is the Prince of peace. Isa.9:6, For a child shall be born unto us, a Son is given to us, He is the Prince of peace. This was a prophecy of Isaiah and we can see that it came to pass for Jesus Christ was born just like God said He would. Phil.4:9, Do the things that you have seen, heard and received of Me and the God of peace shall be with you. In order to have this peace that God gives we have to be obedient to Him. The God of peace shall sanctify you wholly if you will depart from from sin and evil and do good, seek peace and pursue it. Let the peace of God rule in your hearts in which you were called. God is our peace for no man or nothing can give you the peace that God gives. Rom.5:1, Therefore being fustified by faith we have peace with God through Jesus Christ our Lord. The just shall live by faith and not by feelings or anything else. Have faith in God for all your answers for without faith you cannot please Him. Phil. 4: 7, And the peace of God which passes all understanding shall keep your hearts and minds through Jesus Christ. Jesus is the Word, the truth and the life whether you believe it or not. Just because some may not believe all of this it doesn't change the fact that He is all of this and He never changes. Acts 10:36, The Word which God sent unto the children of Israel preaching peace by Jesus Christ was this, He is Lord of all. Rom.16:20, The God of peace will bruise the devil under our feet shortly. His final destimation is coming soon, hell fire forever for the unbelievers. Now may the peace of God be with you forever. Amen

Jesus is the Water of life. Isa.12:3, Therefore shall you draw water out of the well of salvation. There is joy in serving the Lord, there is joy and peace in studying and reading of His Word for His water never runs out and you will never thirst again, His fountain is always running and is always full. If you drink this water you will never thirst again for He is your fulfillment. John 4:14, The water that I give you shall be in him a well of water springing up into everlasting life, it's eternal. The inward well becomes a flowing river of blessings, after the baptism of the Holy Ghost. There is power now, love and joy in the Holy Ghost. You need this power to make it through this life and have life more abundantly as Jesus has promised. It's not all about speaking in other tongues but it's the power that you need and can have in the Holy Ghost. If you have never been baptized in the Holy Ghost then you need to pray and ask God to baptise you. There is a baptizing of water after you are born again and receive Jesus in your heart and life. You have Jesus living within you now but you need the power of the Holy Ghost that only God can give. If you remember, in the upper room when Jesus told them to tarry until the Holy Ghost came, this is what He was talking about. When Jesus was ascended up into Heaven to be with His Father, He left the comforter, the Holy Spirit to lead and guide His children. Rev.22:17, Jesus invites all to come to this living water, He said to take of it freely. He gave His life so it's paid in full to all who will believe and accept it, Jesus is this living water.

Jesus is the Light of the world. John 8:12, Jesus said, I am the light of the world, and they that follow Me shall not walk in darkness but shall have the light of life. In Him there is no darkness. In Him there is light and the life of all who will follow Him. We are to let our light shine for Him wherever we are to everyone. The Lord is my light and my salvation and it can be yours if you will accept Him. Epe.5; 14, Awake you that sleep and rise from the dead and Christ shall give you light. He is saying, be alive, trust Me, get up and do something. We are to walk in the light and always let out light shine for Him so that the world can see Him in us. Rev.21:23, In New Jerusalem there will be no need for the sun, moon or stars for the glory of God will lighten it, and the Lamb Jesus Christ is the light thereof. There will be no night there, no darkness at all.

Jesus Christ is the Word. John 1:1-2 and 14, In the beginning was the Word and the Word was with God and the Word was God.The same was in the beginning with God. And the Word became flesh and dwelled among us. We know that Jesus and the Father are One. They are not as one but they are One. When you have seen Jesus you have seen the Father. If you know Jesus then you know the Father also. Jesus told Phillip, he that has seen the Father has seen Me. Thomas said to Jesus, my Lord and my God. Jesus said, they that has My Word and believes on Him that has sent Me has everlasting life and shall not come into condemnation but has passed from death to life. Man does not live by bread alone but by every Word that proceeds out of the mouth of the Lord.

Jesus is the good and Great Shepherd. Ps.23:1, The Lord is my shepherd I shall not want. He will give us our every need and much more. He feeds His flock just like a shepherd does his sheep. Jesus said, I am the good Shepherd, the good Shepherd gives His life for the sheep. We are the sheep of His pasture and He is our Shepherd. Where He leads I will follow, so should all of His followers. I like David have made up my heart and mind, for my heart is fixed on Him. If you do not follow Him you will go astray and fall away. Do you know what they say about sheep? They say that sheep are the most stubborn animal of all and we are called the sheep. We can get very stubborn at times but please, never get so stubborn that you deny Jesus Christ as your Savior and Lord. Follow Him and He will keep you from harm and will feed and give you the food and living water that will never run out. Heb.13:20, The God of peace that brought again from the dead, our Lord Jesus Christ, that Great Shepherd of the sheep through the blood of the everlasting covenant. I Pet.5:4, When the chief Shepherd shall appear you shall receive a crown of glory that does not fade away. Jesus is coming soon for His children that are ready for Him and are looking for Him. Are you looking for Him? Praise God for He is going to take us out of here and live happily forever more. Please be ready for death could take you first, for none of us know when that will come or when He's coming but we know the time is coming and we need to stay ready. Remember, Jesus is the Prince of life and it's eternal to all who will follow and be obedient to Him. We have to endure to the end to be saved. You can't start this life with Him and then quit and expect to enter into the Kingdom of Heaven. We must run this race to the very end with Him. Jesus never gave up on us so we should never give up on Him. He's been patient and longsuffering and full of love, mercy and grace toward us. When we make mistakes and ask forgiveness He forgives, forgets and keeps on loving us. This is the same pattern we should use for all others also. He has shown us the way and we are to follow all of His instructions. Jesus gave us all that He had and that's all He wants from you and me is our all to Him. He gave us His very best and not the left overs so we are to give Him our best. Do as the song says, Give of the best to the Master. Jesus is our Lord and our Master.

Saints are a delight to the Lord

Ps.16:3, But to the saints that are in the earth and to the excellent in whom is all My delight. If you are saved and being obedient to the Lord then we are His saints and we are a delight to Him. Ps.37:23-26, The steps of a good man is ordered by the Lord and He delights in his ways. We are delighted in Him just as He is of us. Even though we may fall many times we will not be cast down because the Lord holds us with His right hand. That's love, real genuine, agape love of God. As long as we are delighting in Him and are heeding His leading He will keep us in His care. David said, I am old and I have never seen the righteous or His seed forsaken or begging for bread. His seed is blessed for He is merciful. God said that He would meet all of our needs according to His riches in glory and He owns it all. He said to give and it shall be given unto you. What you give to others will be returned back to you. You don't give because you want it back but that's one of God's promises so you can expect things back. He wants your first fruits and you tithes of ter percent and then He said that He would take care of all your needs and He will for it has been proven over and over again to me. You can never out give God. Ps.34:15, The eyes of the Lord are upon the righteous and His ears are open to their cry. Don't think for a moment that He doesn't know where you are and what you need. Ps.92:12, The righteous shall flourish like palm trees, they shall grow like a cedar in Lebanon. They shall be strong in the Lord as long as they stay in Him. Our strength is in the Lord and our joy is in the strength of the Lord. Have you lost your joy? If so then you best check yourself to see what the problem is. We may not always have happiness but we can always have the joy of the Lord as long as we have Him in our hearts and lives. He is joy and unspeakable and full of glory and where there is glory there is joy. Ps.97:10, God preserves the souls of the saints and delivers them out of the hands of the wicked. The Lord will never forsake His saints for they are preserved forever. God keeps us and He keeps our salvation also. He's the one who can keep you from falling from grace for we can't keep ourselves. Matt.13:43, then the righteous shine forth as the sun in the Kingdom of their Father. Who has ears let them hear? This is how much the Lord delights in His saints. He always desires the best for His children. He has promised us much and He will provide what he promises. He even takes His children through death with peace and joy. Ps.119:15, Precious in the sight of the Lord is the death of His saints. Ps.91:14, Because you have loved Me I will deliver you, I will set you on high because you have knowm My name. You are Mine says the Lord. Isa.58:14, Delight yourself in the Lord and He will cause you to ride on high places on the earth and feed you with the heritage of Jacob your father, for the Lord has spoken. He was speaking about Israel here but I believe it goes for us today as well. God has a lot of wealth and He wants to give it to all of His children. We may be poor in this world's goods but we can be rich in Him. We have riches that will never fade away or that can be taken away from us, for they are eternally secured as long as you stay in Him. We have peace that the world cannot give and we have the love of God that the world and no one else can give and no one can take those away. We have a hope that the world cannot give and a God that cannot be found no other place and He is eternal and will never change. He will never leave or forsake His children. We would be foolish to walk away from all of these things. It would be a terrible mistake to lose all of the spiritual wealth that God has given you and He still has more to give. Hab.3:19, The Lord is my strength and He will make my feet like hinds feet and He will make me walk upon high places. I'd like to encourage each one this, when you read and study God's Word to always put your name in the place when God is making promises, for they are all for His children. He does not respect one over the other for He loves all the same.

Our future delight and exaltations and rewards of God

Matt.19:28-29, Jesus said, Verily I say unto you, you that have followed Me shall set upon twelve thrones judging the twelve tribes of Israel. Everyone that has left houses, brothers, sisters, fathers, mothers, wife and children or lands for My sake shall receive as hundred fold and shall inherit everlasting life. Praise the Lord. Do you know that the saints will judge the world? Paul tells us about this in I Cor.6:2-3, He said we are to be judging the small things here on earth. He said we would be judging the angels. We are to help one another in matters of this life especially in the church. We should be able to make decisions and corrections without having to go to a court of law. Paul is saying, we have the Spirit of God so we do have the strength and knowledge. Verse 17, They are join to the Lord are one spirit. Rev.3:21, To them that overcome I will grant to sit with Me in My throne even as I overcame and set down with My Father in His throne, this is Jesus speaking to His saints, which is all of His children. We have to deny and forsake ourselves to be worthy, live godly, righteous and holy in Him to remain His. You are a new person in Him when you accept Him in your heart and life, it's a new beginning for old things are passed away behold all things become new in you through Jesus Christ. You are to live God's way now, a life that's pleasing to Him. He's our Savior Lord and Master and He's your guide, healer, keeper of your salvation and the giver of all things. You have to learn to trust Him in all things. He will give you the wisdom and knowledge to choose all of the right things in this life. Sometimes we fail and take the wrong direction but He will always be there to stir you back in the right direction if you call upon Him. I praise Him for chastising and nudging me when I am slipping in the wrong direction. Many times we can even have a bad thought and He will put in our spirit that we need to correct that. We have to be careful for we will reap what we sow whether good or bad. Isa.3:10, To the righteous it shall be well with you and you shall eat of the fruit of your doings. If you do righteous things then you will reap righteous things. If you do wrong things then you will reap bad things. What you say is what you get, for the Bible says that we shall eat of the fruit of our mouth. So we need to be careful what we say, what we do and where we go, for we will reap if we faint not. If you're going to faint make sure you faint for doing good and not evil.

There is going to be an Eternal Heaven

Isa.65:17, For behold I create new heavens and new earth, the former things shall not be remembered nor come into mind. We won't remember the past and what's going on now after we get to Heaveen. This is the Word of God, praise the Lord. All past will be wiped aways never to be remembered anymore. We will be like Christ for we will be changed to be like Him forevermore. Rev.21:1, John said, I saw a new Heaven for the first Heaven and earth was passed away and there was no more sea. All things will be made completely new. Jesus said, My Words are faithful and true. Heaven is the final home for the saints of God. You can say that Heaven is a safe deposit place for treasures and we are the treasure. We now have come forth as gold for we have been tried and we have passed the test and we have made it. Matt.6:20, Lay up your treasures in Heaven where moth nor rust corrupts and where thieves cannot break through and steal. We can rejoice because our names are written in the Lamb's book of life in Heaven. If Christians would just realize what God has in store for His children I believe they would all try harder to be able to enter in. Also, if they really knew God for who He really is I believe everyone would be closer to Him. They would have a greater relationship with Him. God is so good to us and many times we are so ungrateful and we take so much for granite. We need to show Him how much we love Him and do everything to please Him. Do you know that your name is written down in the Lamb's book of life? You can know, and if you have any doubts then you should make sure for He is coming soon.

John 14:2, Jesus said, in My Father's house are many mansions and I go to prepare a place for you, then I will come again and get you, that where I am you will be also. What a promise to look forward to. He's preparing that place for us now, for all of His children. Just as

He is preparing a place for you then you should be preparing yourself now to be ready to go when He comes for His children. There's no preparing after death, for your preparing time is now while you are living here on this earth. There are only two places to go for your final home and that's Heaven or hell. Obedience is one of the conditions to be able to enter into Heaven. Rev.22; 14, Blessed are they that do His commandments that they may have the right to the tree of life and may enter the gates to the city. Only those who believe in the Lord Jesus Christ and are following Him are going there. You are saved by grace, through faith in Jesus and you have to live here for Him to be able to go to Heaven. Those that are counted worthy will be there. We are worthy only through Jesus Christ for our righteousness is as filthy rags and we stand in His righteousness. Phil.3:21, He will fashion our body like His glorious body and we will be changed to be like Him. A new body to go to Heaven in, what more can you ask? When Christ who is our life shall appear here, we will appear with Him in glory. John says, if anyone shall follow Jesus then wherever He is, we will be also. Whether you go through death or in the rapture you will be with Him. II Cor.5:8, We are confident I say, to be abesnt from the body is to be present with the Lord. There is a hell to lose and a Heaven to gain so prepare to meet the Lord and go to Heaven.

Man is crowned with glory and honor by God

Ps.8:4-6, What is man? Man is a tenant in a house of clay, why are You mindful of him? Also, what is the Son of man that You have visited him? David is asking God thease questions. You have made man a little lower than the angels and crowned him with glory and honor. You made him to have domonion over the works of Your hands and put all things under his feet. Job 4:19, Man's foundation is made out of the dust of the earth. He is a tenant made of clay. Gen.2:7, The Lord formed man out of the dust of the earth and breathed into his nostrils the breath of life and man became a living soul. Gen.1:26-27, God created man in His own image, male and female He created them. He made them after His own likeness and gave them dominion over the whole earth and everything in it. Man has dominion over all the earth and everything in it. Gen.1:28, God blessed them and said, be fruitful and increase in number, fill the earth and subdue it. We are to use what God has made for He made all things good and everything that we need. He made the meats, vegetables and fruits for our food to eat and enjoy. Humans are God's representatives and image bearers. He made us unique to rule His creation for He made us in His own image. God's image involves the Spiritual man and the physical man. Job 32:8, Our spirit can commune with His. We are to exhibit godly character, holiness, righteousness and justice. God made everything perfect, even human beings but Adam and Eve messed that up by sinning. The Garden of Eden was Heaven on earth for it was all perfect made by God. Ps.8:5, God made man a little lower than the angels but over everything else. Humans are under the watchful care of the Lord. Isa.41:14 Fear not for I will help you, God said. David said the Lord is my shield, my strength and my heart trust in Him and I am helped and my heart rejoices. Praise God that He is ever watching His children and caring for us. He is a very present help in time of troubles. This means that He is always with us even before troubles starts. Isa.41:10, Fear not for I am with you, I am your God and I will strengthen you and I will help you. I will uphold you with My right hand of My righteousness. Heb.13:6, We can boldly say, the Lord is my helper and I will not be afraid or fear what man can do unto me for I stand in His care forever.

God paid the ultimate price for man. John 3:16, For God so loved the world that He gave His only begotten Son that whosoever believes on Him should not perish but have everlasting life. Jesus Christ died that awful death on the cross at Calvary to save us because He loved us that much. There has never been such love as this before and will never be again. For Christ died once and for all. You have to believe it, accept it and repent of your sin to have eternal life. He did His part now you have to do yours. It's each and everyone's choice whom they will serve. Joshua said, but for me and my house we will serve the Lord. That's what Leon and I have said and we are doing everything we can to abide by the Words of God and to trust Him, be faithful to Him and obedient to Him. We are careful of what goes on in our home for we want to please God and be a good testimony to and for Him. I Cor.6:20, For we were bought with a price, so we should glorify God in our body and in our spirit, which are God's. We were bought with the precious blood of Jesus. We've been washed in His blood and He has cleansed us from our sins, so we have to live holy and righteous in order to please Him. The just shall live by faith, withour faith you cannot please God. Of everything that God made He honors man most. After man and woman sinned in the beginning God made another way to have Him a perfect people. We know we aren't perfect now but we are striving to be perfect just as Jesus was perfect. He was the only person that was completely perfect. You can live free of sin because of the death and resurrection of Jesus Christ. He has redeemed us and justified all who will follow Him to the end. Thank God, when we do make mistakes He will forgive us when we ask. We are not to go back and repeat the same mistakes. We are not saved to sin but we are saved from sin. One day we will have a perfect body and we will never sin or make anymore mistakes but until then we have to be careful to keep our entire body under subjection to Jesus Christ. He said, draw near to Me and I will draw near to you. Resist the devil and he will have to flee. When things come against you, come against it in the name of Jesus Christ. It's going to be a battle as long as we live in this body of flesh on this earth for the flesh is warring againt the Spirit of God that's in us. Our flesh can get us in a lot of problems so that's why we have to take control over our flesh. Follow the Spirit of God in you and you won't you won't give in to the fleshly lusts. Make sure that God is proud of you and He will crown you with glory and honor.

CHAPTER ELEVEN

Paul's Last Warning To The Obstinate Sinner

CHAPTER 11

Paul's Last Warning to the Obstinate Sinner

II Cor.13:1-11, An obstinate person is one who is determined to do it their way no matter what. It means to be persistent, determined, and self willed or persuaded to do what you want to do. It can be good or bad but in this case it was bad because Paul is trying to convince the Corinthians of their sins and to stop sinning and do what's right. This is the last warning to the Corinthians about living right, being true believers and being motivated by faith, by Paul the apostle of Jesus Christ. He warned them to turn from false teachers and away from their own selfish ambitions and desires. They had been influenced by the false teachers and led astray. Paul told them, on my return I will not spare you who are still sinning in the same way. He told them, you are doubting that I speak from Christ Jesus. He told them to examine themselves to see if they were in the faith, test yourselves, he was saying. If you fail the test then Jesus is not living in you. You need to know for sure that you are standing solid in the faith. You need a checkup often, if your life hasn't changed for the better then you have failed the test and Jesus is not living in you. Just as you get checkups physically you need to do the same spiritually. Paul was telling them these things and warning them so that when he came back to them he wouldn't have to say a word to them about doing wrong and sinning. The authority that the Master gave him was to bring people together not separating them and he wanted to get on with his commission and not have to spend his time on reprimanding them. I want to build you up and not tear you down and I don't want to have to deal with you harshly. This is a picture of the rapture of the church when Jesus comes back in the clouds to get His bride, the church. Those who are ready will rise to meet Him in the clouds. You have to be ready and free of sin to go with Him. He has warned us through out His entire Word on how to live and how to be ready for His coming. You won't have time to change when He comes we'll be gone in a twinkling of an eye.

Verse 11-13, Paul encourages them to be cheerful, keep all things in good repair, keep their spirits up, stay in unity and harmony, be agreeable, aim for perfection, and live in peace with each other and to rejoice. Change all of your sinful ways and to encourage each other in Christ Jesus. Jesus warns all to live holy and live by faith. Our old life dies and a new life begins when you come to Christ. Gal.2:20, I am crucified with Christ, never the less I live, yet not I but Christ lives in me and the life I now live in the flesh by the faith of the Son of God who loved me and gave Himself for me. We have to die daily to self and live by the Spirit of God in this new life. If we please ourselves then we don't please God. Epe.3:17-19, That Christ may dwell in your heart by faith that you being rooted and grounded in love, may be able to comprehend with all of the saints what is the breadth, length, depth and heights. And to know the love of Christ which passes knowledge. Obedience is a command. Whosoever keeps His commandments dwells in Christ and He in them. We are to keep our temples clean and holy. He will not live in a body that's dirty with sin and no sin will enter into the Kingdom of Heaven. Please take His warnings and keep yourselves free from all sin and live holy and righteous in Him. I Cor.3:16, Know ye not that your body is the temple of the Lord and that the Spirit of God dwells in you. 6:19, Know ye not that your body is the temple of the Holy Spirit which is in you, which you have of God and you are not your own. You were bought with a price and your body doesn't belong to you anymore for it is God's. Jesus gave His life for you and me so we could have eternal life with Him. II Cor.6; 16, God said, I will dwell in them and walk with them, I will be their God and they shall be My people. He will dwell in you as long as you are serving Him and living for Him. If you walk away then He is no longer your God for you will be serving the god of this world which is the devil. I Pet.2:5, You are a living stone built upon a spiritual house, a holy priesthood to offer up spiritul sacrifices acceptable unto God by Jesus Christ. Jesus is coming back soon and we need to be ready for we don't know when He is coming, but one thing we know for sure that He is coming. When He comes back He won't be telling you about your sins and what you should be doing for He will come in a twinkling of an eye to get His children. He said He was coming back for those who are waiting and watching for Him. If you're not ready then you will be left here to go through the seven year great tribulation period. You don't want to miss the rapture for there's going to be a time here worse than ever before and will never happen again. The time in unknown when He is coming but it's going to be quick. Luke 12:40, Be ready for the Son comes at a time when you think not. Rev.16:15, Behold I come as a thief in the night, blessed are they that are watching and keeps their garments clean. Rev.3:11, I come quickly so hold on and don't let anyone lure you away from the truth. Be ready always, don't miss out.

Here are some categories and meaning of being obstinate. Check yourselves to see if you fall into any of these. Hardheaded, hard hearted, head strong, opinionated, perverse, self willed, stubborn, willful, narrow minded, wayward, disobedient, uncooperative, unmanageable, unruly, defiant or demanding. If you fall into any of these then you need to make a change in your mind, heart and life. You cannot be a child of God and hold on to these things for these traits will lead you to hell. These are not traits of the Lord and you have to be like Him. If you hold on to these things then you are failing the test as Paul had told the Corinthians. You have to discipline yourself to be like Christ. You have to shun all appearance of evil and crucify your flesh daily. Let God's Spirit lead and guide you for He will never lead you astray. Holding on to these traits are not worth losing out on the opportunity to go with Jesus in the rapture and live forever. Nothing is worth losing what He has for you. Many Christians see the outward faults and sin but over look the inward sins. There are many opportunities that are missed that you can never recover, but that's the one opportunity you don't want to miss, the Rapture, for it will never happen again. You have to think about going through death as well. After death there is no other chance of making things right with the Lord and no one knows the time of death for each one of us but God Himself.

Opportunities missed that can't be recovered

Gal.6:10, As we have therefore opportunity let us do good unto all people especially to those in the household of faith. There are times when we may see people only once in our life so be good to them for we will never have this chance again. We need to use every opportunity that we have to be good to everyone. Jer.8:20, The harvest is past and the summer gone and we are not saved. These sinners had lost their opportunity to get saved in these two seasons. There are many who miss out on the opportunity to get saved and they never have another chance. Today is the day of salvation for tomorrow may never come for many and yesterday is gone forever. Many have had a chance to accept Jesus Christ as their Savior and didn't and died before there was another chance. We are not promised tomorrow for all we know that we know we have is right now, this moment. Matt.25:10, And when they went up to buy oil the Bridegroom came and they that were ready went into the wedding and marriage supper and the doors were close. This talks about the ten virgins, five were wise and five were foolish. The wise ones had oil in their lamps and were ready when the bridegroom came but the foolish ones had no oil for thay had not prepared for the wedding and they were left outside and couldn't go in. This was a lost opportunity for these foolish virgins and it could not be recovered. Prov.1:24, Behold I have called and you refused. Don't put your calling off because there may not be another chance, it may be a lost opportunity forever for you to get saved for you could be called through death or the rapture may appear before you have another chance.

Ezek.3:20, If you do not give a person warning to turn from their sin and then they die, I will hold you accountable. His blood will I require upon your hands. We have neglected out duty is we neglect to tell everyone about their sin, death, Heaven and hell and about Jesus. There have been many that died that have never known about Him and how to live holy and righteous. Jesus said to go out on the highways and byways and tell them about the gospel to everyone. Another thing is this, words spoken can never be recovered. Matt.12:36, Every idle word that you speak shall be given account of in the Day of Judgment. When we speak a word of a tale bearer thay are as wounds and they shall go down into the innermost parts of the belly. Words hurt a person very deeply. People will forgive but the words spoken many times are never forgotten. You can never take words back for once it leaves your lips it has been spoken out. In anger people say words that they really don't mean but never the less, they have been spoken and the person that it was spoken to have been hurt. The tongue is like a fire, a world of iniquity is the tongue among our members, it defiles the whole body and sets on fire the course of nature and it is set on fire of hell. We are to speak no evil of no one or to no one, especially our Christian family. James says, if you keep your tongue you can keep your life. We should all have this motto, if we can't say anything good then never say anything at all. Now we do have to correct one another so we all can live a godly life and we have to lift each other up so we all can grow stronger in unity of the Lord Jesus Christ our Lord.

Gal.1:3-15, Paul said, you have heard how in the past how I persecuted the church of God and how I wasted it. But God called me to preach the gospel to the heathens. He said that he responded immediately. He couldn't change what he had done in the past but he was forgiven and was called of God to do a great ministry for Him. The time is past and gone, lost and can't be recovered. The time is short and we need to do all we can for the Lord and His work. Whatevcer He's called you to do, do it with all your mind, heart and strength. Don't miss out on what He's called you to do. Whatever talent you have, use it for the gospel and the Lord's sake. The old saying is, if you don't use it then you will lose it. Use what God has given you for there are many callings. Epe.5:15-16, See that you walk circumspectly, careful, attentively not as fools but be wise, redeeming the time because the days are evil. Use your time very wisely and do all you can for the cause of Christ. Remember, you can't recover the past, the time that you have already lost but you can start now doing all you can in the time now and that's ahead of you. Life goes quickly for it's like a vapor. The night is far spent and the day of the Lord is at hand, it's time to be serious and stop playing around with Christianity. Don't waste your time on worldly things and worldly people unless you are ministering to them about the Lord Jesus Christ. We know that we are going to reap what we sow so let's sow good seeds so we can reap a good harvest for the Lord. All of God's works and plans are perfect for He never lost anything nor did He lose any time or opportunities. Gen.6:3, God said, My Spirit will not always strive with man. Don't put off until tomorrow what you can do today, right now. Don't be foolish and wait until another time for the time may never come. God is calling now, listen and heed to His call. If you wait and miss the opportunity it could be the worse mistake you have ever made and it won't be recovered. You can't get saved anytime you want to for the Holy Spirit has to draw you and call you. To reject Jesus Christ and to deny Him is the blaspheming of the Holy Ghost and that will never be forgiven for. All sin will be forgiven except the blaspheming of the Holy Ghost. Whatever you do please don't reject His call.

A life after it's been taken cannot be recovered. Gen.4:8-15, Cain killed his brother Abel because of hatred and jealousy so he died and can't be recoved by Cain. Then Cain went from the presence of the Lord so now his life can't be recovered. The sixth commandment is, Thou shall not kill. God does forgive but a person's suffering for committing murder for taking a person's life will be a tormented on most of the time. A stone thrown away can't be recovered. That stone could make you come up short of one stone when you need it and you can't recover it. That may sould like a very small thing but one stone could mean a job isn't complete without it. Ecc.3:5, There is a time to cast stones and a time to gather stones. Be careful of stones that you throw. Jesus said, they that are without sin cast the first stone. We can call criticism stones. We are not to criticise our brothers and sisters in the Lord. Words are as stones and they can hurt and mar the body, mind and soul many times. These stones cannot be recovered, forgiven but not recovered. Prov.18:19, A brother offended is harder to to be won than a strong city and their contentions or feelings are like the bars of a castle. Their feelings cannot be broken for the hurt is so deep. Verse 14, Who can bear a crushed spirit? Have you ever had your feelings hurt? Have you ever been accused of things that you didn't do? Do you remember how badly that it hurt? Be careful of stones that you throw. We need to be careful of doing things that can't be recovered if needed to be recovered. Let us not be an obstinate sinner but let's be an obstinate child of God. We need to be set in His ways; doing all the things He wants us to do. We need to be grounded in His Word so we will never sway from it. We need to be grounded in love for one another so that we will never hurt anyone. We need to be determined to follow Jesus no matter the cost. We are to be sold out to Him forever, be a soul winner for God. We need to be all we can and waste no time, for time is important and short. Work today for the time is coming when our work will be done. I want Jesus to say to me, Come on in My good and faithful servant, you have been faithful over a few things and I will make you ruler over much. Don't you want Him to say that to you? Let the redeemed of the Lord say so. He alone is worthy to be praised. Praise the Lord forever.

Cunning ways of the devil

Prov.7:6-7, The adulterous woman looked out her window and saw these foolish young men. She noticed that one of them had no wisdom. The rest of the story tells of how she lured him into her evil scheme. She approached him as he was walking toward her house. She was dressed like a prostitute and she planned to trick him. This man had to know what she was by the way she was dressed and by her actions but he was weak, foolish and had no wisdom of God. Jezebel encouraged the people to worship false gods and many died because of listening to her. Many men have fallen into the same trap and are still doing the same thing. Many have died because of having sex with many women. They either had venereal diseases of from another man or woman killing them over jealousy. An adulterous woman way and her house is on the way to hell or death. If she doesn't repent and change her life and the way she lives she will end up in hell and destruction and those that follow as well. Whosoever leads God's people from serving Him to serve other gods and leads them down the road to destruction is like Jezebel. You are going to be responsible for the ones you lead astray. The devil is roaring around everywhere seeking who he can devour. He's a liar and the father of it, a thief and a murderer. He came to steal, kill and destroy all that he can. He knows he's going to hell for eternity and he wants all he can get to go with him. He is looking for the weak and young Christians before they get the understanding and wisdom of God. Of course, he will trick anyone that will heed to him. He always comes around when one is weak and troubled. He will do to you what the adulterous did to that young man if you let him. You can resist him like the Word says. Draw near to God and He will draw near to you, resist the devil and he will flee from you in Jesus name. He will make things look good for a while until he pulls you in and then he will leave you for a while. He's unlike God, for God will never leave or forsake you if you follow Him and are obedient to Him. He's a very present help in time of trouble. You can always lean and trust him for He cares for you. Be careful for your sins can and will separate you from the Lord and He will not hear or answer your prayers. Verse 12 tells us that this woman is out on the streets and is in wait at every corner. This is how the devil is for he is lurking, looking and waiting to find someone he can deceive. You need to keep watch for him always and be on your guard against him and his deceitful schemes. He will come at your weakest moment to tempt and pull you away from doing what you should. You can't see him but if you are wise you can feel him and know he's around.

Verses 13-15, 21, 26-27, She kissed this young man and said unto him. I have peace offering with me today, this day I have paid my vows. I came forth to meet you diligently, to seek your face and I have found you. She had paid her vows because she had made her bed with good smelling linen sheets and had everything in order for the Goodman of the house was gone on a journey. Isn't that like the devil, he makes everything look good and so many fall for it. This woman had succeeded in what she wanted just like the devil does to many people. Now that she has his attention she will do to him what she wants to do. That's the way of the devil always. He's out for pleasure seekers those who are trying to find something to satisfy their desires of the flesh. They are looking in all the wrong places. Only Jesus can satisfy your longings and your souls. People look for so long and all they need is Jesus Christ in their lives. He's all you need. Seek ye first the kingdom of God and His righteousness and everything else will be added unto you. That's the Word of God. Jesus said, Trust, try and prove Me and see if I won't do whay I have promised you. Don't follow the ways of the cunning and sly ways of the devil for his end is death and hell and he will burn forever in the lake of fire filled with fire and brimstones. Follow Jesus and you will have eternal life with Him in complete happiness. With all of her much fair speech she caused this young man to yield to her temptation. With her fair lips she forced him, for she wouldn't give up on him. Isn't that like the devil? He keeps on until lots of people give in to him for it seems the easy way. The easy way is not always the best way. Without the wisdom of God it could be easy to fall into temptation and sin. The evil woman will cast down, wound and hurt you for many strong men have been slain by her. The other young man was a weak and foolish man but this kind of woman has done this to strong men as well. We have seen this happen even to men in the ministry, preachers in the pulpit. You may wonder how this can be for some of these men have been baptized in the Holy Ghost and they know the Word of God, they know right from wrong. The Bible teaches, watch lest you fall. Pride always comes before a fall. Some of these that have fallen have had great ministry and a great following and maybe money got in the way. Only God knows what happened but we are not their judge, just beware lest you fall the Word of God says. We are never to condone sin but pray for the fallen, lift them up to God for they need help. No one in their right mind at the time would do what they sometimes do. We are to have mercy on them because only by the grace of God we could be in the same situation. Some would say, oh it will never happen to me. WATCH lest you fall also. Many have fallen and have come back and repented but it has left a scar that many won't forget and neither will they. It does hurt your testimony. God forgives and forgets but people don't, they may forgive but not forget.

Rom.6:23, For the wages of sin is death. If you don't repent of your sins and come to Jesus Christ there is no other way to have eternal life. It will cause you your life forever for death and hell is the penalty of sin if not forgiven. Prov.11:9, They that look at and does evil brings death it their life and soul. Paul said in Thessalonians to shun all appearances of evil, don't look upon any sin. Ezek.18:4, The soul that sins shall surely die. Ps.66:18, If I regard or keep sin in my heart the Lord will not hear me. I spoke about this earlier in the book. God will not hear or answer your prayers if you have sin in your heart and life. There are so many that say they pray all of the time but little do they realize that God does not hear them because of sin in their lives. God hears other Christians that are praying for them, for the Bible says that the prayer of a righteous man prevails much. Isa.59:2 Make sure your sins find you out. Don't let your heart decline and grow weak in the Lord, don't go astray in these last days. We are living in evil days but you can be strong in the Lord for He is your strength. He's your divine keeper for He's your salvation. Proc.7:24-25, Jesus Christ is pleading with His children, Hearken unto Me. Now therefore, oh you children and attend, listen to the Words of My mouth. Do not let your hearts go the way of that woman, do not go astray in the evil paths. The devil makes many evil paths but Jesus Christ has warned us not to follow down those paths. There are only two roads to follow. One is the straight and narrow road that leads to everlasting life and the other road is the broad road that leads to death, hell and destruction. There are only two leaders, Jesus Christ our Lord and Savior and the other one is the devil. Which one are you following? Rom.6:23, The gift of God is eternal life through Jesus Christ our Lord. He's the only way to escape the wiles of the devil and have everlasting life. Choose Jesus today and the way will be much brighter, your load will be much lighter.

Cup of suffering, waters of affliction

The saints will drink of the cup of suffering and the waters of affliction. Things will come to all who follow Christ. Some are tested of the Lord, often blessings in disguise, to refine Christians to be patient and teach them to learn control. Most people think of trials we go through comes from the devil but not so. Some does come from the devil and some we bring on ourselves. But the Bible teaches us that God chastises us for our own good and growth in Him. Chastisement is a mark of God's love toward His children. We love our children so we chastise them and correct them when needed to be better children. So how much more will God the Father chastise His children? Job 23:10, Job said, He knows the way that I take, when He has tried me I shall come forth as gold. Ps.66:10, David said, you have tried and proved us as silver is tried. Isa.48:10, Isaiah said, I have refined you but not with silver, I have chosen you in the furnace of afflictions. We grow stronger out of our trials and testings. If we never had a problem we wouldn't know that God could solve them. Jesus was tested and tried in the wilderness by the devil when He walked on earth as man, but He never gave in to him nor did He fall. He taught us the way and we too can endure just as He did without falling into temptations. He was human just as you and I are when He walked this earth. He was God and man, but His human side was tested to show us the way to walk in this flesh and mortal body. We have to be tested and tried, for Paul said all who follow Jesus will have troubles and trials all the days of your life but God will make a way for us that we can bear whatever we have to go through. Job said to be happy when God corrests and chastises us for He does it because He loves us and wants to spare us from going the wrong way, so be thankful to Him and praise Him for this. Job 33:28, God knows our heart and life and He knows what it takes to keep us from going astray. He will do everything He can to keep us on the right path and to keep us in the light. Sometimes problems of this life will keep us from going the wrong way for we look to God for help and then He shows us the way. Ps.119:67, David said. Before I was afflicted I went astray but now I have kept the Word. David made many mistakes that brought troubles and afflictions on himself but he always came back to God. Ps.94:12, Blessed are the ones You chastise O Lord and teach them Your laws. God has given us His laws written by Moses, the other prophets and disciples in the Bible. We are without excuse for not following them. In order to know the commandments you have to read and study the Word of God. The Bible tells everything you need to know how to live what to do and not do. One thing that He did not promise His children and that is this. He never promised us that we would never have any problems if we follow Him. He told us that we would go through many trials and tribulations if we followed Him but He would make a way of escape that we could bear them.

John 15:2, Every branch that does not bear fruit will be cut off and every branch that bears fruit He purges it so that it may bear more fruit. Christians are to bear fruit for the Lord. The fruit that He is talking about are the good things we do for Him. We are to bear the fruit of the Spirit which are, love, joy, peace, longsuffering, gentleness, patience and kindness. If we don't bear these fruit then we are none of His and He will cut us off. We are to be like Jesus for He has all of these fruit. Rev.3:19, As many as I love I rebuke and chasten, be earnest and repent. Now the chastening of the Lord here and now is not joyous for it is grievous, but afterwards it yields the peaceable fruit of righteousness unto them that heed to Him. I Pet.1:7, That the trial of your faith being much more precious than the gold that perishes, though it be tried with the fire might be found unto praise, honor and glory at the appearing of Jesus Christ. I Pet.4:12, Beloved, think it not strange concerning the fiery trial which is to try you, as some strange thing has happened to you. True Christians does not faint under the pressures of chastisement. They are thankful to God for whatever it takes to make them stronger in Him. II Cor.4:16 and 21, For which cause we faint not, though out outward person perish yet the inward person is renewed everyday. Seeing therefore we have this ministry as we have received mercy, we faint not. God will not call us where He will not keep us. If He brings you to it He will carry you through it. We need to always put our trust in Him in all things. We can do nothing on our own but we can do all things through Him who gives uf strength. Rev.2:3, Jesus said, I see what you've done, your hard work and your refusal to quit for My name sake and you have not fainted. God knows everything about you and me. He's knows our weakness and our strength and how to keep us on the right way. Let Him lead you in the way He wants and trust Him, be faithful and obedient to Him.

The simple people

Simple means, or indicates a person who is open, a vulnerable, easy to influence person. One who falls for just about anything. If you will read Prov.7:6-27 you will see the warning of adultery. It talks about the simple people and a youth who lack judgment. This young man here walked right into the snares of evil right from the devil. He never thought about right or wrong for he was a simple person who would fall for anything. The devil is always snooping around looking for these kinds of people for they are easy targets. In order to avoid walking into the wrong path you need to walk alert and purposely through life aiming and striving to be like Jesus. There are people who will fall for almost anything for they believe everything they hear. God said to test the spirits to see if they are of God or not. If what you hear doesn't line up with the Word of God then never believe it. Of course, if you don't know the Word of God then you are in darkness. No Christian should ever be labeled a simple person, for you have the Spirit of God living in you and you have the mind of Jesus Christ. You know right from wrong so do it. Phil.3:10 and 14, I want to know Christ and the power of His resurrection and the fellowship of sharing His sufferings, becoming like Him in death. I press on toward the goal of the high calling to win the prize of eternal life for which Jesus has called me. You are in this Christian race if you are one of His children. He has called us and we are to strive hard everyday and night to win this race. To win you have to endure to the end. You can't start and then stop when things get rough and hard but you have to press on to the end. You have to be willing to give up all to follow Christ and to gain eternal life.

Spiritual adultery

Prov.6:31, Whosoever commits adultery lacks judgment and whoever does this destroys themselves. You can commit spiritual adultery as well as physical adultery. Spiritual adultery is sin committed against God, you'll not only destroy your body but your soul if you commit spiritual adultery, Jesus Christ is your spiritual husband and you are to stay true to Him, be faithful, loving and obedient to Him. Ps.106:39, Thus were the defiled with their own works and went whoring with their own inventions. These are the ones who follow after what they want and their own makings. They refuse to follow Christ and keep His ways. This is Spiritual adultery. I Tim.4:1-4, Now the Spirit speaks of these in latter times, some shall depart from the faith giving heed to seducing spirits and doctrines of devils. Speaking lies in hypocrisy having their conscience seared with a hot iron. For the time will come when they will not endure sound doctrine but after their own lusts shall they heap to themselves teachers having itching ears from the truth and shall be turned into fables. They will look for something to amuse themselves instead of wanting to hear the truth. They will believe a lie and be damned. Heb.3:12, Take heed brethren lest there be any among you that has an evil heart of unbelief in departing from the living God. Don't fall from serving the only true God. God won't leave you but you can leave Him. He will not live in a body that doesn't want Him or one who won't be obedient and faithful to Him. He will not live where there is sin. II Pet.3:17-18, Brethren,seeing that you know these things before, beware lest you also being lead away with the error of the wicked fall from your own steadfastness. But grow in grace and the knowledge of our Lord and Savior Jesus Christ. To Him be glory bith now and forever. Rev.22:14-15, Blessed are they that do His commandments that they might have right to the tree of life and may enter in through the gates of the city. For without are dogs, sorcerers, whoremongers, murderers, idolaters and liars. The evil people are the dogs and they will not enter. The sorcerers are the witchcraft, magicians and those who follow horoscopes and things that are of the devil for they shall not enter. No sin will enter into the Kingdom of God. Don't be among the simple people that are so easily led astray for not serving God. Stay true to the only true God and Father Jesus Christ is Lord of all so follow Him.

Summary

God will make a way, for He will never leave or forsake you no matter what situation you may be in. You may feel you cannot handle something but always know that He can. Trust Him in all things. I Cor.10:13, There has no temptation taken you but such as is common to man, but God is faithful who will not suffer you to be tempted above that you are able, but with the temptation also make a way to escape that you may be able to stand. He promised never to leave or forsake His children, just believe this. Job 5:1, He shall deliver you from six troubles, yes, in seven there shall no evil touch you. David said, surely He shall deliver you from the fowler and from the noisome pestilence, offenses, displeasures, and disgust. Ps.91:3, God promised His children many, many times that He would take care of us if we would just put our trust in Him and follow Him. He said to put all our trust in Him for He cares for us. Can't you see how much easier it would be to put everything in His hands and listen to Him and be obedient to Him? Worry is sin, doubt is sin, grumblind and complaining will get you no place so why do it? II Tim.4:18 And the Lord shall deliver me from all evil work and will preserve me unto His Heavenly Kingdom to who be glory forever. Oh my goodness, what a promise from our Lord God Almighty. Why can't we trust Him to do what He says He will do? He said He would make a way where there seem to be no way. If we will do our part you can rest assure that He will do His. His Word is true and He never lies for He cannot lie. II Pet.4:18, The Lord knows how to deliver the godly out of temptation and to reserve the unjust unto the Day of Judgment to be judged and punished.

Here are few examples in the Bible of God's deliverances. He delivered Lot from burning in Sodom and Gomorrah. He delivered David out of the power of the lion, the bear and out of the hands of the Philistine, the three Hebrew children from the fiery furnace. He saved Daniel from the mouth of the lion. He rescued Jonah from the belly of the whale. There were Paul and Silas who He made the chains fall off and the doors of the prison were open. He saved Paul and other passengers on the ship out in the storm on the sea and they all escaped safely on the land. There are many of us today that God has kept us safe from many things. I know there are many times that He has kept me safe in bad situations. I could have died several times but God spared my life and kept me safe. My husband, Leon was healed and saved from death several times. He healed one of my daughters of cancer many years ago. We don't know how many times that He has saved us from something. It seems we take so much for granite but we need to be aware that God is still working in our favor and for our good. I would not want to get up a day of my life without God being there with me. He's the very breath that we breathe, He's our strength, salvation, healer, keeper, comforter, peace, joy, strong tower, and the solid Rock that we lean on. He's my everything for He's my all in all. Praise him forever.

We go through grief, pain and sorrow with much weeping and mourning but joy comes in the morning. There's light at the end of the tunnel and that light is Jesus Christ. John 16:20-22, I tell you the truth, you will weep and mourn while the world rejoices. You will grieve but your grief will turn to joy. David said, now is your time of grief but I will see you again and you will rejoice and no one will take away your joy. Going through trials and tribulations and problems are not easy but when you make it through them you can rejoice. Rom.5:3-5. We rejoice in our sufferings because we know that sufferings produce perseverance, character, hope and hope does not disappoint us because God has poured out His love into our hearts by the Holy Spirit whom He had given us. Be careful not to bring troubles on yourself for wrong doings. Epe.5:6, Let no one deceive you with vain words for because of these things, disobedience, unrighteousness, contentions, indignation, wrath and any sin. From sin comes the wrath of God upon the children of disobedience. Rom.1:18, For the wrath of God is revealed from Heaven against all ungodliness and unrighteousness of all people who hold the truth in righteousness. If you know to do good and doeth it not it is sin, and if you continue to commit sin then the wrath of God will be upon you. Ps.38:1, David said, remove Your wrath from me, for I am overcome by the blow of Your hand. He was talking to God, he said that he was changed because of the chastisement of God. Ps.32:4, He said, my strength was zapped while I was under Your chastisemnet O Lord but now he has overcome and has the joy of the Lord. We need to learn from God's corrections and chastisements in our lives just as David did. The quicker we learn will be the better for us. I'm so glad that He is still working on me to make me what I ought to be, and that He never gave up on me. My desire is to be closer to Him and to know Him even better. I thank Him and praise Him for what He means to me and what I mean to Him. I'm so glad that I'm a part of the family of God.

CONCLUSION

One Thing I Ask of Myself And Every Child of God Should Also

CONCLUSION

One thing I ask of myself and every child of God should also

Ps.27:4-5, One thing I ask of the Lord. This is what I seek, that I may dwell in the house of the Lord all the days of my life, to gaze upon the beauty of the Lord and to seek Him in the temple. He will hide me in the shelter of His tabernacle and set me high upon a rock. This is a Spiritual foundation that David is talking about. He expresses his desire to be with the Lord always and he wants to be in His presence always. Verse 13-14, I am still confident of this, I will see the goodness of the Lord in the land of living. David said that he would have fainted or fallen if he hadn't believed this. When David wasn't talking to God directly he was talking about Him. He spoke out loud so that his heart and soul would know what he was thinking. When you place your hope and faith in God you will never be disappointed. Wait on the Lord, be strong, take heart and wait on the Lord. Ps.40:1, David said, I waited patiently for the Lord and He turned to me and heard my cry. Everyday we are faced with options on how we're going to spend our time and where we're going to put our focus. Our decisions reveal what we value the most in our lives. What's the most important thing in your life? Who is the most important person? God has to be number one, above everyone and all else. He will not take second place. Luke 41:42, Jesus tells His friend Martha, you are worried and upset about many things, but only one thing is needed. Mary her sister had chosen what is better and it will never be taken away from her. Mary was washing Jesus's feet and listening to Him and Martha was upset with her because she wasn't busy helping her to fix a meal for Jesus to eat. She told Mary that she had left all of the work for her to do and Martha was very upset with her. Verse 40, Martha even ask the Lord, don't You care that she's not helping me? Jesus told her that Mary was doing the most important thing for she had chosen to be with Him. Mary had put Jesus first. Have you chosen to give Him first place in your heart and life? Mary was learning from Jesus and she was making memories that no one could ever take away from her.

Prov.16:3, Commit your works (and ways) unto the Lord and your thoughts shall be established. There are three steps to victory over the flesh. Walk in honesty, walk of death and walk in the Spirit of God. God doesn't reform old nature, the natural person but He regenerates and makes a new person. When we got saved, we were saved and delivered from the old nature or person and now we have to die to self daily and walk with Jesus Christ and be led by the Holy Spirit of God. Now we can claim the victory through Jesus. Rom.6:6, Knowing this, that our old person was crucified with Him that the body of sin might be destroyed, that henceforth we should not serve sin. We must walk in the Spirit of God and not walk after the lusts of the flesh. Our new life or person has good fruit now for we have the fruit of the Spirit which is, love, joy, peace, patience, kindness, goodness, faithfulness, gentleness and self control. This is my desire to show forth the fruit of the Spirit always. There are nine different fruits of the ONE FRUIT of the Spirit. The Holy Spirit will never lead us to believe anything or to engage in anything that is contrary to God's will.

We need always to be on guard for the devil, for anyone who is doing a work for the Lord, the devil is going to try to do anything he can to cause problems. You are a special target for him if you are working for the Lord. You know, it's not the praying sheep that he fears but it's the presence of the Shepherd, Jesus Christ. Those who are in vital communion and fellowship with Christ are the very ones who must face this enemy in his most devious strategies. That's why we must put on and wear the whole armor of God everyday so we can fight our enemy the devil. A Christian should never be defeated for we have the Spirit of God living in us. We are covered by the blood of Jesus. Draw near to God and you can resist the devil in Jesus name and he will have to flee from you. Every Word of God has been given to His children not just to know, but to use it for the victory and for the glory of God. There's life and power in the Word of God. Today is a new day for you, it is a valuable day and not one minute must be wasted. Live today like it was your last day on earth, enjoy it and enjoy the Lord while you have breath. Jesus said that we could have life and have it more abundantly here on earth and then eternal life with him in His Kingdom. I want to be like David, I want to be in His presence, for there's nothing that compares with being in the presence of the Lord. I want to love Him with all of my heart, soul, mind and strength. I want Him to say to me, Well done My faithful servant you have been faithful over a few things and I will make you ruler over much. God has many blessings to pour out on His children if they will serve Him, be obedient to Him and be faithful to Him. David said that the steps of a righteous person are ordered of the Lord. I pray that God will lead me and keep me in the steps that He has planned for me. God may have steps that we may not want to walk at times but I don't want to walk any other way but what He has planned for me. My prayer and desire is that I will stay in His will and endure to the end. I never want my name to be blotted out of the Lamb's book of life and I want to hear Him say to me, enter in my good and faithful servant into My kingdom that I have for you.

About the Author

I was borned in a little place in the country of Virginia called Alton. I was raised in a Christian home and I praise God for that. My parents were loving and caring and they raised seven children on a farm there. They were married for seventy four years. They now have both gone to be with the Lord, my dad in March 2006, he was 96, and my mother July 2008, she was 94.

I was saved and baptized at the age of 9 in a little Baptist church. I had a calling on my life at the age of 11 to do a work for the Lord. I always loved church, reading God's Word and singing for the Lord. Of course, I didn't heed the call of God and was married at an early age. I had, and raised 5 beautiful girls. Four of them and I started singing Southern Gospel music when the youngest was age five. We went to a lot of churches and outings and anywhere the Lord opened the doors to sing for Him. When they all grew up and left home I joined other groups and continued to sing. When my youngest daughter was 5 she began to sing with me. We started a mother/daughter duet and had a prison ministry and sang in many churches. When I married my husband Leon, we continued to sing with my daughter, Julie. When she became about fifteen she wanted to resign from singing so Leon and I continued and we are still in the music ministry. We are both ordained ministers and love to evangelize. Anywhere the Lord opens the doors we will go.

I missed my calling at the age of eleven and I can't turn back the clock but I can go forward now in what God has called me to do. God says that He does not repent of His calling. We are members of Shiloh P.H. Church in Richmond, Va. And are in the music ministry there at the present time along with going where God calls us to go. We have written about fifty gospel songs, which are anointed of God, that we sing ourselves. Our names aren't in the know or bright lights but God knows who we are and that's what counts. God has performed many miracles in our lives. He brought my husband from death to life in 2002. He kept me from death several times that I know of and I praise Him for these.

No, I don't have a PHD, B.A. or a Master's degree in anything, but I do have a B.A.H.G.E., BORNED AGAIN HOLY GHOST EXPERIENCE with God. I like John, received my education and teaching from the Father through the Holy Spirit by reading and studying the Holy Bible. Of course, I learned a lot from preachers and teachers over the years. I've taken several Bible courses. The best Teacher yet is the Holy Spirit for He will lead and guide you in all truth. I love the Word of God and I believe God has called me into the writing ministry. I know this book is ordained as well as the first one, "There's No Room for Doubt" I pray that it will bless all who reads this book as it did as I was studying God's Word preparing to write it. It's not about me but about Him and all the blessing He has for His children, those who follow, serve Him and do His will. I do thank God for my husband, a true man of God who puts God first and then me second place in his life. God said, if you will delight yourself in Me, I will give you the desires of your heart. God gave me the desire on my heart when He sent me Leon, my husband over twenty six years ago. We truly are a great team together. He's been so patient with me as I have been writing these books. I have another one that I want to start on soon. God keeps giving me more to write and I praise Him for that. My real desire is to be able to help people spiritually. I want to see as many saved as possible and show people they can live an abundant life here and then have eternal life to come. Jesus loves you and so do I.

If you would like to contact me you can email me at, clhmb7@yahoo.com You can write me also at. H.Marie Barton, 1766 Cook Rd. Powhatan, Va. 23139. You can also call me at, 804-598-2660

PERSONAL NOTES

PERSONAL NOTES

PERSONAL NOTES

PERSONAL NOTES

PERSONAL NOTES

PERSONAL NOTES

Another Book by

Hilda Marie Barton

THERE'S NO ROOM FOR DOUBT

Fear is the rejection of faith and it brings worry. Worry robs the body of rest spiritually and physically. Worry and doubt has no place in a Christian's life for the just shall live by faith. In this book you will find it shows the path to conquering fear, worry and doubt through Jesus Christ. Through the Word of God Jesus shows us the roadmap to finding our way through problems away from grief and misery and toward feeling whole and renewed in Him. There are many problems that we will face but there is one solution for everyone, stand in faith in Jesus Christ. When you walk with God and feel His strength and love there is truly no room for doubt for He has it all in control and He will sustain you. You can believe and stand on this.

The river of life flows freely, you shall live and not die. And He showed me a pure river of water clear as crystal proceeding out of the throne of God and of the Lamb. (Rev.22:1)

Whosoever drinks of this water that I give shall never thrist, but the water that I give shall be in them a well of water springing up into everlasting life. (John 4:14)

And the Spirit and the bride say come and let them that hear say come. Let them that are thirsty come. Let whosoever will come take the water of life freely. (Rev.22:17)

There is life in this water for there's life in the Word, Jesus Christ is this water for He is the Word.